I Tatti Studies in
Italian Renaissance History

Sponsored by Villa I Tatti
Harvard University Center for Italian Renaissance Studies
Florence, Italy

The Return of Lucretius to Renaissance Florence

Alison Brown

HARVARD UNIVERSITY PRESS
Cambridge, Massachusetts, and London, England
2010

Copyright © 2010 by the President and Fellows of Harvard College

ALL RIGHTS RESERVED

Printed in the United States of America

Library of Congress Cataloging-in-Publication Data
Brown, Alison, 1934–
The return of Lucretius to Renaissance Florence / Alison Brown.
    p. cm.—(I Tatti studies in Italian Renaissance history)
    Includes bibliographical references (p.) and index.
    ISBN 978-0-674-05032-7 (alk. paper)
 1. Lucretius Carus, Titus. De rerum natura.   2. Philosophy—Italy—Florence—
History.   3. Florence (Italy)—Intellectual life.   4. Scala, Bartolomeo, 1430–1497.
    5. Adriani, Marcello, 1464–1521.   6. Machiavelli, Niccolò, 1469–1527.   I. Title.
                            B776.I8B76 2010
                            187—dc22   2009035766v

Contents

Preface	*vii*
Abbreviations	*xv*
1. The Epicurean Revival in Florence and Italy	1
2. Medicean Florence: Marsilio Ficino and Bartolomeo Scala	16
3. Republican Florence: The University Lectures of Marcello Adriani	42
4. Machiavelli and the Influence of Lucretius	68
5. Lucretian Networks in the Late Fifteenth and Early Sixteenth Centuries	88
Appendix: Notes on Machiavelli's Transcription of MS Vat. Rossi 884	113
Select Bibliography	*123*
Index	*129*

Preface

This book reflects my longstanding interest in Lucretius and the attraction he held for Florentines in the hundred years after the rediscovery of his poem *De rerum natura (On the nature of things)* in 1417. He was a dangerous author to admire. As a follower of the Greek philosopher Epicurus, he challenged Christian belief in a providential universe and an afterlife, and in 1516–1517 his work was prohibited in Florentine schools. Between 1417 and 1517, however, *De rerum natura* was copied in numerous manuscripts in Florence and then printed in several different editions in Italy, raising the question of what drew so many readers to this long and difficult poem. One of these readers was Bartolomeo Scala, a miller's son from the provinces who became chancellor of Florence in 1465. When writing his biography in the 1970s, I had been intrigued by the fascination that Lucretius held for Scala throughout his life, despite the critical stance he initially adopted towards this Roman poet in his public role as chancellor. Although love—Venus as the "delight" or *voluptas* of men and gods in its famous opening line—is *De rerum natura*'s most attractive and obvious theme, this was not Scala's principal interest in the poem, nor that of other, noncurialist, Florentines. Instead, they were drawn by three themes that are more intrinsic to its argument: fear of death, evolutionary primitivism, and atomism, with its theory of chance or fortune in life. In the chapters that follow, I explore the way in which these themes provide a link between the early revival of Lucretius and the humanists most interested in his philosophy in Florence—that is, Scala; his successor as chancellor of Florence, Marcello Adriani; and Adriani's assistant in the chancery, Niccolò Machiavelli. They help to explain the wider—and perhaps surprising—interest in this author in mercantile Florence, as well as the interest of a later, post-1494 generation of young Florentines who belonged to families alienated from the Medici and found in Lucretius a voice to express their antiauthoritarianism.

The appeal of Lucretius was not so much (initially) his Epicurean philosophical beliefs in themselves as their moral and religious implications. He believed that the universe was composed only of space and matter, whose atoms interlocked through randomly swerving from the direct pull of gravity, to create multiple worlds that dissolved in time like their inhabitants; and although he accepted the existence of gods, he thought they were totally disinterested in human affairs and played no providential or judgmental role in the world. One of Lucretius's aims was to rid people of their fear of death and the retribution that it threatened. This was also one of his attractions, as well as one of the most dangerous implications of his philosophy, in removing the sanctions of the afterlife that rewarded the good and punished the wicked. Another apparent attraction to merchants and explorers, then discovering new peoples and new worlds in Africa and America, was his evolutionary account of civilization, which made sense to them in narrowing the gap between humans and animals—as Darwinism does today—despite contradicting the biblical account of creation. Lucretius's theory of the swerve that allowed for the play of fortune in life and the possibility of individual free will was equally subversive—and equally plausible to the same people, for whom random chance at sea and in business was an everyday experience. This theory, too, went against Christian orthodox belief in a providential, God-dominated world.

So although Lucretius cannot be called an atheist—since he accepted the existence of gods—*De rerum natura* is nevertheless an intriguing and dangerous text whose impact on Renaissance readers is difficult and controversial to interpret. Christians had always lived with classical texts, and it seemed that the second wave of ancient writings recovered in the fifteenth century would be safely contained in the scholastic syntheses of St. Thomas Aquinas and Albert the Great, which had accommodated the thirteenth-century recovery of Aristotle within a Christian framework. For this reason, the nineteenth-century view that antiquity exercised unbounded influence in the fifteenth century has given way to a more restricted view of its influence. Writing after Lucien Febvre, who declared in 1942 that it was impossible to be an unbeliever during the Renaissance period, in the sixteenth as well as in the fifteenth century, Paul Oskar Kristeller summed up what is probably still the attitude of many scholars today, in arguing in 1953 that there were "probably few real atheists" and fewer pantheists in the Renaissance, the main threat to religious orthodoxy being the steady growth of nonreligious intellectual interests that competed with religion for attention.[1] Nevertheless, not everyone agrees with this view. David Wootton disagrees with Febvre that people had "little choice but to believe" during this period, arguing that because of the need for dissimulation, it may be difficult to pin down and quantify unbelief, but there is no doubt that it existed. Nicholas Davidson, too, finds clear evidence of unbelief in Italy during the Renaissance period.[2] And it is wrong to argue, as Kristeller does, that Christian convictions were "never really challenged" in this period, or, as Michael Reeve has written, that Italian humanists like Petrarch, Salutati, and Valla failed to make "any distinction of principle between pagan and Christian writers."[3] Instead, a different approach has to be adopted. The difficulty of proving nonbelief has recently led another scholar, Christopher Celenza, to redefine the problem as one of distinguishing orthodoxy not from paganism, but from heterodoxy, where the boundary was much more porous and fluctuating.[4] We know what the Church regarded as heretical from the charges it leveled against teachers and writers in the fifteenth

---

[1] Lucien Febvre, *The Problem of Unbelief in the Sixteenth Century: The Religion of Rabelais* (1942, trans. Cambridge, MA, 1982); Paul Oskar Kristeller, "Paganism and Christianity," in *Renaissance Thought: The Classic, Scholastic and Humanist Strains* (1955, repr. New York, 1961), 71–72, reiterated recently by John Monfasani, "Platonic Paganism in the Fifteenth Century," in *Reconsidering the Renaissance*, ed. Mario di Cesare (Binghamton, 1992), 46. Cf. Jacob Burckhardt, *The Civilisation of the Renaissance in Italy*, trans. Samuel Middlemore (London, 1950), 121.

[2] David Wootton, "Lucien Febvre and the Problem of Unbelief in the Early Modern Period," *Journal of Modern History* 60 (1988): 695–730, and "New Histories of Atheism," in *Atheism from the Reformation to the Enlightenment*, ed. Michael Hunter and David Wootton (Oxford, 1992), 13–53, esp. 16–17, 9, 27, 31; Nicholas Davidson, "Unbelief and Atheism in Italy, 1500–1700," ibid., 55–85, esp. 61–62.

[3] Kristeller, "Paganism and Christianity," 73; Michael Reeve, "Classical Scholarship," in *The Cambridge Companion to Renaissance Humanism*, ed. Jill Kraye (Cambridge, 1996), 24 (contrasting with Poggio's view, cited in chap. 1, p. 00).

[4] Christopher Celenza, "Pythagoras in the Renaissance: The Case of Marsilio Ficino," *Renaissance Quarterly* 52 (1999): 668–69, note 6; id., "Late Antiquity and Florentine Platonism: The 'Post-Plotinian' Ficino," in *Marsilio Ficino: His Theology, His Philosophy, His Legacy*, ed. Michael Allen and Valery Rees (Leiden, 2002), 72–73, cf. Allen's introduction, ibid., xx–xxi.

PREFACE

century, who included a grammar teacher in Borgo San Sepolcro, accused of heresy in 1404 for teaching pagan authors like Seneca, Ovid, and Lucan, as well as Giovanni Pico della Mirandola in the 1480s for his nine hundred *Conclusiones* and his *Heptaplus*.[5] This suggests that it remained troubled by the danger of ancient pagan texts, despite the reconciliation achieved by the Scholastics and by Renaissance syncretists (such as Pico), who argued for the compatibility of ancient and Christian philosophies. That these texts remained dangerous is also suggested by the way Marsilio Ficino and Bartolomeo Scala—two of the earliest initial followers of Lucretius in Florence—referred to his philosophy. Even allowing for their use of poetic license, Ficino's determined assault on the "obstreperous" voice of the Epicureans in his *Platonic Theology* and Scala's reference in one of his fables to their beliefs "circulating everywhere" by the 1480s imply that they may have been more widespread and threatening than we have been led to believe.

This explains the approach I adopt in the chapters that follow, in which I explore—as a "prowler"[6]—the revived interest in Lucretius and Epicurus as one ill-defined area on the frontier dividing orthodoxy from heterodoxy. For even if we cannot speak about individual belief, careful rereading of the evidence shows how these texts helped to change the boundary markers. I have been careful always to track the influence of Lucretius through quotations from *De rerum natura* itself. Far from being filtered, secondhand, through Cicero or through Christian critics like Lactantius, as some scholars suggest, these often lengthy and unfamiliar quotations are primary evidence that the rediscovered text itself was being read—and by men whose interest was not primarily philological, like that of the scholars Poliziano, Pontano, Pomponio Leto, and Michele Marullo, but was, as I have already suggested, more wide ranging. My approach is unashamedly contextual in its attempt to answer the question of why so many ordinary Florentines appeared to be interested in this text—which was my starting point in 1999, in an inaugural lecture in which I first asked the question. It could be argued that this is not a question

---

5 Cited by James Banker, *The Culture of San Sepolcro During the Youth of Piero della Francesca* (Ann Arbor, 2003), 71–76 (with thanks to Donal Cooper for the reference); on Pico's heresy, Alison Brown, "New Light on the Papal Condemnation of Pico's Theses," *Rinascimento* 42 (2006): 357–72.

6 Michel De Certeau's evocative image of the historian, in *The Writing of History* (1975), trans. Tom Conley (New York, 1988). See also Celenza, "Pythagoras in the Renaissance," including 669 on "different antiquities."

we are capable of answering, and that it is the recovery itself, as the quarry pursued by avid "book hunters" in old libraries throughout Europe, that is important. I disagree, since I think it is possible to trace a deeper connection between *De rerum natura* and the interests of its readers, especially the three chancery humanists I devote most attention to, whose curiosity was aroused not by new words or poetic tropes, but by new ideas. This is a short book because I wanted to follow Lucretius's trail through men whose work I am familiar with, where I think I can detect his discreet (and often unnamed) influence on their thinking over a long and sustained period. In each case, however, it is *De rerum natura* itself that provides their starting point, as the source of their interest and inspiration.

The opening chapter of this book describes the awakening interest in Epicureanism before the fifteenth-century discoveries, and then the importance of Florence as a center of interest in Lucretius and Epicurus, after the rediscovery of *De rerum natura* in 1417 and the translation of Diogenes Laertius's *Lives,* including the *Life of Epicurus,* in 1433. The central chapters discuss in turn the importance of the three men (with Marsilio Ficino), whose writings and lectures reveal a shared interest in specific Lucretian themes concerning death, evolution, and the role of fortune. As laymen working in the chancery, Scala, Adriani, and Machiavelli were evidently not inhibited by the concerns of their fellow humanists, scholars like Ficino, Poliziano, and Bartolomeo Fonzio, who we know were worried about the limitations placed on their work by their clerical status. As a result, the chancery humanists evidently felt freer than other humanists to develop their interest in the special topics that interested them. These three chapters are based on previously published material,[7] but here they form a sequential narrative that illustrates the close interweaving of ideas and events in the developing interest in Lucretius among these chancery men.

The first of these central chapters, Chapter 2, describes the early interest in Epicureanism of Ficino and Scala, who were the first Florentines to engage extensively with *De rerum natura* and *The Life of Epicurus,* probably using the

---

[7] "Lucretius and the Epicureans in the Social and Political Context of Renaissance Florence," *I Tatti Studies* 9 (2001): 11–62; "Reinterpeting Renaissance Humanism: Marcello Adriani and the Recovery of Lucretius," in *Interpretations of Renaissance Humanism,* ed. Angelo Mazzocco (Leyden, 2006), 267–91; and "Philosophy and Religion in Machiavelli," in *The Cambridge Companion to Machiavelli,* ed. John Najemy (Cambridge), forthcoming.

texts in Cosimo de' Medici's library; and although it was only Scala who remained an adherent, not Ficino, there are clear signs of Scala's continuing interest in Lucretius, if we look carefully for them, in his writings and fables (illustrated in the frieze decorating his Borgo Pinti palace). This interest he then transmitted to the next generation of scholars in Florence, to Marcello Adriani (who succeeded Scala as first chancellor of Florence in 1498), and then to Niccolò Machiavelli. As I describe in Chapter 3, Adriani revealed Lucretius's influence in the still-unpublished inaugural lectures that he delivered as Angelo Poliziano's successor in the chair of Poetry and Oratory in Florence's university after 1494; and although Lucretius is not always named in them—especially after Savonarola's onslaught on the person who taught that the world was made by atoms, "those tiniest of particles that fly through the air"—he is nevertheless a hitherto undetected presence, if not a leitmotif, running through these annual prolusions that Adriani delivered publicly to the young men of Florence and their parents for twenty-five years. Adriani in turn leads to Machiavelli, who was probably a student of Adriani's and was certainly his close colleague in the Florentine chancery. Lucretius's influence on Machiavelli is the subject of Chapter 4, for which the textual evidence is Machiavelli's autograph transcription of *De rerum natura* in the late 1490s, now Vatican MS Rossi 884, first attributed to Machiavelli by Sergio Bertelli in 1961. Although the manuscript has slowly been generating interest since then, the extent of Lucretius's influence on Machiavelli is still undervalued, partly, perhaps, because Machiavelli never cited him by name and rarely quoted from his poem openly, due to the situation in which he was writing.[8] Considered in the context that I have described, however, it is clear that Lucretius provides an invaluable key to understanding Machiavelli's views about man's nature, religion, and the cosmos.

The approach of these three men to Lucretius stands in contrast to that of humanists like Ficino, Poliziano, and Fonzio, as I describe in Chapter 5,

---

8 Sergio Bertelli, "Notarelle Machiavelliane: un codice di Lucrezio e di Terenzio," *Rivista storica italiana* 73 (1961): 544–53, id., "Ancora su Lucrezio e Machiavelli," ibid., 76 (1964): 774–92. See most recently, Paul Rahe, to whom I am grateful for exchanges of writings and ideas at a late stage of both of our work on the subject: "In the Shadow of Lucretius: The Epicurean Foundations of Machiavelli's Political Thought," *History of Political Thought* 28 (2007): 30–55, rev. in *Against Throne and Altar: Machiavelli and Political Theory under the English Republic* (Cambridge, 2008), 32–34; cf. Jérémie Barthas, "Au fondement intellectuel de l'irréligion machiavélienne, Lucrèce?" in *Sources Antiques de l'Irréligion moderne*, ed. Didier Foucault and Jean-Pierre Cavaillée (Toulouse, 2001), and the recent PhD diss. of Ada Palmer, "Reading Lucretius in the Renaissance" (Harvard University, 2009), which I have not seen.

before going on in this chapter to trace the expanding interest in Lucretius among a network of younger Florentines after 1494. At the center of this network was Lorenzo di Pierfrancesco de' Medici, the son of Scala's first employer and a patron himself of Scala in Scala's old age, closing the circle—as Scala put it, in an unfinished poem *On Trees* that he dedicated to Lorenzo shortly before he died—by returning him "to the port" whence he set out forty years earlier.[9] Lorenzo di Pierfrancesco was also a patron of the Lucretian scholar Michele Marullo, who married Scala's daughter shortly before Scala's death in 1497. Returning to Florence after the revolution in 1494, Lorenzo and his brother Giovanni promoted an alternative culture to replace the Platonizing idealism of his ousted cousins' regime, helping to make Lucretius fashionable among his circle of friends at the same time as Adriani was lecturing on him in the university. Many of Lorenzo di Pierfrancesco's friends were the alienated offspring of former Miceans, and they enable us to map the wider social network of people interested in Lucretius in the late 1490s to early 1500s, artists, writers, and perhaps some libertines or *godenti* as well. One of these friends, Piero Martelli, owned an important printed edition of *De rerum natura* annotated by Marullo (now in Paris; it is described in the concluding Appendix, together with all the other texts I have used in my discussion there of Machiavelli's transcription and its place in the textual tradition); other friends included Tommaso Soderini, who had Lucretian works dedicated to him. Together they document the growing influence of Lucretius and the Epicureans on wider circles in Florence, social and political as well as cultural.

In the course of writing about Lucretius, I have incurred very many debts to institutions, friends, and scholars who have responded to my interest with great generosity. My first debts are owed to my alma mater, London University, where I was first introduced to the Renaissance as an undergraduate—especially by Marion Tooley at Bedford College and by Ernst Gombrich at

---

9 Alison Brown, *Bartolomeo Scala, 1430–1497, Chancellor of Florence* (Princeton, 1979), 273; *De arboribus*, in *Bartolomeo Scala: Humanistic and Political Writings*, ed. Alison Brown (Tempe, AZ, 1997), 426, lines 7–11: "portum indulgere carinae . . . A te principium studiorum et prima iuventa; Haec quoque debentur tibi iam et postrema senectus."

the Warburg Institute—and where, at Royal Holloway, I later spent most of my teaching life and delivered my inaugural lecture, "Civilizing the Centaur: The Evolution of Renaissance Man," in 1999. I am also greatly indebted to the Harvard Center for Italian Renaissance Studies at the Villa I Tatti, which has nourished and supported my work over many years under its directors Walter Kaiser and Joseph Connors. So I am very pleased that I can, like Scala, publish this work at Harvard under the aegis of I Tatti as the port that helped to launch it and has now steered it safely into print—thanks in no small part to the series' editor, Edward Muir, and especially to the editorial skills and dedication of Jennifer Snodgrass, Liz Duvall, and Justine Rathbun. I also owe a debt of gratitude to the libraries holding Lucretius's manuscripts and their librarians, especially those at the Biblioteca Laurenziana, the Biblioteca Riccardiana, and the Biblioteca Nationale in Florence; the Vatican library in Rome; and the British Library in London. In addition, I have received help from librarians at the Bibliothèque Nationale in Paris, the Staatsbibliotek in Munich, and from François Quiviger at the Warburg Institute in London. Among the many friends and scholars who have helped me in my work on Lucretius, I must particularly thank the editors of my first essay on Lucretius for *I Tatti Studies,* Caroline Elam, Bill Kent, and David Quint; my second editor, Angelo Mazzocco, for the scrupulous care with which he edited my contribution to his book; and especially John Najemy, who has always shared my interest in Lucretius and whom I would especially like to thank for the stimulus he has given me and for the care he has devoted to editing my work for the *Cambridge Companion to Machiavelli.* Foremost among the other scholars who share this interest and have provided me with help in important ways is James Hankins, who enabled me to read his recent work on Ficino before its publication (see p. 92, note 12 below) and, more importantly, has given me invaluable help through his many constructive comments on this book, especially concerning Renaissance philosophy, and through his helpful suggestions for clarifying and improving it. Luca Boschetto is another friend I want to thank, especially for the information he gave about Epicureanism in the papal court in the 1430s. I am similarly grateful to David Marsh, Jonathan Nelson, Jonathan Davies, Jill Burke, and my daughter Charlotte Brown, an expert on incunabula, all of whom—and many others—have given me generous help in writing this book.

Abbreviations

ASF	*Archivio di Stato, Florence*
ASI	*Archivio storico italiano*
BNF	*Biblioteca Nazionale, Florence*
CTC	*Catalogus Translationum et Commentariorum*
DBI	*Dizionario biografico degli italiani (Rome, 1960–)*
GC	*Ginori Conti Archive in the Biblioteca Nazionale, Florence*
JWCI	*Journal of the Warburg and Courtauld Institutes*
MAP	*Fondo Mediceo avanti il Principato, Archivio di Stato, Florence*
L	*Florence, Biblioteca Laurenziana, MS Laur. 90, sup. 39*
N	*BNF, MS II, V. 78*
R	*Florence, Biblioteca Riccardiana, MS 811*

THE RETURN OF LUCRETIUS TO RENAISSANCE FLORENCE

I

The Epicurean Revival in Florence and Italy

The story of the recovery of Lucretius and Epicureanism in the fifteenth century has long been familiar in outline. Following a brief Carolingian renaissance, Lucretius "went underground" for about five hundred years before being unearthed by Poggio Bracciolini in 1417; after an anxious period in which the manuscript of *De rerum natura* he lent to his friend Niccolò Niccoli disappeared, it was then copied in sufficient manuscripts (fifty-five survive today) and printed editions to ensure that it never disappeared again.[1] Another source that helped to recover knowledge of Epicurean philosophy was Diogenes Laertius's biography of Epicurus, which was contained in the manuscript of his *Lives of Eminent Philosophers*, brought from Constantinople in 1416. After being translated into Latin by Ambrogio Tra-

---

1 Poggio Bracciolini, *Lettere*, ed. Helene Harth (Florence, 1984), 1: 89, 103, 142, 144, 149, 172, 187; Leighton Reynolds, *Texts and Transmissions: A Survey of the Latin Classics* (Oxford, 1982), 220; Michael Reeve, "The Italian Tradition of Lucretius Revisited," *Aevum* 79 (2005) (Reeve [II]): 121, updating Reeve [I] and followed by Reeve [III], all listed in the bibliography below). Cosmo Gordon lists four different printed editions before the Florentine Giunti edition of 1512, in *A Bibliography of Lucretius* (London, 1962), 49–53.

versari in 1433, it too was repeatedly copied and printed (forty-eight fifteenth-century manuscripts survive, with seven different printed editions between 1472 and 1497).[2] Together, we are told, these texts sparked the "radical naturalism" and "new vision of the world" that has traditionally marked the Renaissance period, Lucretius's opening invocation to Venus, goddess of love and mother of burgeoning nature, being an inspiration not only to Virgil in his own day but to Renaissance poets and artists as well.[3]

We now know a little more of the whereabouts of *De rerum natura* before it was rediscovered by Poggio. It was listed in only two Carolingian libraries, at Murbach and Bobbio, and in three libraries in France in the twelfth century, including St. Bertin, the home of one of the two surviving ninth-century manuscripts now at Leiden (the other is in Mainz). Nevertheless, it remains true that "it was seldom read in the Middle Ages"—a "striking example," we are told, "of how a text can circulate in the ninth century and then virtually disappear from sight for the rest of the Middle Ages," when it was known mainly through some fragments in Vienna and Copenhagen, and through Priscian, Isidore of Seville, and some medieval florilegia.[4] Epicurus was more familiar, thanks to the influence of Seneca's *Letters,* Cicero's dialogues *in utramque partem,* and the more critical patristic writings of St. Augustine and Lactantius.[5] Despite a few countervailing voices asserting his his-

---

[2] Marcello Gigante, "Ambrogio Traversari interprete di Diogene Laerzio," in *Ambrogio Traversari nel VI centenario della nascita*, ed. Gian Carlo Garfagnini (Florence, 1988), 367–459; Agostino Sottili, "Il Laerzio latino e greco e altri autografi di Ambrogio Traversari," in *Vestigia: Studi in onore di Giuseppe Billanovich*, ed. Rino Avesani et al. (Rome, 1984), 2: 704–7 and note 21; Maria Pagnoni, "Prime note sulla tradizione medioevale ed umanistica di Epicuro," *Annali della Scuola Normale Superiore di Pisa* s. 3, 44 (1974): 1143–77, at 1459, note 74.

[3] Eugenio Garin, "Ricerche sull' Epicureismo del Quattrocento," in id., *La Cultura filosofica del Rinascimento italiano* (Florence, 1979), 75, 77, 85–86; Richard Jenkyns, *Virgil's Experience. Nature and History: Times, Names and Places* (Oxford, 1998), 211–15.

[4] David Ganz, "Lucretius in the Carolingian Age: The Leiden Manuscripts and Their Carolingian Readers," in *Medieval Manuscripts of the Latin Classics: Production and Use*, ed. Claudine Chavannes-Mazel and Margaret Smith (London, 1996), 91–92, 100 (it was used "to learn how to scan Latin words"); cf. Wolfgang Fleischmann, in *Catalogus translationum et Commentariorum*, ed. Paul Oskar Kristeller and Ferdinand Cranz (Washington, DC, 1971), 1: 349–65; Monte Johnson and Catherine Wilson, "Lucretius and the History of Science," in *Cambridge Companion to Lucretius*, ed. Stuart Gillespie and Philip Hardie (Cambridge, 2007), 131–48 at 132 (referring to William of Conches in the twelfth century); Michael Reeve, "Lucretius in the Middle Ages and Early Renaissance," ibid., 205–13; George Hadzsits, *Lucretius and His Influence* (London, 1935). I quote Leighton Reynolds and Nigel Wilson, *Scribes & Scholars: A Guide to the Transmission of Greek and Latin Literature*. 3rd ed. (Oxford, 1991), 112.

[5] Pagnoni, "Prime note," 1454–55, citing the positive evaluation of Thomas Aquinas, *In X libros Ethicorum Aristotelis ad Nicomachum expositio*, I.1.5; Alexander Murray, "The Epicureans," in *Intellectuals and Writers in Fourteenth-Century Europe*, ed. Piero Boitani and Anna Torti (Cambridge, 1986), 138–63;

torical persona, it was Epicurus's posthumous reputation for hedonism that dominated his—and Lucretius's—medieval reception, transmitted through sources like Horace's letters, where he refers to himself (ironically) as one of "the pigs from Epicurus's herd."[6] What made these writers even more threatening to believing Christians were their underlying ideas about the universe, which, as we have seen, contradicted the biblical account of creation and the afterlife, with its promise of due retribution for good and bad behavior in this life.[7] Not surprisingly, then, Dante buried the Epicureans apart from the other heretics in Book 10 of *The Divine Comedy*, since they alone believed "that man's soul, when his body does, will die," and this, as Cristoforo Landino explained in his influential 1481 *Commentary* on Dante, "removes every basis for right living in civil society and for true religion."[8]

Despite this, a new interest in Epicurus was developing even before the recovery of these texts, especially in thirteenth- and fourteenth-century Florence. Even if the earlier pleasure-loving sensuality described by the historian Giovanni Villani hardly constituted an Epicurean cult or "sect," there was undoubtedly a shift in attitude in the course of the fourteenth century. A recent subtle rereading of Boccaccio's approach to Epicurus in four of his writings—in the poem "Phylostropos," in two stories in *The Decameron*, and in his commentary on Dante—shows how Boccaccio challenged the predominant perception of Epicurus by pointing up the values he espoused of friendship and moral probity against the vulgar Aristippean hedonism attributed to him, warning us as readers not to be deceived by "mistaken opinions."[9] Another sign of a more balanced assessment of Epicurus comes from a late-

---

Riccardo Fubini, "Note su Lorenzo Valla e la composizione del 'De voluptate,'" in *I Classici nel Medievo e nell'Umanesimo: Miscellanea filologica* (Genoa, 1975), esp. 22–44 (discussing Cicero's *De finibus* as a source for reevaluating Epicurus on 24–25, 35). Cf. Cicero, *Tusc. Disp.*, 3, xx, 46, that Epicurus spoke "multa severe, multa praeclare."

6 Horace, *Epist.*, 1, 5, 16: "Epicuri de grege porcum."

7 See Lucretius, *De rerum natura* (subsequently, Lucretius) 2: 180–81: "nequaquam nobis divinitus esse creatam / naturam mundi"; 3: 161–62: "naturam animi atque animai / corpoream docet esse"; 470: "quare animum quoque dissolui fateare necessest"; and the introduction above.

8 Dante, *Divine Comedy* 10: 1–15: "da questa parte hanno / con Epicuro tutti i suoi seguaci, / che l'anima col corpo morta fanno"; Landino, *Commentary* (Florence: Nicholas Alamannus, 1481), fol. g6r, ed. Paolo Procaccioli (Rome, 2001), 2: 581: "Imperoché chi pone l'anima mortale toglie ogni fondamento al giusto vivere civile et alla vera religione."

9 Zygmunt Baranski, "Boccaccio and Epicurus," in *Caro Vitto: Essays in Memory of Vittore Branca*, ed. Jill Kraye and Laura Lepschy (London, 2007), 10–27, "da oppinione ingannati" (19); he cites *Buccolicum carmen* (eclogue 15 in *Tutte le opere*, Milan, 1964–), 5: ii, 880–93, *Decameron*, ed. Vittore Branca (Turin, 1987), 6: 9 and 10: 8; *Esposizioni sopra la Comedia di Dante, Tutte le opere* 6: 515–16.

fourteenth-century manuscript owned by Zanobi Guasconi, a Dominican friar at Santa Maria Novella, which contains a not unsympathetic account of Epicurus among its alphabetically arranged lives of philosophers.[10] For although the life of Epicurus stated that he erred "more than all the other philosophers" in his beliefs—which it accurately summarized as believing that the gods were indifferent to human affairs, the world was everlasting and not ruled by divine providence, the soul died with the body, and pleasure was the highest good—it nevertheless marks a new approach in expressing its admiration for Epicurus's "many notable writings."[11]

Boccaccio's rehabilitation of Epicurus in this new reading shows how delicately we too have to tread in recovering the "new" Epicurus from his "complex, confused and contradictory" medieval reception.[12] For although on one hand there is clear evidence of a growing interest in Epicurus in humanist circles in the early fifteenth century, we also know that this was a period of "marked clericalization" in which—as we have seen—it was unthinkable not to have been a Christian. For this reason, it is argued that in Naples the scholars at the center of another Lucretian network—Pontano, Marullo, and Lorenzo Bonincontri, who wrote scientific poems and *Hymns to Nature*—all exploited Epicureanism "by recalling Lucretius and then by deliberately rejecting Epicurean arguments to reinforce their own Christian positions."[13] The Church provided a career structure for nearly all Renaissance scholars, including Poggio Bracciolini, who, after reading Antonio Beccadelli's (Panormita) *Hermaphroditus*, reprimanded him by telling him that "the same license, you know, is not given to us Christians as was given to the poets of old who did not know God."[14] As well as working in the papal curia as secretaries and

---

10 BNF, Conventi Soppressi G. 4. 1111, referred to by Christopher Celenza, "Pythagoras in the Renaissance: The Case of Marsilio Ficino," *Renaissance Quarterly* 52 (1999): 680–81.

11 MS cit., fol. 45v: "Epicurus atheniensis philosophus quavis multa preclara documenta reliquentur multa etiam notabilia scripserit, plusquam omnes alios tamen philosophos erravit," going on to quote Seneca and Lactantius.

12 Baranski, "Boccaccio and Epicurus," 19–20, 14.

13 Charlotte Goddard, "Epicureanism and the Poetry of Lucretius in the Renaissance," PhD diss., Cambridge University (1991), 3, ead., "Pontano's Use of the Didactic Genre: Rhetoric, Irony and the Manipulation of Lucretius in *Urania*," *Renaissance Studies* 5 (1991): 257; cf. Jill Kraye, "Epicureanism," in *The Cambridge Companion to Renaissance Philosophy*, ed. James Hankins (Cambridge, 2007): 102–6. Riccardo Fubini calls the period "un'epoca di già spiccata clericalizzazione della cultura" in "Ficino e i Medici all'avvento di Lorenzo il Magnifico," *Rinascimento* 24 (1984): 13, repr. in id., *Quattrocento Fiorentino: politica, diplomazia, cultura* (Pisa, 1996), 245.

14 Cited by Eugene O'Connor, "Panormita's Reply to His Critics: The *Hermaphroditus* and the

abbreviators, humanists were often given benefices with the cure of souls as a form of academic patronage, to enable them to continue their studies. In 1510, one of these humanists, Bartolomeo Fonzio, reflected on the problem this created for beneficed humanists like himself, Angelo Poliziano, and Marsilio Ficino, and how different things were for "Scala, Landino, Pico, Nesi, and Crinito," who could publish what they wanted, unimpeded by religion. "We ministers of God," he went on, "*can* indeed publish what we wrote when we were still laymen, but whether we *should* do so, with a sound conscience, I don't know."[15]

The fact that religion was seen to be an impediment to humanist studies suggests that there was more tension between Christianity and ancient philosophy than historians like Kristeller suggest, at least by the early sixteenth century. A century earlier, at the time of what George Holmes calls the "Humanist Avant-garde" in Florence, the situation was rather different, due to the Schism and later the ten-year residency of the Roman pope in Florence. Familiarity, if not breeding contempt, bred a spirit of nonsubservience and "equivocal disillusionment" towards the papacy, according to Holmes, that helped the new ideas of the avant-garde to grow.[16] This is the context in which a new interest in Epicurean *voluptas* began to develop in the early fifteenth century. The first evidence of change is provided by Leonardo Bruni's *Isagogicon*, written between 1424 and 1426, in which he argued that there was little to distinguish Epicurus's views on the close relationship between pleasure and the good moral life from those of the other two major philosophical sects, the Aristotelians and the Stoics.[17] Although there was no obvious connection between Bruni's *Isagogicon* and the "robustly hedonistic" *Defense of Epicurus*

Literary Defense," *Renaissance Quarterly* 50 (1997): 997: "Scis enim non licere idem nobis, qui Christiani sumus, quod olim poetis qui Deum ignorabant." Traversari's scruples about translating Diogenes Laertius and his means of resolving them are discussed by Gigante, "Ambrogio Traversari," 394–404.

15 Bartolomeo Fonzio to Ioanfrancesco Zeffio, 11 September 1510, *Epistolarum libri III*, ed. Laszio Juhasz (Budapest, 1931), 49: "Nam Politiani Ficinique exceptis . . . longe alia fuit ratio Schalae, Landini, Pici, Nesii et Criniti, qui dare in lucem quae poterant etiam debebant, nulla religione impediente. Nos vero ministri Dei possumus quidem, sed nescio quae saeculares adhuc lusimus an salva conscientia debeamus."

16 George Holmes, *The Florentine Enlightenment, 1400–50* (London, 1969), at 53, cf. 63, 67.

17 *Isagogicon*, ed. Hans Baron, in *Humanistisch-philosophische Schriften* (Leipzig-Berlin, 1928), 23–28, trans. and discussed by James Hankins in *The Humanism of Leonardo Bruni*, ed. Gordon Griffiths, Jim Hankins, and David Thompson (Binghamton, 1987), 257–58, 270–73; cf. Fubini, "Note sul Lorenzo Valla," 24–28.

written around 1429 by the Cremonese Cosma Raimondi, both used Cicero's discussion of ancient sects in *De finibus* as a starting point, even if the influence of Aristotelian-Averroist naturalism made Raimondi's Epicureanism more openly irreligious than Bruni's.[18] Raimondi's *Defense* in turn influenced the better-known *De voluptate* (later *De vero bono*) of Lorenzo Valla, who was teaching in Pavia at the same time as Raimondi in 1430–1431.[19] In Valla's dialogue, the Epicurean interlocutor is given the name of "Panormita," a suitable protagonist of a dialogue about pleasure in view of his *Hermaphroditus*, referred to above, a collection of lascivious epigrams that initially received warm support from scholars and patrons like Cosimo de' Medici (to whom it was dedicated in 1425) before a backlash condemned it to the flames.[20] Beccadelli also provides a tenuous link to Lucretius and the later Lucretianism of the academy in Naples that he helped to found, since it seems that in 1427 he had enjoyed an early sighting of Poggio's Lucretius in Florence, when it was still in Niccoli's possession and before he himself owned a copy of Lucretius in the early 1440s.[21]

Once the papal court was established in Florence in 1434, we have evidence that other humanists had access to Poggio's Lucretius or to copies made from it. A letter written by Lapo da Castilionchio to the apostolic protonotary Gregorio Correr reveals that Correr had criticized him for referring to fortune in his letters, which he believed was wicked for Christians even to mention.[22] In responding to Correr that he was far from being "one of those who attribute everything to fortune and believe that no world is moved by a single controller—as one poet, I don't know who, has it," Lapo makes it clear that the poet was Lucretius, whom he also cites in his *De curiae commodis*,

---

18 Fubini, "Note sul Lorenzo Valla," 37–39; Martin Davies, "Cosma Raimondi's Defence of Epicurus," *Rinascimento* 27 (1987): 123–39.

19 Fubini, "Note," especially 40–44; cf. Pagnoni, "Prime note," 1461–67, and Maristella Lorch, "The Epicurean in Lorenzo Valla's *On Pleasure*," in *Atoms, Pneuma, and Tranquillity: Epicurean and Stoic Themes in European Thought*, ed. Margaret Osler (Cambridge, 1991), 89–114.

20 On Beccadelli, see Gianvito Resta in *DBI* 7 (Rome, 1965): 400–406; Michael de Cossart, *Antonio Beccadelli and the Hermaphrodite* (Liverpool, 1984), preface to his translation.

21 Goddard, "Epicureanism," 30–31.

22 Lapo to Gregorio Correr, 7 July [1436], replying to Correr's letter of 1 July, in *Opere di Gregorio Correr*, ed. Aldo Onorato (Messina, 1994), 2: 457, 460–61. For this reference, I am indebted to Luca Boschetto, who generously told me about this letter and about recent work on Alberti (referred to in note 24 below); see his forthcoming book, *"Quando Papa Eugenio fu a Firenze": Cortegiani, mercanti e umanisti nella Citta' del Concilio, 1434–1443* (Rome).

written just before his death in 1438.²³ Another reader of Lucretius attached to the papal court is Lapo's friend Leon Battista Alberti. According to a recent account, Alberti's library is not "an obvious library" in that it contained many newly discovered texts, such as Lucretius, which he utilized "in a very precocious way."²⁴ Although there are only two direct quotations from *De rerum natura* in his writings—a passage about old age in the *Theogenius* (where he is quoted, interestingly, in Italian), and one in *De re aedificatoria*—there are numerous other allusions that show Lucretius's influence, as well as many direct references to Epicurus taken from Diogenes Laertius's *Life*.²⁵ Most striking are Alberti's descriptions of the force of animal love and desire to copulate in the *Libri della famiglia*, written in the 1430s, and his later ironic reflections in the *Theogenius* about the limited achievements of civilization: not only is man always subjected to the force and power of animals, despite being born nude and learning through his intelligence to survive and rule over them, but he alone is responsible for adulterating nature by excavating metals and gems, and then gashing them to create new forms, and by cutting and grafting trees to make new species—the latter providing a link to the same theme in Bartolomeo Scala's long poem *On Trees*, discussed in Chapter 2.²⁶ His satire on the gods, *Momus*, also contains many allusions to Epicurean ideas about the

---

23 Ibid., 461: "Verum nolim opineris me ex illis esse, qui fortune sub casibus omnia ponant et nullum credant mundum rectore moveri, ut est apud poetam nescio quem . . . longe ego aliter sentio" (cf. Lucretius 2: 180, 251–57, etc.); *De curiae commodis*, 8, 46–47 (cf. Lucretius 5: 1275–78), ed. Christopher Celenza, *Renaissance Humanism and the Papal Curia* (Ann Arbor, 1999), 213, who refers to it as "a Lucretianizing passage" (75), 8–51; Riccardo Fubini, in *DBI* 22 (Rome, 1979): 47.

24 Mariangela Regoliosi, "Per un catalogo degli *auctores* latini dell'Alberti," in *Leon Battista Alberti: La Biblioteca di un umanista*, ed. Roberto Cardini (Florence, 2005), 107: it is not "una biblioteca 'ovvia' . . . Lucrezio . . . è utilizzato in un modo precocissimo," 110; cf. Scheda 88 (by Nicholetta Marcelli), listing citations from Lucretius, ibid., 448–49.

25 Lucretius 3: 451–54, quoted in *Theogenius, Opere volgari*, ed. Cecil Grayson (Bari, 1966), 2: 101; cf. Susanna Gambino, "Alberti Lettore di Lucrezio: Motivi lucreziani nel Theogenius," *Albertiana* 4 (2001): 82–83 and Lucretius 2: 24–26 (on golden statues of youths holding flaming torches in the house), quoted in *De re aedificatoria* 9: 1. Epicurus is quoted in Alberti, *Libri della Famiglia*, ed. Grayson, cit., 1: 91–92, 103–4, 131, 337; in *Theogenius*, ibid., 2: 75, 102; and in *Profugiorum ab aerumna* 2: 126; Gambino, 77–79.

26 Alberti, *della Famiglia* 1: 87–88; Lucretius 1: 1–5, 14–20; 4: 1052–56; *Theogenius*, ibid., 2: 89–90, 92–93; Lucretius 5: 222–34, 1241–76, 1297–340; cf. Gambino, "Alberti lettore di Lucrezio," 79–82; Regoliosi, "Per un catalogo," 110. The passage on the force of love is discussed more fully by John Najemy, "Alberti on Love: Musings on Transgression and Discipline," in *Public Life, Gender and Private Conduct across the Early Modern and Modern World: Essays in Honour of Richard C. Trexler*, ed. Peter Arnade and Michael Rocke (Toronto, 2008), 139–40, first presented in a paper given in 2000.

chance creation of the world and the minimal role in it played by the gods, which are drawn from both Lucretius and Diogenes Laertius.[27]

As a priest enjoying a benefice with the cure of souls in San Martino at Gangalandi near Florence, Alberti is unlikely to have needed Poggio's warning about the dangers of unorthodoxy—any more than Poggio did himself, the rediscoverer of Lucretius, who was a papal secretary from 1423 until 1453, in minor orders until his marriage in 1436, and subsequently chancellor of Florence.[28] Like Alberti, Poggio seldom quoted Lucretius directly, but his world-weary writings reveal many of the same attitudes as Alberti's, and they are drawn from many of the same sources. The dialogue *De infelicitate principum* contains several Lucretian references—to man's blindness, for example, and to happiness residing not in gold and silver but in looking down on others' miseries while totally free from care and ambition oneself—and so does his later *De miseria conditionis humanae*.[29] But it is his *Historia de varietate fortunae*, begun in the early 1430s and completed in 1448, that best represents what has been described as Poggio's distinctive outlook or "voice": his relativistic view of the world as a theater subject to the play of fortune, which is illustrated in the last book of this *History* by the accounts of several travelers who came to Florence for the Ecumenical Council in 1439, "from almost outside the world itself."[30] His discussion of fortune does not in itself make him a Lucretian, although, in the case of Lapo da Castilionchio, its mention was sufficient, as we saw, to suggest Lucretian impiety. Another hint of Lucretius's influence comes from Poggio's view of the world as a theater, recalling Lucretius's vivid depictions of the Roman theater bathed in the light reflected from its tent coverings, which Lucretius used to teach lessons not only about

---

27 *Momus* 2: 75, 79, 80, 86; 4: 10, trans. and ed. Sarah Knight with Virginia Brown (Cambridge, MA, 2003), 155, 159, 388–89 (notes 12, 13, 14, 17).
28 See Riccardo Fubini, "Umanesimo e società civile in Poggio Bracciolini," in id., *Quattrocento fiorentino*, 222, 224–25.
29 *De infelicitate principum*, ed. David Canfora (Rome, 1998), 6, 22, 58, 60, reflecting Lucretius 2: 14, 45–46, 48; 1: 54–56, 127–35; 2: 6–16; 3: 58; *De miseria conditionis humanae*, Opera omnia 1 (1538, repr. Turin, 1964): 93, 101–2, 110, reflecting Lucretius 1: 93; 5: 821–22; 2: 598–99.
30 *Opera omnia* 2, ed. Riccardo Fubini (Turin, 1966): 628: "ab extremis orbis finibus." Fubini describes "la peculiarità della sua voce" and his empiricism and relativism in "Il 'Teatro del mondo' nelle prospettive morali e storico-politiche di Poggio Bracciolini," in *Poggio Bracciolini, 1380–1980 nel VI centenario della nascita* (Florence, 1982), 1, 10; on the "schietti motivi epicurei" in his writings (though not in *De varietate*), 26–27. According to Martin Davies, "Poggio never quotes Lucretius" ("Cosma Raimondi," 124, note 7).

sensory perception—"reality" being in fact merely a "theatrical" sequence of *simulacra*—but also about Epicurean ethics, according to which the only wise ethical stance is to see life at a safe distance, as if it were a theater show.³¹

Poggio provides a link between the world of the curial humanists who read and referred allusively to Lucretius in the 1430s and 1440s and the secular world of Florentine merchants and travelers, who were already open to these new ideas. In the absence of a well-established university in Florence, the impetus for the new learning came from the interchange of ideas between scholars and merchants in squares and piazzas, in private homes, in monasteries, and in the cathedral. Antedating the arrival of the curialists in Florence in the 1430s, an established "seminar group" (as it has been called) already existed in the city, a circle of men who gathered to learn Greek from Manuel Chrysoloras around 1400. By including a cross section of the new intelligentsia—mathematicians, artists, merchants, theologians, and humanist administrators—it ensured that the newly recovered book of Ptolemy's *Geography* served not only as a language manual for learning Greek, but also as a stimulus to artists to learn the science of perspective and to explorers to envisage an encompassable world. Florentine merchants were already sailing the world, and shortly after acquiring the ports of Porto Pisano and Livorno in 1421, the city established its own maritime fleet under the control of six sea consuls, intensifying the city's interest in travel and exploration.³² The interest in Ptolemy's *Geography* in this environment rapidly transformed the city into a center for cartographic and geographical study, ensuring that books became the medium through which the scholarly pursuits of curialists became integrated with the business and trading life of Florence.³³

So it was perhaps not surprising that it was the fourth book of Poggio Bracciolini's *De varietate fortunae* that won immediate popularity, being translated and then widely diffused as a separate volume. It was this book that contained his account of the far-flung travels of several visitors to the 1439

---

31 See John Godwin, *Lucretius* (Bristol, 2004), especially 96–97, 104–11; Lucretius 4: 75–89, 29, and ff.; 2: 1–15, 37–58; 3: 58.

32 Michael Mallett, *The Florentine Galleys in the Fifteenth Century* (Oxford, 1967), 21–23.

33 Samuel Edgerton, *The Renaissance Rediscovery of Linear Perspective* (New York, 1975), 93–94, 97–99; also *Firenze e la scoperta dell' America: umanesimo e geografia nell'400 Fiorentino*, ed. Sebastiano Gentile (Florence, 1992), the catalog listing many of these manuscripts, including the *Cosmographia* probably given to Palla Strozzi by Chrysoloras, 77–90 (no. 38, cf. 37 and 43); Jerry Brotton, *Trading Territories: Mapping the Early Modern World* (London, 1997), 87–90, 93–94.

Council, including a Venetian merchant home from India, a northern Indian (understood through an Armenian interpreter), and some Ethiopians, who reported the existence of peoples beyond the limits of the world recognized by Ptolemy. They were all interviewed by Poggio, who found Conti's account of his journey "to such remote peoples, where they were sited, their different customs, and especially about their animals and trees" so gripping and so credible that he decided to record what he had heard as "worthy of being known."[34]

The subject of Poggio's book, "the variety of fortune," was itself a topic that interested Florence's merchants, who were all too aware of the sudden changes fortune could bring to their businesses through storms at sea (the other meaning of *fortuna* in Latin and Italian) and through financial crashes. Some years before Machiavelli famously wrote about the power of fortune in *The Prince* (with a different emphasis, as we shall see), the Florentine merchant Giovanni Rucellai set down his own opinion for the benefit of his children—that although good sense and prudence can mostly resist fortune, yielding to its force may be the best policy. But because "philosophers and authors" had opposing views about it (which he carefully described for his children), he also asked Marsilio Ficino for his opinion, which he then copied into his commonplace book as well. Interestingly, Lucretius was not among the authors he cited, showing that in the mid-fifteenth century, *De rerum natura* was not part of the culture of merchants like Rucellai, although it was soon to enter their world.[35]

Another facet of this openness was Florence's religious heterodoxy, which encouraged the early outburst of hedonism and Epicureanism, as well as Catharism, in the thirteenth and fourteenth centuries. Nor was skepticism about revealed religion confined to upper-class families like the Pulci, since Italian city dwellers were as distrustful as the peasants in Montaillou of ideas that ran counter to their everyday experience. A Dominican sermon in Flor-

---

34 Poggio, *Opera omnia* 2: 628: "ad tam remotas gentes, de Indorum situ, ac moribus variis, praeterea animantibus atque arboribus . . . scite graviterque disseruit, ut non fingere, sed vera referre appareret," 651: "digna scitu visa sunt, quae litteris mandarentur," and note 30 above; cf. *Firenze e la scoperta*, ed. Gentile, 168–73 (nos. 81 and 82).

35 "Cos'è Fortuna," in *Giovanni Rucellai ed il suo Zibaldone*, ed. Alessandro Perosa (London, 1960), 1: 103–16, cf. id. (London, 1981), 2: 140. It is discussed, together with the banker Francesco Sassetti's will, by Aby Warburg, *The Renewal of Pagan Antiquity* (1932, trans. Los Angeles, 1999), 223–62, esp. 240–42 and 255–58. Sassetti did own a copy of *De rerum natura* (see chap. 5 below), but it is not referred to by Warburg.

ence's cathedral in 1305 claimed that people no longer believed either in paradise or in hell, and six years earlier a businessman of Tuscan origin denied the possibility of resurrection.[36] Although this is not the same as denying God altogether, it may—as Susan Reynolds has said—be just as serious, in implying the possibility of unbelief; for if people say that they do not believe in important Christian doctrines, "then unbelief was not impossible for them."[37] And what was true of the thirteenth and fourteenth centuries is also true of the fifteenth. Among the heresies that Cristoforo Landino listed as alive in his day, in his 1481 Dante *Commentary*, was the Patarine belief that "our bodies won't rise again," that it is "a mortal sin to kill any animal excepting fish, fleas and lice," and that "usury is not a sin if done without fraud"—suggesting perhaps some continuity between the early Catharism of merchant and banking families in Florence like the Pulci and the heretical views of the Medici poet Luigi Pulci in the fifteenth century, who was deprived of a Christian burial *ob scripta prophana prophano in loco*, that is, for decrying miracles and describing the soul as "no more than a pine nut in hot white bread."[38] We are also told that the chancellor Carlo Marsuppini, who taught Greek oratory and poetry in the university, died in 1453 "without confessing and communion and not as a good Christian." This, another Florentine, Francesco Giovanni, wrote in his diary, made it difficult to record anything about "the matter of his soul," especially since he also left no instructions about "the distribution of his possessions"; that someone could be "so farsighted in life and then so totally blind when he came to die" was a cause for amazement among the people: "May God let him rest in peace if it pleases him to do so."[39]

---

36 Alexander Murray, "Piety and Impiety in Thirteenth-Century Italy," *Studies in Church History* 8 (1972): 101; id., "The Epicureans," 149–50; cf. Carol Lansing, *Power and Purity: Cathar Heresy in Medieval Italy* (New York, 1998), 96–105; and John Stephens, "Heresy in Medieval and Renaissance Florence," *Past and Present* 54 (1972): 26–36, 59.

37 Susan Reynolds, "Social Mentalities and the Case of Medieval Scepticism," *Transactions of the Royal Historical Society*, ser. 6, 1 (1991): 36: "even if their grounds for doubting were not the same as those of, for instance, Lucien Febvre."

38 Landino, *Commentary*, fol. g3v, ed. Procaccioli, 2: 572–73; Paolo Orvieto, "A proposito del Sonetto *Costor che fan sì gran disputazione* e dei sonetti responsivi," *Interpres* 4 (1981–1982): 400–13: "L'anima è sol . . . in un pan bianco caldo un pinocchiato" (with the reply, "Tu nneghi l'anima essere immortale"), who now attributes it to Bartolomeo Dei, "forse ricorrendo alla consulenza poetica del Pulci" (409); cf. Lorenz Böninger, "Notes on the Last Years of Luigi Pulci (1477–1484)," *Rinascimento* 27 (1987): 261, 271; Constance Jordan, *Pulci's Morgante: Poetry and History in Fifteenth-Century Florence* (Washington, DC, 1986), 38–42; Lansing, *Power and Purity*, 71–78.

39 Giovanni Cambi, *Istorie*, in *Delizie degli eruditi toscani*, ed. Ildefonso di San Luigi (Florence, 1785), 20: 311: "Dio l'abia honorato in Cielo, se l'à meritato, che non si stima perché morì senza chon-

Neither Marsuppini nor Pulci typify popular unbelief in Florence, since one was a learned humanist and the other an irreverent parodist of the recondite debates in Medici circles in the 1470s about the soul, "where it enters and where it leaves." Yet Pulci belongs to the tradition of versifying represented by Burchiello that does throw light on popular attitudes towards religion. The lines in Pulci's *Morgante,* for instance—"but what rises, in the end descends . . . while one rises, another falls, as perhaps happens with Christianity"—are reflected in the verse, or *frottola,* with which a printed pamphlet attacking Savonarola in 1496 ends: "He who hasn't too much faith doesn't sin or fail too much, when dead he returns afloat; who is dead goes to the bottom, and this is what happens in the world."[40] Forty years later, Bartolomeo Cerretani documented the same fatalism in his *Dialogo della mutatione di Firenze,* where he wrote that most people went to church out of shame and fear, but neither they, nor the prelates who ministered to them, believed in God and in the incarnation of his son, but instead "that the world has always existed, exists, and will exist . . . and that once dead, everything is over for man."[41]

Florentine skepticism about religion and openness to novelty was nevertheless counterbalanced by religious traditionalism and the hostility of friars trained since the thirteenth century to combat unorthodoxy—such as Giovanni Dominici and later Savonarola, both of whom vigorously attacked the new learning with threats of spiritual retribution in the next world. Fueled by mendicant sermons and repeated cycles of plague, sin and fear were domi-

---

fessione e chomunione, e non come buono christiano"; Francesco di Tommaso Giovanni, *Ricordanze,* ASF Carte Strozziane, ser. 2, 16 bis, fol. 16v: "Circha il fatto dell'anima pocha memoria si può farne, et per lo simile nessuno ordine lasciò circa la stributione di sue sustanze. Delle quali cose admiratione maxime dette al popolo, essendo sì antiveduto [sic] in vita et poi sì acecato in tutto in morte. Idio lo ripose in pace se è suo piacere . . ."

40 Luigi Pulci, *Il Morgante,* XXVI, ed. Domenico De Robertis (Florence, 1962), 31: 785: "Ma ciò che sale, alfin vien poi in bassezza . . . mentre l'una sormonta, un'altra cade: così fia forse di cristianitade"; *Epistola consolatoria de' Caldi, Freddi & Tiepidi & una frottola insieme* (Florence, Lorenzo Morgiani, 1496): "chi non ha troppa fede / troppo non pecca o falla / morto ritorna a ghalla / chi morto è ito al fondo / così interviene al mondo," discussed by Alison Brown, "Ideology and Faction in Savonarolan Florence," in *The World of Savonarola,* ed. Stella Fletcher and Christine Shaw (Aldershot, 2000), 38–39, repr. in *Medicean and Savonarolan Florence,* chap. 8.

41 Bartolomeo Cerretani, *Dialogo della mutatione di Firenze,* ed. Giuliana Berti (Florence, 1993), 16 (Girolamo): "ma che il mondo sia sempre stato, sia et habbia a essere . . . et che morto questo huomo sia finita ogni cosa per lui," cit. Adriano Prosperi, "Intellettuali e Chiesa all'inizio dell'età moderna," in *Storia d'Italia: Annali,* ed. Corrado Vivanti (Turin, 1981) 4: 179.

nant themes in late medieval society, especially in Florence, where plague was recurrent throughout the fifteenth century and its merchants were vulnerable to an additional "malaise of soul" due to their dubious entrepreneurial activities and noted unwillingness to enter a church.[42] It was in Florence in 1439—at the ecumenical Church council already referred to, which was famous for bringing together scholars from East and West and (according to Marsilio Ficino) inspiring the Platonic revival—that the decree of a much earlier council was reenacted, promising that "those souls who die in the state of Deadly Sin, or with the sole Original Sin, will go down into Hell."[43] The message was later reinforced by sermons of the Mendicants and Savonarola on "the art of dying well," which urged people to "go often to see the dead being buried" and to take pleasure in watching relatives die and be buried. Although the "explosion of masses" in Florence and elsewhere in the later fifteenth century demonstrated the evident success of this campaign to save souls, it is also evidence of heightened anxiety about death.[44] One young woman in Bologna (wife of Giovanni degli Arienti) admitted on her deathbed in the 1480s that despite putting all her hope in God, "I yet fear fear itself, because I don't know where I am going," and in Florence the doom-laden sermons of the friars in 1492 are known to have frightened other devout women. Filippo da Gagliano, the Medici banker, wrote to a friend, "These women are so scared and freaked out by these threats that they can't be reassured, nor they can be dug out of these churches and from the feet of these friars."[45]

---

[42] Peter Howard, "Entrepreneurial Ne'er-do-wells: Sin and Fear in Renaissance Florence," *Memorie Domenicane*, n.s. 25 (1994): 246; Jean Delumeau, *Sin and Fear: The Emergence of a Western Guilt Culture, 13th–18th Centuries* (1983, trans. New York, 1990).

[43] Delumeau, *Sin and Fear*, 276, also cited by Howard, "Entrepreneurial Ne'er-do-wells," 248; Ficino, preface to his translation of ten Platonic dialogues in 1464, ed. Paul Oskar Kristeller, *Supplementum ficinianum* (Florence, 1937), 2, 105.

[44] Savonarola, *Predica dell'arte del ben morire* (Florence, four editions between 1496 and 1500); see Lorenzo Polizzotto, "The Piagnone Way of Death, 1494–1545," *I Tatti Studies* 3 (1989): 27; Donald Weinstein, "*The Art of Dying Well* and Popular Piety in the Preaching and Thought of Girolamo Savonarola," in *Life and Death in Fifteenth-Century Florence*, ed. Marcel Tetel et al. (Durham, NC, 1989), 88–104. On the "heightened sense of spiritual anxiety" in the later fifteenth century, see Sharon Strocchia, *Death and Ritual in Renaissance Florence* (Baltimore, 1992), 204, 208.

[45] Carolyn James, *Giovanni Sabadino degli Arienti: A Literary Career* (Florence, 1996), 70: "ho pur paura de la paura perché non so dove me vada"; Filippo da Gagliano to Niccolò Michelozzi, 8 May 1492 (BNF, GC, 29, 69, fol. 47): "Queste donne sono tanto impaurite e spaventate da questi minacci che non si possono rasichurare e non si possono chavare de queste chiexe né da pie di questi frati" (cf. chap. 3 below).

Together these tensions created the "precarious" but "dynamic" equilibrium that helps to explain the unusual context in which interest in Lucretius and Epicureanism developed in fifteenth-century Florence.[46] It has been suggested as "likely, though . . . difficult to prove" that Poggio was an important influence on Marsilio Ficino, who turned towards an Epicurean understanding of human misery and happiness in the mid-1450s, perhaps as a result of Poggio's empirical and concrete approach to philosophy in his writings.[47] From Ficino, interest in Lucretius spread to the laity outside papal circles in Florence, who generated a surge in manuscript copies of *De rerum natura* in the fifteenth century. It seemed that the text would never again be at risk. Almost one hundred years after Poggio rediscovered *De rerum natura*, however, Lucretius was prohibited as "reading in our schools" by the Florentine synod in December 1516, because it was "a lascivious and wicked work, in which every effort is used to demonstrate the mortality of the soul."[48] And although Lucretius escaped being listed in the *Index of Prohibited Books* by the intervention in 1549 of cardinal Marcello Cervini, he was nevertheless listed by the commissary general of the Inquisition, Michele Ghislieri, as the author of one of many pagan books to be read as fables and not to be taken seriously.[49] So we are presented with a paradox, a text that multiplied more than fifty-fold in the course of the fifteenth century and yet whose readers, and their motives for reading Lucretius, remain largely unknown. The popularity of the text seems confirmed by the need to prohibit it from being read in school, but because of the danger that Lucretius presented, it is as difficult to discover how Lucretius was read as it is to discover who read him.

This paradox explains my approach in the chapters that follow. If we rely on the textual route to understanding Lucretius in the fifteenth century, we

---

46 Timothy Verdon, "Christianity, the Renaissance, and the Study of History," introduction to *Christianity and the Renaissance: Image and Religious Imagination in the Quattrocento*, ed. Verdon and John Henderson (Syracuse, NY, 1990), 2.

47 Arthur Field, *The Origins of the Platonic Academy of Florence* (Princeton, NJ, 1988), 186–89.

48 "Opera lasciva et impia, quale est Lucretii poema, ubi animae mortalitatem totis viribus ostendere nititur," cit. Fleischmann, *CTC*, 352; Maria Fubini Leuzzi, "Note sulle costituzioni sinodali fiorentine del 1517," in *I ceti dirigenti in Firenze dal gonfalonierato di giustizia a vita all'avvento del ducato*, ed. Elisabetta Insabato (Lecce, 1999), 184–85.

49 Valentina Prosperi, *"Di soavi licor gli orli del vaso." La fortuna di Lucrezio dall'Umanesimo alla Controriforma* (Turin, 2004), 99–100; *Index des livres interdits*, ed. Jesus De Bujanda (Geneva, 1990), 8: 32, 245 (no. 00147); cf. Ludwig von Pastor, *Storia dei Papi dalla fine del Medio Evo*, ed. Angelo Mercati (Rome, 1963), 6: 491 (with thanks to Humfrey Butters).

have to agree that his influence was restricted to a group of scholars who liked the medium of his poetry but not his message. But was this really how the fifteenth century responded to the bold and imaginative Lucretius, who wrote so movingly about the human condition: about love, mental fear *(terror animi),* and that "hidden power" *(vis abdita quaedam)* that grinds down humanity, as well as about the evolution of mankind from primitive naturalism to the uncertain benefits of civilized society?[50] It has recently been suggested that the importance of certain texts and writings depends less on their novelty than on their ability to give reality and concreteness to "hybrid and . . . unsystematic clusters of useful ideas," by localizing them and giving them a relevance that they might not otherwise have had.[51] This may be a useful approach to Lucretius, whose poem contains many "hybrid and unsystematic clusters of useful ideas" that in differing ways reflected contemporary concerns. By helping to articulate them, his poem gave them a "reality and concreteness" in a fifteenth-century context that has hitherto gone unnoticed.

50 Lucretius 1: 146–48: "Hunc igitur terrorem animi tenebrasque necessest / non radii solis neque lucida tela diei / discutiant, sed naturae species ratioque," and 5: 1233–34: "res humanas vis abdita quaedam / obterit," translated by Charles Segal as "a certain dark force," in *Lucretius on Death and Anxiety: Poetry and Philosophy in De rerum natura* (Princeton, 1990), 227; on the fear of death to which Lucretius offered a therapy, 19–25.

51 Germaine Greer, *Shakespeare* (Oxford, 1986), 59–60, cited by Peter Howard, "The Preacher and the Holy in Renaissance Florence," in *Models of Holiness in Medieval Sermons,* ed. Beverly Kienzle et al. (Louvain-la-Neuve, 1996), 355–56.

2

Medicean Florence:
Marsilio Ficino and Bartolomeo Scala

Lucretius and Epicurus had returned to Florence by the 1440s. Copies of Poggio's newly discovered manuscript of *De rerum natura* and of Traversari's translated *Life of Epicurus* were circulating among—and even being discreetly mentioned by—humanists at the papal court, then resident in Florence. As yet, however, nobody had apparently quoted it outright or openly praised it within these circles. The first people to do so were two young men from the provinces who were completing their education in Florence's university in the late 1440s–early 1450s, Marsilio Ficino and Bartolomeo Scala. Ficino was the son of Cosimo de' Medici's doctor from Figline, in the upper Arno valley, and Scala was a miller's son from Colle Val d'Elsa in southwest Tuscany. Of the two, Ficino was perhaps better prepared economically to pursue the life of the scholar, although both became dependent on Medici patronage, Ficino being employed by Cosimo to translate his newly acquired Greek manuscripts while Scala was appointed secretary to Cosimo's nephew Pierfrancesco in 1457—then becoming chancellor of the Guelf Party and first chancellor of Florence in 1465. In the mid-1450s, however, both young men were unemployed, for although in 1456 Scala had been shortlisted to be an assistant of Poggio's in the chancery (which Poggio now headed), he had failed to be appointed and, like Ficino, was suffering "the misery of the human condition" that Poggio was writing about at the time.

It has been suggested that it was Poggio who now encouraged Ficino to turn from the abstract scholasticism of his earlier writings towards a more empirical interest in ancient philosophers, like Plato and Lucretius. Ficino wrote first about Plato in 1456 (in his *Platonic Institutions,* now lost), and after completing it, the following year he turned to Lucretius as his guide to happiness and freedom from fear.[1] Lucretius's desire to rid people of their fear of death and the afterlife is one of the principal themes of *De rerum natura.* Of all the themes that were relevant to fifteenth-century Florentines, this is the one that perhaps had the widest resonance, especially when approached via Virgil, who had praised Lucretius (though unnamed) in his *Georgics.* He was that enlightened man, Virgil wrote, who through knowing "the causes of things" had "trampled underfoot" our ungrounded fear about death ("all fear and inexorable fate and the roar of greedy Acheron")—or, as Lucretius himself described it, this "terror of the mind," which was no more to be feared, in the daylight of reason, than the dreams that make "little boys shiver in the dark."[2] This is the context in which to understand the first Florentines who repeatedly—and openly—quoted chunks of Lucretius in their writings.

It was in 1457 that Ficino started to write to his friends about Lucretius. Asked by Michele Mercati to explain Lucretius's philosophy to him, he responded on October 15 with a brief outline of his philosophy, prefaced by eight lines from *De rerum natura* (1: 402–9) in which Lucretius promises his friend Memmius to give him enough of the scent to enable him to pursue his quarry himself:

> But, for a keen scented mind, these little tracks
> Are enough to enable you to recognize the others for yourself.
> For as hounds very often find the leaf-hidden resting place
> Of the mountain-ranging quarry by their scent
> When once they have found certain traces of their path,
> So you will be able for yourself to see one thing

---

1 Field, *Origins,* 178–90, esp. 183, on his "curious turn" towards Epicureanism in 1457; Paul Oskar Kristeller, *Studies in Renaissance Thought and Letters* (Rome, 1969), 200–203; James Hankins, *Plato in the Italian Renaissance* (Leiden, 1990), 2: 457.

2 Lucretius 2: 55–58; cf. Segal, *Lucretius on Death and Anxiety,* 3–4, and Jenkyns, *Virgil's Experience,* 374, quoting Virgil, *Georg.* 2: 490–92.

> After another in such matters as these
> And to penetrate all unseen hiding places
> And draw forth the truth from them.

Six weeks later, when asked by another friend, Antonio Serafico, what "Democritean and Epicurean philosophers" thought about man's highest good, he replied, "assuredly, they all want peace and tranquility." This time he quoted four lines from the second book of "the most famous of Epicurean philosophers, our Lucretius" (2: 18–21), that we are blind not to see that what our nature craves is

> ... this alone, that the body
> Be free of pain and that the mind should enjoy
> The sense of pleasure, free from care and fear.
> So we see how little our bodies need,
> Only such things as ease the pain away.

And to answer Serafico's question more precisely, since Lucretius—he said—copied Epicurus, and Epicurus drew from Democritus, Ficino then quoted five lines from Lucretius's famous eulogy of Epicurus in Book 6 for dispelling mental terror by illuminating nature's appearance and laws. He was the man who

> ... purged men's hearts with his truth-telling words
> and set a limit to desire and fear.
> He showed the highest good, to which we all strive,
> What it was, and the narrow path
> By which we might directly reach it.[3]

At the end of that year, Ficino quoted many more lines from Lucretius in a long treatise on pleasure, his *Epistola de voluptate*, completed in Figline on December 29–30, 1457. The opening of the letter suggests that it is going to

---

3 Ficino, letters to Michele Mercati (15 October 1457), quoting Lucretius 1: 402–9, and to Antonio Serafico (29 November 1457): "omnes autem magnopere quietem ac tranquillitatem expetere nemo dubitat. Atque ideo Lucretius ille noster Epicureorum philosophorum clarissimus nihil aliud desiderare naturam disseruit" (82), quoting Lucretius 2: 18–21, and 6: 24–28: "ex morali epitomate Epicuri ad verbum usurpatum est, quod ipse quoque Epicurus ex Democriti fontibus hausit" (83), ed. Kristeller, *Supplementum* 2: 81–84; the second passage is translated in Field, *Origins*, 185. I mainly follow William Rouse's translation in the Loeb edition (Cambridge, MA, repr. 1982), but I also use Anthony Esolen, *On the Nature of Things* (Baltimore, 1995).

MEDICEAN FLORENCE: FICINO AND SCALA

be a comparison of the views of ancient philosophers on pleasure, especially those of Plato and Aristotle, who dominate the first fifteen chapters. Despite this, the tenth chapter contains a four-line quotation from *De rerum natura* (4: 1057–60), on the sweetness of Venus before the chill sets in, to illustrate Aristotle's view of happiness as the anticipation of pleasure:

> For his dumb desire presages delight.
> This is our Venus, from this also comes love's name.
> From this first trickled into the heart
> That dewdrop of Venus's sweetness.
> And then followed the freezing chill.

When the Epicureans are finally broached, they have the last two long chapters to themselves, with several long quotations from *De rerum natura*, as well as references to Epicurus's letter to Menoeceus in Diogenes Laertius's *Life*. Three of these quotations relate to atomism by illustrating how different shapes of atoms can cause pain or pleasure: how "smooth and round" atoms give pleasure, whereas hooked atoms "tear open their way into our senses"; how bodies feel pain when attacked by atoms and pleasure when they desist, whereas atoms themselves feel nothing; and how atoms that are neither smooth nor completely hooked tickle our senses rather than hurt them (2: 402–7, 963–72, 426–30). When Ficino returned in the final chapter to the theme of his earlier letters, that the end of pleasure is tranquility and the absence of grief and disturbance, he referred frequently to Epicurus's letters and the theme of tranquility, concluding the treatise with six lines from Lucretius (2: 14–19):

> O wretched minds of men! O blinded hearts!
> In what darkness life, with what great perils,
> Life, such as it is, is spent!
> Not to see that all life yelps for is this, that the body
> Be free of pain and that the mind should enjoy
> The sense of pleasure, free from care and fear."[4]

So although the letter started out as a formal scholastic debate centering on Plato and Aristotle, it ends on an almost personal note in its emphasis on

---

4 Ficino, *Opera omnia* (1576, repr. Turin, 1962), 1: 1017–42, quoting Lucretius on 1033, 1039–40, 1042; Kristeller, *Supplementum* 1: cxv. Cf. Diog. Laert., *Lives* 10: 128.

Epicurean moral philosophy. This would presumably have been the focus of his lost "Commentariola in Lucretium," which must have been written at this time, "when still a boy," before he "consigned it to the flames" when more mature.[5] Although we can only guess at its contents, a commentary presupposes familiarity with the whole text and is in itself evidence of Ficino's precocious interest in Lucretius. He quoted from *De rerum natura* once more in this early period of his life, this time in an undated letter to Clemente Fortini, "On the four philosophical sects," in which he compared the views of Platonists, Aristotelians, Stoics, and Epicureans on God, the world, the human mind, and the highest good. The first quotation, six lines from Book 2 of "the most noble Lucretius Carus, the Epicurean," describes the nature of the gods as "most blessed":

> For the very nature of divinity must necessarily enjoy
> Immortal life in the deepest peace,
> Far removed and distant from our affairs.
> Deprived of all pain, without danger,
> It is powerful through its own resources, not needing us at all,
> Not indebted to our propitiations, nor touched by wrath.

The second quotation, seven lines from Book 3, describes the human mind as a unity made up of different elements, including a nonmaterial spirit or soul:

> So heat and air and the invisible power of breath
> Commingled form one nature, together with that
> Quickest of elements that moves the others,
> Carrying movement via the senses through our flesh.
> For this nature lies deep down, hidden more deeply
> Than anything else in our body.
> It is the soul itself of all the soul.[6]

Since a letter on the same topic was written by Bartolomeo Scala on April 24, 1458, it seems likely that both letters were written at the same time as exercises, probably in connection with the lectures on Cicero's *Tusculan Dispu-*

---

5 "neque commentariolis in Lucretium meis, quae puer adhuc . . . commentabar, deinde pepercerim; haec enim. . . . Vulcano dedi," in letter to Martinus Uranus, 1492, *Opera* 1: 963 (*Epist.* 11), discussed and translated by Hankins, *Plato*, 457; cf. Kristeller, *Supplementum* 1: clxiii.

6 *De quatuor sectis philosophorum*, ed. Kristeller, *Supplementum*, 2: 7–11, quoting Lucretius, 2: 646–651, 3: 269–75; cf. Hankins, *Plato*, 2: 457, note 17.

tations that Cristoforo Landino was giving at the university.⁷ Although not dissimilar from Giannozzo Manetti's slightly earlier account of these sects in his 1454 *Adversus iudeos et gentes,* which used Diogenes Laertius's *Lives* and Cicero's *De natura deorum* as its principal sources for Epicureanism, Scala's and Ficino's letters differ from Manetti in quoting directly from Lucretius.⁸ Since they also differ from each other in the words and passages they quote, they were evidently written independently of each other—although within the same context. Ficino's letter is much shorter than Scala's, but with more on Epicurus than in Scala's pithy, but accurate, summary of his philosophy. Scala's letter includes a long historical introduction and more on the pre-Socratics (including Democritus and Empedocles) before it turns to analyze the tenets of the four principal sects. Despite being shorter than Ficino's, Scala's discussion of Epicurus is more accurate in describing Epicurus's negative view of the gods and the soul, which he "strips of its dignity," according to Scala. Scala's one direct reference to Lucretius in this early work is to quote his description of Anaxagoras's use of the word *"homoeomeria,* as the Greeks call it" ("homogeneousness of elements," or first principles), and unlike Ficino, Scala quotes from Virgil, not Lucretius, to describe Epicurus's indifferent gods, "as if their peaceful state were touched with human fate.⁹ He may have been less innovative than Eugenio Garin believed in concluding that "some things were written by Epicurus quite divinely" (despite the pagan philosophers, he said, being wrong about many things), but his parting shot was nevertheless an early sign of his interest in this philosophy.¹⁰

---

7 *Epistola de sectis philosophorum,* in Scala, *Writings,* ed. Brown, 251–61, repr. and trans. Renée Watkins, in Scala, *Essays and Dialogues* (Cambridge, MA, 2008), 2–33 (subsequently distinguished as "ed. Brown" and "trans. Watkins"). On Landino's inaugural lecture in early 1458 on Cicero, who "frees us from the fear of death with his divine arguments," Field, *Origins,* 236, 244. Landino was never apparently influenced by Lucretius.

8 *Adversus iudeos* is in Città del Vaticano, MS Urb. lat. 154, dated 1454 by Charles Trinkaus, *In Our Image and Likeness* (London, 1970), 2: 582, 726–34; cf. Alfonso De Petris, "L'*Adversus Iudaeos et Gentes* di Giannozzo Manetti," in *Rinascimento* ser. 2, 16 (1976): 198. Despite his negative view of Epicurus as a hedonist here, Manetti had given "un giudizio positivo" in *De illustribus longevis* (ivi), and he cited Lucretius in his late *De terremotu;* Daniela Pagliara, "Annotazioni storico-culturali a proposito del *De terremotu,*" in *Dignitas et excellentia hominis,* ed. Stefano Baldassarri (Florence, 2008), 271.

9 *Epistola de sectis,* ed. Brown, 254, 257–58, trans. Watkins, 10–11, 20–23: "expoliavit omni dignitate," quoting Lucretius 1: 830, and Virgil, *Aen.,* 4: 379–80: "scilicet is superis labor est, ea cura quietos sollicitat."

10 "nonnulla etiam ab Epicuro scripta sane divinitus. Aberrarunt etiam in multis," in *Epistola de sectis,* ed. Brown, 261, trans. Watkins, 32–33; Garin, "Ricerche sull' Epicureismo," 72–75: "un motivo fortemente innovatore" (75); see, however, the fourteenth-century life of Epicurus quoted in chap. 1

If Ficino's and Scala's letters on philosophical sects were written as a student exercise set by Landino, it must have been due to their privileged position as intimates of the Medici palace that these two young scholars, and especially Ficino, quoted so directly from Lucretius's still-elusive text. As the son of the Medici's doctor, Ficino had been acquainted with Cosimo—if not already "philosophizing" with him, as Ficino later put it—since 1452; he showed Cosimo his *Platonic Institutions* in 1456 (and may have taught his son Giovanni), and after being advised by Cosimo not to publish until he had learnt more Greek, he accepted the villa in Careggi in 1463 that enabled him to devote himself to translating the newly recovered writings that Cosimo wanted to read before he died.[11] The same period saw Scala entering Cosimo's orbit. By 1455 he, too, was acquainted with Giovanni de' Medici, and two years later he became secretary to Giovanni's cousin Pierfrancesco, through whom he would have had easy access to Cosimo's new palace in Via Larga. There, like Ficino, we know he spent time with the dying Cosimo, reading to him notes on Argyropoulos's lectures on Aristotle's *Ethics*.[12] As well as owning the Platonic and Hermetic texts that Scala (on the evidence of his 1463 *Dialogue of Consolation*) worked on with Ficino, Cosimo also possessed manuscripts of Traversari's translation of Diogenes Laertius's *Lives* and Lucretius's *De rerum natura*, which may have provided the theme of the courtyard medallions in Cosimo's palace that were being completed around 1460.[13] Since Ficino acknowledged the help he had received from Scala (among others) in translating the early Platonic dialogues for Cosimo, the two humanists doubtless also shared each other's interest in the other newly available texts in the Medici library.[14]

---

above. In quoting from both letters, Garin, following Ludwig Stein, wrongly attributed Scala's letter to Giovanni Battista Buoninsegni.

11 Kristeller, *Studies*, 197; *Supplementum* 1: cxli–ii, 2: 79–80; cf. Arnaldo della Torre, *Storia dell'Accademia platonica di Firenze* (Florence, 1902), 527–29; Field, *Origins*, 178, 200, note 96.

12 Brown, *Scala*, 36. Scala was listed as part of the Medici household upon Cosimo's death in 1464, honored (like Piero de' Medici) with fourteen *braccie* of cloth for the funeral, ibid.

13 Laur. 65: 21 and 35: 27, listed by Albinia de la Mare, "Cosimo and His Books," in *Cosimo "il Vecchio" de' Medici, 1389–1464*, ed. Francis Ames-Lewis (Oxford, 1992), 147, 151–52. Laur. 35: 27 was inherited by Piero; see Ames Lewis, "The Inventories of Piero di Cosimo de' Medici's Library," *La Bibliofilia* 84 (1982): 121, 134 (other Medici manuscripts of Lucretius are discussed in the appendix below). On the medallions, see Ursula Wester and Erika Simon, "Die Reliefmedaillons im Hofe des Palazzo Medici zu Florenz," *Jahrbuch d. Berliner Museen* 7 (1965): 15–91.

14 Ficino, preface to the *Editio princeps* of his translation of Plato (Florence, 1484), cited in Brown, *Scala*, 207, note 43.

In view of Ficino's lengthy quotations from Lucretius and his early commentary on *De rerum natura*, it seems likely that he was the person responsible for interesting Scala in this novel writer. But whereas Scala continued to develop what I have called his "lifelong love-hate relationship" with Lucretius, Ficino seems to have suffered some sort of a religious crisis in the late 1450s, which was associated with his interest in Lucretius, as well as in Plato.[15] He was apparently warned of the dangers of studying pagan thought, and significantly—in view of Bartolomeo Fonzio's later remarks about the dangers of humanists in holy orders publishing what they wrote in their youth—the *Institutiones Platonicae disciplinae* that Ficino wrote in 1456 has disappeared, together with his *Commentariola in Lucretium*. After he became a priest and a dedicated Platonist in the 1470s, he referred to Lucretius only to attack him, but the care he then devoted in the *Platonic Theology* to refuting Lucretius's arguments against immortality shows how powerful Lucretius's impact on Ficino as a young man had been.

So it was Scala who continued to engage with Lucretius and Epicureanism in the later 1450s and the early 1460s, although always in a dialogic context that protected his own orthodoxy—like St. Basil, he said, he imitated the bees in visiting all the flowers to choose the best for making honey.[16] In differing ways, his writings in this period—the letter *On whether a Wise Man Should Marry*, his *Elegy* praising Pius II, and his *Dialogue of Consolation*—all reflect his engagement with Epicurean themes. Unlike earlier writings on marriage—such as Francesco Barbaro's *De re uxoria*, dedicated to Cosimo de' Medici's brother Lorenzo on the occasion of his marriage in 1416—Scala's treatise was an exercise in arguing *in utramque partem*, continuing the earlier discussion of ancient wisdom in his letter "On the philosophical sects" and quoting from Cicero, Juvenal, and St. Jerome, as well as borrowing the topic itself from Quintilian and from Diogenes Laertius's *Life of Epicurus*. For the question of whether a wise man should marry was in fact proposed for debate by Epicurus, whom Scala took as his starting point, arguing (initially, before reversing the argument) that as Epicurus placed marriage on the borderline between

---

15 Ibid., 313. On Ficino's crisis, Hankins, *Plato*, 2, Appendix 16, 454–59 (cf. 1: 279–80), who argues that Kristeller (*Studies*, 204) minimalizes the episode in suggesting that even in his comments on Lucretius, Ficino was "always a Christian." For Hankins's essays on Ficino's critique of Lucretius, see chap. 5 below.

16 *Epistola de sectis*, ed. Brown, 261, trans. Watkins, 30–31.

good and evil, a wise man should not marry because he should never be in doubt.¹⁷ And although Scala ostensibly rejected Epicurus's position on account of his reputation for hedonism (which Scala had already shown he knew to be false), it is clear that he cites him as one voice in a two-sided debate.

The same is true of his reappearance in Scala's *Elegy* to Pope Pius II, written around 1459–1460, which criticized the Epicureans for their views about the gods and the random behavior of atoms: "Will Epicurus persist in abolishing the carefree gods, while he denies they watch over or listen to even the prayers of the just, since they treat just and unjust alike?" Quoting from the poem of "the learned Lucretius Carus," that "it is necessarily the very nature of divinity" to live in peace, remote from our affairs (2: 646), Scala went on to contrast Lucretius with the "masculine sect" of the Stoic Zeno, who believed in a world governed by reason and in gods who looked down on us kindly, a boon not provided "by the random behavior of atoms."¹⁸ Since Pius II wrote two epitaphs, one for and the other against Epicurus, Scala's lines may allude to the pope's known interest in Epicureanism, but they also document Scala's own careful balancing of the merits and demerits of this philosophy.¹⁹

Scala's next writing, the *Dialogue of Consolation,* on the death of Cosimo's son Giovanni in 1463, continues this process. In it, the dialogue form enabled him to present the Stoic-Epicurean debate openly as two opposing arguments in a very real and topical discussion about fear and death. Whereas consolatory letters normally advocated accepting grief with Stoic fortitude, Scala used Cosimo's voice to counter his own Stoicism with a sympathetic reevaluation of Epicureanism, having heard that the Epicureans regarded grief as the worst of evils and much less tolerable than it was for the Stoics. For despite Scala's attempt to emphasize the dangerous public implications of Epi-

---

17 *Ducendane sit uxor sapienti,* dedicated to Piero de' Medici, [1457–59?], ed. Brown, 262–73 at 263, trans. Watkins, 34–67 at 36–37; cf. Diogenes Laertius, 10: 119, trans. Traversari, fol. 177r: "Uxorem tamen ducturum ac liberos procreaturum sapientem, ut Epicurus in Ambiguis et in libros de Natura. Ceterum pro vite interdum in conditione ducturum uxorem."

18 *Elegia in laudem Pii II Pontificis Maximi, Writings,* ed. Brown, 413–14, lines 61–74: "Et persistet adhuc Epicurus tollere divos, dum quid securos invigilare negat Aut voces audire aliquas vel iusta precantum, Quod paribus spectent aequa et iniquae modis"; quoting "docti Lucreti carmina Cari," 2: 646: "Omnis enim per se divum natura necessest" (also quoted by Ficino, *De quatuor sectis,* ed. Kristeller, *Supplementum,* 2: 9).

19 Pius II's two epitaphs on Epicurus, for and against him, are in *Enee Silvii Piccolomini Carmina,* ed. Adriano Van Heck (Città del Vaticano, 1994), 109–10 (at 109, note 1).

curean morality by asking if Epicurus would really have been prepared to burn his country and profane the sacred temples of the gods to escape grief —"surely not!"—Cosimo responds by identifying his own plight with that of the rich man described by "Lucretius in the highly elegant verses of his poem *De rerum natura*":[20]

> Nor will hot fevers leave the body more quickly
> If you toss upon a floral quilt or purple gown
> Than if you lie in a poor man's clothing.

For it is true, he went on, that

> The fears and anxieties that dog the human breast
> Do not fear the sound of arms, nor savage weapons,
> Nor are they awestruck by the gleam of gold
> Nor by the bright splendor of purple robes,
> But mingle boldly among kings and potentates.

And after citing a string of feats achieved by famous ancient heroes, Cosimo is forced to exclaim "with Lucretius" that life is, indeed, very miserable:

> O wretched minds of men! O blinded hearts!
> In what darkness life, with what great perils,
> Life, such as it is, is spent!

According to his biographer, Vespasiano da Bisticci, Cosimo was burdened with guilt not only on account of his "dubiously acquired" wealth, but also because of his political activities and ambition, so he could well have experienced the vivid fears described by Lucretius that Scala puts into his mouth.[21]

The *Dialogue* ranged widely over many other topics before ending on a note of Christian resignation. Since we know that Scala spent time reading to Cosimo in the year before he died in August 1464,[22] its argument may reflect the drift of the two men's conversation—especially since it refers to the excit-

---

20 *Dialogus de consolatione*, ed. Brown, 286–87, 290–91, 294, trans. Watkins, 104–5, 114–17, 126–27, citing Lucretius 2: 34–36, 48–52, 14–16 (only the last of these quotations was also in Ficino's *De voluptate*; see note 4 above). The *Dialogue* was sent to Lorenzo de' Medici in December 1463, ed. Brown, 10 (letter 13).

21 Vespasiano da Bisticci, *Le vite*, ed. Aulo Greco (Florence, 1976), 2: 177: "danari di non molto buono aquisto."

22 Brown, *Scala*, 36.

ing new acquisitions in the Medici library that would have encouraged open debate about religion and the human condition. Most relevant to the theme of Lucretius and Epicureanism—in addition to the passages quoted above—is the *Dialogue*'s opening discussion concerning primitive man. Attempting to lift Cosimo from his gloom by talking about the gods' gifts to man, Scala professed to agree with Cicero in *De legibus* that the gods created man in their image, not from mud or stones as Ovid and the myths of Pandora, Pyrrha, and Deucalion would have us believe; for when the poets said that man was made out of hard wood and trunks, they surely intended to describe primitive man's emergence, "nude and hairy," from the protective shelter of tree trunks in the early days when he lived without hearth or home, wandering freely through the woods. In referring to Ovid, Scala must have been thinking of his account of the Golden Age, when man was either created by the gods out of their own substance or molded from earth and water into the form of gods. But this Golden Age man was very different from the primitive man whom Scala describes, since Ovid's man was born erect and made of "finer stuff" than animals, and he was also capable of behaving morally without the force of law—like Cicero's early man, who though made from earth was nevertheless upright and endowed with reason. Perhaps reflecting the theme of the courtyard medallions, the primitivism described in Scala's *Dialogue* is drawn more obviously from Lucretius and the hard primitivists, who unlike Ovid regarded this first stage of human life as far from golden.[23]

Primitivism and man's evolution is the second theme that made Lucretius relevant to fifteenth-century Florentines, who—as we have seen—showed an early interest in Ptolemy's *Geography*, which they put to practical use as traders and explorers. Just before Scala wrote his *Consolation*, he became closely involved in maritime affairs in Florence for the brief period (from 1459 to 1462) during which they fell under the control of the Guelf Party. This coincided with Scala's appointment as the party's chancellor, when his employer, Pierfrancesco, and Pierfrancesco's cousin Giovanni de' Medici also became closely involved in the Guelf Party as its bankers. The party's influence was immediately reflected in Scala's letters, which became filled with news about

---

23 *Dialogus de consolatione*, ed. Brown, 276, trans. Watkins, 72–75; cf. Lucretius 5: 932, 955–57. Scala quotes Ovid, *Metamorphoses* I: 76–90 (who refers to the "Aurea . . . aetas" on line 89), and Cicero, *De legibus* 1: vii, 22, 1, x, 30. On "hard" and "soft" primitivism, see Arthur Lovejoy and George Boas, *Primitivism and Related Ideas in Antiquity* (Baltimore, 1935, repr. 1997), especially 9–11, 43ff., 225ff., 257.

the movements of the Florentine galleys at this time.[24] We now know, too, that in 1480, shortly before describing the cultural practices of distant countries in his *Dialogue on Laws and Legal Judgments,* Scala acquired two spheres of the heavens and the earth, a "Zodiac" and a "Mappamundi," which he bought in Florence from the heirs of Donnus Nicolaus Germanus, the printer and astrologer famous for his new trapezoid projections of Ptolemy's *Geography.*[25] So it is not stretching the evidence to link Scala's early interest in foreign places and primitivism to his later writings, in which Lucretius remained a steady, if still understated, influence.

After Scala was appointed first chancellor of Florence in 1465, he had little time for private scholarship until the conclusion of the Pazzi War more than fifteen years later. His continuing interest in Lucretius is attested by a few small but revealing pieces of evidence. The first is the presence of the opening five lines of *De rerum natura* copied by Scala himself in the margin of a page of draft poems; although the poems belong to his early period of writing, the Lucretian lines may have been added to the page around the same time or, since the miscellany contains writings dating from 1458 to 1496, they could have been added at any later moment. The second piece of evidence, a now-lost poem by Scala, "modeled on Lucretius," was seen by Michele Verino before his early death in 1487, which must be its latest date.[26] And Lucretius's influence can be fleetingly seen even in his chancery letters that refer to "a minimal particle" or "an atom of time."[27]

Scala's most substantial writings in the second, mature, phase of his literary career are his 1483 *Dialogue on Laws and Legal Judgments* and his *Defense against the Detractors of Florence,* printed in 1496 as a public vindication of Savonarola and the new popular regime.[28] Seemingly unrelated to the discussion of Epicureanism in his earlier writings, these later works neverthe-

---

24 Brown, *Scala,* 28; ead., "The Guelf Party in Fifteenth-Century Florence," *Rinascimento* 20 (1980): 55–58, repr. in Alison Brown, *The Medici in Florence* (Princeton, 1992), 117–20.

25 See Brown, introduction to Scala, *Essays and Dialogues,* xii.

26 Modena, Bibl. Estense, Racc. Campori Appendice 235 (Gamma P.2.5) (described in Scala, *Writings,* ed. Brown, xxviii), 20v: marginal note headed "Lucretius" and quoting 1: 1–5. On his "carmen de rebus naturalibus [al. "moralibus"] instar Lucretii," see Brown, *Scala,* 209–10, note 49.

27 ASF, Legazioni e Commissarie 16, fol. 7v (1 Aug. 1465): "una minima particella"; Minutarii 12, fol. 318r (13 June 1482): "uno athomo di tempo."

28 *De legibus et iudiciis dialogus,* in Scala, *Writings,* ed. Brown, 338–64, trans. David Marsh in Scala, *Essays and Dialogues,* 158–231; *Apologia contra vituperatores civitatis Florentiae,* ed. Brown, 394–411, trans. Watkins, 232–79.

less show how the mature Scala integrated Epicurean ethics and primitivism into a new public morality, especially in the *Dialogue*, which demonstrates the naturalistic direction of his public thinking about law and morality in the 1480s. The argument of the dialogue is presented in the form of a debate between Scala and Bernardo Machiavelli, father of the more famous Niccolò, on whether law should be codified as the embodiment of unchanging reason or whether it should adjust flexibly to changing circumstances. Given immediacy by the recent translation of Plato's *Minos* as well as by the presence in Florence of the ancient manuscript of Justinian's *Codex*, "Bernardo" argued in favor of retaining Roman civil law and Gratian's canon law as the firm, rational basis for our secular and religious lives, whereas "Scala" opposed him by preferring law to be flexible, based on the universal law of nature and administered by a good man or judge.

The relevance of this Platonic argument for allowing the good man freedom to rule flexibly—in contrast to Aristotle's preference for laws to act as a constraint—is obvious, since at the time the Medici were flexibly adjusting the laws to increase their power.[29] It was also topical in discussing the more pragmatic question of how litigation could be speeded up (a common complaint, then as now) and how it should respond to the different practices of the countries where Florentines were trading—like Turkey, or "the new islands and hitherto unknown peoples" in Africa, recently discovered by king John of Portugal. In Turkey, justice was administered by pashas who suffered death if their sentences were found by the sultan to be unjust, whereas in the islands discovered by the king of Portugal there were unlettered inhabitants living "completely without laws, like beasts obeying nature"—yet even they enjoyed a law, Scala wrote, the law of nature that is set before us as "a sign to keep us from swerving from what is right and honorable," which is identical to the law taught by Christ (in his Sermon on the Mount).[30] This was Scala's argument for flexible government according to a universal moral standard. It was opposed by Bernardo, partly on the grounds that a law code like Justinian's, interpreted by prestigious jurists, was far preferable to unwritten law, and also because the customs of people from other parts of the world, far

---

29 See Brown, "Platonism in Fifteenth-Century Florence," *Journal of Modern History* 58 (1986), repr. in *Medici in Florence*, 219, ead., *Scala*, 288–94, 336–42; cf. Plato, *The Laws* 4: 711–12; Aristotle, *Politics*, 1287a–b.

30 *De legibus*, ed. Brown, 343–44, trans. Marsh, 173–75; see note 32 below.

from reflecting a universal law of nature, were often in conflict. Nor was it true that primitive peoples had no written law, since even animals used signs, "as a sort of alphabet," but even if such people existed, should we model ourselves on them? So he concluded that written laws were needed, and since they were all divine in origin—as Homer, as well as the Bible, tell us, in describing how Minos and Moses received their laws—they helped to make people "more obedient by invoking the authority of the gods . . . by means of fables invented for this purpose."[31]

The overall argument seems clear enough: one protagonist following a Platonic argument in favor of flexible laws based on a universal law of nature, the other, like Aristotle and the legists, preferring the sanctions imposed by legislated law derived ultimately from God. Yet it is complicated by the presence of Lucretius and Epicurus in the debate, who sometimes appear on Scala's side of the argument, sometimes on Bernardo's. Scala's discussion of natural law is indebted to the Epicureans, as we can see from his reference to the law of nature as "a sign to keep us from swerving from what is right and honorable." "Do nothing to another person, nature says, that you do not wish to be done to you." Although he went on to say that "our Saviour teaches us the same thing" ("Do unto others as you would have others do unto to you"), a clue to his initial source is the word *sign (signum)*. *Sign* was the word used in Traversari's translation of Epicurus's natural precepts or maxims in Diogenes Laertius's *Life,* where the law of nature is described as "a sign of expedience, that you should not harm another or be harmed."[32] The expedient use of religion to enforce obedience is another Epicurean tenet present in the dialogue, this time put into Bernardo's mouth, as is Lucretius's definition of religion, which comes—he tells us—from *religare,* to bind, hence his desire to "free our minds from tight bondage to religion."[33]

It is Bernardo, too, who opposes Scala's idea that primitive people are

---

31 Ibid., ed. Brown, 352–53, 357, trans. Marsh, 198–99, 210–11.

32 Ibid., ed. Brown, 344, trans. Marsh 174–75: "nisi signum natura proposuisset . . . quod in te nolis (inquit natura) in alium ne feceris," quoting Matth. 22: 37, 39; cf. Diog. Laer., *Lives,* 10, 150, trans. Ambrogio Traversari (Venice, Nicolaus Jenson, 1475, fol. 138r): "Naturae ius utilitatis est signum, ut neque se invicem laedant neque laedantur," maxim 31 in the Loeb edition, trans. Robert Hicks (Cambridge, MA, 1965), 673–75; cf. Lucretius 5: 1020, on the early growth of communities eager "inter se nec laedere nec violari."

33 *De legibus,* ed. Brown, 363, trans. Marsh, 226–27, quoting Lucretius 1: 931–32: "et artis religionum animos nodis exsolvere pergo."

analphabetic with Lucretius's argument, that since animals and even birds had "agreed-on signs as a sort of alphabet," primitive men must have a language, too. For in contrast to Aristotle, who believed that language was an innate faculty that distinguishes us from animals, Lucretius believed it evolved naturally from animal-like cries: "it is madness to think that someone distributed names to things and that from him men learnt their first words." Interestingly, it is this passage that produced the only marginal comment in Piero de' Medici's otherwise pristine Lucretius: "Names are not discovered by reason, but by chance."[34] And although only one of many comments in Bartolomeo Fonzio's transcription of *De rerum natura* for Francesco Sassetti, the general manager of the Medici Bank, it is primitive man, wandering "in the manner of wild beasts," that again evokes interest, as we can see from the marginal note: "on the first kind of man and how wild and uncultivated he was."[35]

So although the insertion of Lucretius and Epicurus in the dialogue might seem to confuse the argument between its protagonists, they make its overall argument clearer, if we consider the dialogue as Scala's piece of writing, not his opponent's, and expressing his ideas. Like his similarly confusing *Dialogue of Consolation*, it shows how much Lucretius and Epicurus contributed to the growing naturalism of Scala's thinking about law and morality, as he moved from his early Platonic idealism to a more realistic approach to law and justice.[36] The topic of primitivism was very much in the air when Scala was writing the dialogue, as we can see from the excitement aroused by breaking news of the Portuguese exploration of Africa three years later. A letter read aloud in the main square of Florence in 1486 reported "the splendid and great

---

34 On language, 360 (trans. 218–19): "quasdam . . . sibi notas quasi litteras constituisse"; cf. Lucretius 5: 1028–32, 1056–61, 1087–90, and the following note; Lucretius 5: 1041–43: "putare aliquem tum nomina distribuisse rebus et inde homines didicisse vocabula prima desiperest" (cf. Aristotle, *Politics* 1253a. 10), commented on in MS Laur. 35: 27, fol. 123v: "vocabula non ratione inventa sed casu." Primitive accounts of the origin of language are discussed by Thomas Cole, *Democritus and the Sources of Greek Anthropology* (Ann Arbor, 1967), 60–69, discussing Lucretius at 61.

35 MS Laur. 35: 28, fols. 108v–9r: "De primo hominum genere et quam incultum et agreste fuerit," commenting on Lucretius 5: 925–75; other marginalia are cited in chap. 5, pp. 95–96.

36 An interesting recent attempt by Robert Fredona to integrate the Platonic and Lucretian themes in the dialogue proposes that it was written as an ironic carnivalesque satire (it was written during the Carnival, which it discusses), which demystifies the Medici philosopher-ruler in a world governed by Lucretian fear, "Carnival of Law: Bartolomeo Scala's Dialogue *De legibus e iudiciis*," *Viator* 39 (2008): 193–214, esp. 213.

news" just arrived from Portugal, that "a great lord of Ghinea" had been baptized, and the king of Portugal had sent experts to teach the natives Portuguese and "train them in good behavior . . . [in order to] introduce them to a human and not a bestial life."[37] For Scala, however, the interest of these lawless peoples lay not in their conversion to a civilized and Christian life but in the fact that they were able to live peaceably as "beasts, obeying nature," employing "signs as a sort of alphabet." The same was true for Amerigo Vespucci, when some years later he described to his patron Lorenzo di Pierfrancesco de' Medici—also patron of another Lucretian scholar, Michele Marullo—the similarly lawless natives he encountered on his voyages to Brazil and the coast of South America.[38] Showing the same "anthropological" interest as Poggio and Scala in the customs of other peoples, he wrote that these people had no churches and no laws: "they live according to nature and can be said to be Epicureans rather than Stoics."[39]

Scala's dialogue *On Laws* provides a bridge to his discussion of religion in his last official writing, his *Defense against the Detractors of Florence,* printed in Florence in 1496. Religion was necessarily a theme of a defense of Savonarola's new popular regime, yet Scala discussed it in entirely naturalistic and anthropological terms, as something common to all people and nations, "none of whom were so barbarous and savage that they lacked religion altogether, since it is born in our bodies with our soul and grows old together with it."[40] Prophecy, or what Scala called "foreknowledge of things to come," was similarly found among almost all peoples, and although admirable and divine, these prophets, or "diviners," were nothing new, since belief in foreknowledge had always existed, whether these prophets were called "seers" (as by

---

37 Lorenzo Tornabuoni to Benedetto Dei, 4 November 1486, ed. Armando Verde, *Lo studio fiorentino* (Pistoia, 1977), 3: 1, 576: "Io udì istamane, sendo in piazza . . . che 'l re v'à mandato molti huomini experti a insegnare loro el linguaggio di Portogallo e amaestrarli in costumi . . . a parte a ridurli alla vita humana et non bestiale," "et è tenuta in questa cità una bella e una magna nuova."

38 On Amerigo, a nephew of Giorgio Antonio Vespucci, a learned scholar who owned a map of Ptolemy and was tutor to both Amerigo and Lorenzo di Pierfrancesco de' Medici, see pp. 89–90 below.

39 Ibid. Cf. Tribaldo de' Rossi's description (in March 1494) of the natives discovered in the West Indies by Columbus: "huomini, done assai, engniudi tutti, cierte frasche intorno ala natura e non altro; e mai vidono più cristiani loro," *Ricordanze*, in *Delizie degli eruditi toscani* (Florence, 1786), 23: 281.

40 *Apologia contra vituperatores civitatis Florentiae*, ed. Brown, 407, trans. Watkins, 266–67: "cum anima simul innascatur in corpus et cum aetate inolescat simul"; although the passage refers here to religion, it follows closely Lucretius's description of how the mind "gigni pariter cum corpore et una crescere sentimus pariterque senescere" (3: 445–46).

the Hebrews), oracles or diviners (as by the Greeks), or augurs (as by the Romans).[41] So despite one reference to "our God, the God of mercies and piety, the God of peace and of all consolation" and an impressive "show of historical knowledge" (as he calls it) of biblical as well as ancient prophets, there is nothing specifically Christian about Scala's defense of Savonarola; on the contrary, its description of religion being "born in our bodies with our soul" and shared by barbarians as well as Christians is perhaps closer to Lucretius's view of the mind being born and growing up with the body than to Christian orthodoxy.[42]

It was at the beginning of this *Defense* that Scala embarked on a disquisition on the power of fortune in life, demonstrating even more directly the continuing influence of Lucretius on his thinking at this time—which is as surprising in this context as the unexpected opening on man's primitive origins was in his 1463 *Dialogue of Consolation*. Digressing with "a few words about fortune, which they say overturns all mortal affairs according to her will and pleasure," Scala went on in the *Defense* to attribute to "that admirable poet Lucretius—whose poem Virgil himself, the king, so to speak, of Latin writers, did not blush to integrate into his own work"—the view that the world originated in "the fortuitous clash of invisible atoms." Although he said he was not "totally convinced" by this view of the power of fortune, he was equally skeptical about those "who remove fortune totally from human affairs," acknowledging that no discipline was so exact that—without God's dispensation—it could deflect nature's impetus when it raged against us, "as has clearly happened to us now" (after Florence's sudden loss of Montepulciano and Pisa).[43] His approach was very different from that of the merchant Giovanni Rucellai referred to in Chapter 1. In describing the destabilizing power of fortune in this way and openly attributing this new view to Lucretius, Scala not only anticipates what became a common theme of writing after the French invasions but provides us with a valuable pointer to Lucre-

---

41 *Apologia*, ed. Brown, 408, trans. Watkins, 270–73 ("Apud omnes ferme gentes [nisi fallor] semper fuit opinio aliqua praescientiae rerum futurarum").

42 Ibid., 410, trans. Watkins, 274–75: "Deus noster," "ad ostentandas historias," and note 40 above. On the Christian position, see Hankins, "Ficino's Theology and the Critique of Lucretius," cited on p. 92, note 12 below.

43 *Apologia*, ed. Brown, 395–96, 397, trans. Watkins, 236–37, 240–41: "principia . . . creatarum rerum fortuitae cuidam concursioni indivisibilium minutorum." On fortune, see Mario Santoro, *Fortuna, ragione e prudenza nella civiltà letteraria del Cinquecento* (Naples, 1967), especially 11–21.

tius's less obvious influence on other humanists, especially his successors in the chancery, Marcello Adriani and Niccolò Machiavelli.

Despite this openness, Scala was nevertheless careful to present these radical ideas as part of a dialogue or debate in which he was able to safeguard his orthodoxy. For a more intimate understanding of the role they played in his personal outlook on life, we have to turn to the fables he wrote throughout this later period. Gathered in two different collections of one hundred fables, dedicated to Lorenzo de' Medici in 1481 and around 1486, and then continued as an "annual tribute" to the Medici until 1492, they were a usefully allusive medium through which to express his views on other more contentious topics associated with the revival of Epicureanism in Florence, especially religion and man's fear of death. Influenced by Leon Battista Alberti's fables, as well as by Lucian and Aesop, they reveal a similarly ironic and skeptical approach to man's nature and superstitious religion.[44] In the fable *Moral Values*, a Cynic, after dining intemperately with an Epicurean, describes his postprandial dream of an upside-down world, fish swimming on dry land and horses carried by men, to which the Epicurean replies that the one marvel missing from his list is that grief and hard work are preferred to pleasure, and cares and worries to leisure and a tranquil life: "You weren't dreaming; believe me, life is lived with upside-down morals."[45] In the fable *Religio*, for example, we are told that the origin of most gods can be ascribed to fear *(timor)*, an argument that he attributed to Lucretius in his 1483 *Dialogue on Laws and Legal Judgments*.[46] The association of fear and death recurs in his second collection of fables in *Death*, in which a traveler is amazed to encounter people with bandaged eyes fleeing the onslaught of Death, portrayed as a wild beast mounted on a black horse striking out at random: "How needlessly they fear and bind their eyes; if this is living, isn't it better to die?"[47]

---

44 *Apologi centum* (I) and *Apologorum liber secundus* (II), ed. Brown, 305–37, 364–93, trans. Marsh, 88–271 (repr. from his *Renaissance Fables*). On the genre, see his introduction, ibid., esp. 25–27, and id., *Lucian and the Latins: Humor and Humanism in the Early Renaissance* (Ann Arbor, 1998), esp. 42–67.

45 "Mores," *Apologi* II: 37, ed. Brown, 378, trans. Marsh, 224–25. I owe to James Hankins the comment that this poetic figure of *adunaton* is particularly associated with Lucretius; see 1: 159ff. and 5: 126ff.

46 *Apologi* I: 22, "Religio," ed. Brown, 312–13, trans. Marsh, 110–11: "origines in timorem." On *De legibus*, note 33 above; in it, Scala contrasted Lucretius's derivation of *religio* with Cicero's, who unlike Lucretius distinguished between superstition and religion in deriving it from *relegere* (to retrace ancient ritual, *De nat. deor.* 2: 28, 71–72).

47 *Apologi* II: 20, "Mors," ed. Brown, 371, trans. Marsh, 206–7: "quam temere timent."

Death is also the subject of Scala's two last fables, which he sent to Piero de' Medici on the first All Souls Day after the death of his father, Lorenzo il Magnifico, in 1492. In the first, the shades are only allowed to return to earth on this one day in the year; moved by overwhelming desire for the light of day, they then flock to visit the living in such numbers that the rulers feel deserted and repeal their concession—in order, Minos explains, to prevent the living from losing their fear of them through familiarity. In the second fable, a persistent shade eventually wins Pluto's permission to visit the living on All Souls Day and encounters a living man, with whom he discusses whether it is better to live in continual fear of death or to lack the good things of life. "The good things of life!" the shade exclaims with loud guffaws. "What is generally believed by us about you is true. You with your possessions are more dead than the dead themselves."[48] An earlier fable on *Death* plays with the same words "more dead than the dead" *(mortui . . . mortui)* and "the living dead" *(vivi mortui)* in describing Icarus's fall from the heavens and burial in a tomb ("to prevent the dead part of him from wandering"); in his fall, he is supported by the Muses, who immortalize him in their verse: "For not only the dead are dead [*mortui . . . mortui*], the living are also dead" *(vivi mortui).*[49]

The immortality bestowed by literature was a commonplace of humanism, of course, and Scala had himself employed it in a letter he wrote to Lorenzo de' Medici in the 1470s. In it, he told Lorenzo he believed that letters—by which, he explained, he meant the discipline of the liberal arts, consisting of the study of human and divine affairs—were far more immortal than other human activities. For, he wrote, everything we do eventually perishes and nothing lasts for long, yet "we are accustomed to speak in this way and to honor whatever is lasting with the name of immortality, which is peculiar to divine things."[50] He also wrote two fables about the immortality of letters. In the first, *Litterae,* Immortality is forced to take refuge against Old Age in a bookstore protected by bronze outer walls and cedar wood inside, whereas in the second, *Immortalitas,* a Christian soul seeking its final immor-

---

48 *Apologi* II: 101, "Inferorum regnum": "minus verebuntur umbras"; II: 102, "Vivi mortui": "vos his bonis quam mortui magis estis mortui," ed. Brown, 393, trans. Marsh, 270–71.

49 *Mortui* II: 47, ed. Brown, 379, trans. Marsh, 232–33.

50 Scala, *Writings,* ed. Brown, 41–42 (no. 47) [April–May 1474]: "Etsi enim occidunt cuncta nostra tandem et diu nihil extat, tamen solemus ita loqui et quae diuturniora sunt immortalitatis quae sua est rerum divinarum nomine honestare." (I owe this translation to David Marsh.)

tal resting place is mocked by an Epicurean for the unhappiness of his plight. Still homeless and pondering on his impure life, he meets the Epicurean, to whom he asserts that he, the Christian, is immortal and that "those fables of yours, which circulate everywhere" cannot change his nature or the truth. To which the Epicurean smilingly replies: "May you even be one of the gods while you are wandering around and being punished." Since Scala made an autograph correction to Luca Ficini's transcription of his fables, deleting the last line, "'But I am immortal,' the soul said, 'and I haven't died,'" he leaves the last word of his emended version with the Epicurean, whose beliefs—casting aspersions on Christian immortality—circulate everywhere.[51]

We know that Scala's first collection of one hundred fables was popular and in demand at the time, read not only by humanists in Florence like Landino and Ficino, who said he was encouraged by them to write more fables of his own, but also outside Florence. The Sienese humanist Giovanni Lorenzo Buoninsegni wanted copies of the first collection, so did cardinal Francesco Gonzaga, and Alessandro Farnese (later Pope Paul III) admired them for mixing humor with seriousness.[52] Less is known about the response to his second collection, however, which marks his shifting attitude towards immortality. Although it is impossible to say with certainty how far the fables reflect his personal beliefs, there is good reason to think that Scala was not traditionally devout. He made no religious bequests in his will and "didn't trouble himself about funeral rites" (as Epicurus also commended), leaving it to his son to institute masses for him and his wife after their deaths. A contemporary account of the miracles of the Virgin at SS. Annunziata suggests that he owed his escape from death in 1474 solely to the pious intercession of his mother-in-law, without which his life, "which he himself had so intemperately neglected," would have come to an end.[53] So the fables may have provided him with a vehicle for expressing more personal and skeptical views about religion than his public writings allowed him to do.

Another—and not unconnected—shift in attitude concerns the relation-

---

51 *Apologi* II: 70 and 80 (cf. the earlier *Immortalitas* I: 18), ed. Brown, 385, 387 (311), trans. Marsh, 248–49, 254–55 (108–9): "illae nos vestrae, quibus omnia completis, fabulae" (trans. Marsh: "all the fables you tell everyone"), "sum immortalis," Anima inquit, "nec interii' *del.*"

52 See Brown, *Scala*, 278–79.

53 Ibid., 319–23; Scala, *Writings*, 483; Diog. Laert., *Lives*, 10: 118, trans. Traversari, fol. 177r: "neque Sepulturae curam habiturum."

ship between men and animals. Unsurprisingly, in a genre modeled on Aesop and Lucian, animals are sometimes used to support the underdog and sometimes to comment cynically on man's pretensions. So in *Man,* a wolf laughs at the lion for being scared of man: "Are you, our king, frightened of specters? If you flee, man is bold; if you act, he flees. Man isn't man, he only seems to be a man." In another, Diogenes the Cynic sees men as animals in an "Animal Farm"—as pigs, foxes, wolves, and Harpies according to their various professions, belying their claim to be superior to animals. This idea is repeated in the fable *Monster,* in which the Cynic comments that humans are just as "monstrous" as the strange animals that amaze people as monsters, since man is equally multiform with the head of a serpent and a human face, the throat of a dog, and hands of Harpies, bent and deformed with nails: "Tell me, if you will, what is a monster if you aren't monsters?"[54]

The same approach to animals can be seen in the fables depicted in the stucco frieze decorating the atrium of Scala's urban villa in Borgo Pinti. As Alessandro Parronchi pointed out some time ago, the fables illustrated in the frieze are, with one exception, all taken from Scala's first (1481) collection of fables; although their overall meaning is still being debated, they must be assumed to have had special significance for their author within his own home.[55] Most of them describe triumphal scenes, as Leon Battista Alberti tells us was the practice of the ancients, with titles like *Praelium, Regnum, Iurgium, Victoria, Imperatoria,* and *Gloria militaris,* interspersed with more autobiographical scenes, like *Negligentia,* describing Scala's success as a new man, or *Quies,* depicting Lorenzo de' Medici as the apparent author of repose. But far from representing a triumphalist progression from vice to virtue, or from animal bestiality towards civilization, as recent accounts of the frieze have suggested, they instead offer a series of pithy and ironic comments on warfare, love, and marriage, influenced more by the cynicism and primitivism of

---

54 *Apologi* II: 24 ("Homo" [II]): "Neque iam homo homo est: videtur homo"; II: 1 ("Homo"); II: 10 ("Monstrum"): "Dic, sodes, quid tandem monstrum est, si vos non estis monstra?" ed. Brown, 372, 365–66, 368, trans. Marsh, 210–11, 192–93, 200–201. On Diogenes and the Cynics, see Michèle Clement, *Le cynicisme à la Renaissance d'Erasme à Montaigne* (Geneva, 2005), esp. 36, 47–50.

55 See Alessandro Parronchi, "The Language of Humanism and the Language of Sculpture," *JWCI* 27 (1964): 108–36, with a plan on 112. It is also described by James Draper, *Bertoldo di Giovanni* (Columbia, 1992), 220–53, and Cristina Acidini Luchinat, "Di Bertoldo e d'altri artisti," in *La Casa del Cancelliere,* ed. Anna Bellinazzi (Florence, 1998), 91–120, figs. 50–76 (the same plan on 94).

Lucretius (and Martial, whose *Epigrams* we know Scala owned) than by the prevailing neoplatonism of Lorenzo's entourage.[56]

Animals are depicted in four panels of the frieze. Three of these are together on the west wall, facing the entrance: *Drunkenness (Ebrietas)*, in which centaurs dismember and devour animals who are being stuffed into a cauldron (the only panel not based on his fables); *Battle (Praelium)*, depicting a battle scene of enmeshed men and animals, some mounted and others freestanding; and *Sovereignty (Regnum)*, another violent scene of men and animals locked in conflict after the animals decide in a council of war to throw off their longstanding yoke of servitude to men. The fourth panel, *Magnanimity (Magnanimitas* or *Mitas)*, is in the center of the north wall, between *Love (Amor)* and *Strife (Iurgium)*; in it, a bull is gored by a lion—but not before the sight of a hare safely sheltering from hounds between the lion's paws gives him hope that he too may be saved. Its moral, that "it is often better to be a weak suppliant than to resist boldly" suggests—like Machiavelli's later poem, *The Golden Ass*, discussed in Chapter 4—that animals are kinder to each other and more virtuous than men.[57] *Praelium* and *Regnum*, like the panels representing military victories, *Gloria militaris*—*Imperatoria* on the south wall and *Victoria* on the east wall—offer a cynical and reductive view of life, in which human triumphs are illusory and animals, by contrast, behave better than men.[58] Overall, the frieze suggests that civilization is at best a mixed blessing, in view of the illusions of war and power struggles, and man's misuse of animals and abuse of his own animal passions through drunkenness, excessive love, and bellicosity.[59]

---

56 See Alison Brown, "The House and Culture of Bartolomeo Scala, Chancellor of Florence" (Colle Val d'Elsa, forthcoming). For other recent accounts, see Draper, *Bertoldo*, 223, and Acidini Luchinat, "Di Bertoldo," 94, and Parronchi, 124–25 (who does, however, acknowledge the "elegaic irony" of the east wall); also André Chastel, who interprets them as a *psychomachie* in *Art et Humanisme à Florence au temps de Laurent le Magnifique* (Paris, 1959), 27.

57 *Apologi* I: 60, *Bellum*, titled *Praelium* in the courtyard; 76, *Regnum*; 54, *Magnanimitas* or *Mitas*, ed. Brown, 324–25, 329–30, 323, trans. Marsh, 150–51, 164–65, 144–45; *Ebrietas* has no corresponding fable. See Parronchi, 113–14, 116–17. They are illustrated ibid., pls. 17a, 20e, 21c, 20a, and in Acidini-Luchinat, figs. 56–58, 60.

58 *Apologi* I: 46, 30, and 29, ed. Brown, 313, 315, trans. Marsh, 112–13, 118–21; illustrated in Parronchi, pls. 19e, 18a, 21a; Acidini-Luchinat, figs. 63, 65, and 66 (the titles of 63 and 66 are reversed).

59 Lucretius 3: 476–85, 1051 (on drunkenness); 4: 1141–1287 (on love and marriage); illustrated in the panels *Ebrietas, Amor, Iurgium,* and *Neglegentia* (which also illustrates the autobiographical theme of escape from poverty by hard work); *Apologi* I: 83, 40, 36, ed. Brown, 331–32, 318, 317, trans. Marsh, 170–73, 130–32, 126–27; in Parronchi, pls. 17a, 22a, 17e, 16a; in Acidini-Lucinat, figs. 56, 59, 61, 55.

These are all, of course, themes of *De rerum natura*. The battle scenes recall Lucretius's description of the pomp of the mock battles of legions "seething over the Campus Martius," and even more his account of the way civilization, "quite unbelievably," made men rebrutalize the very animals they had domesticated by making them engines of war. Together, they reinforce his argument that men have allowed the good instinctual drives they share with animals to be perverted by their growing sophistication, which recoiled against them in the same way that the retrained animals turned against their owners.[60]

The shift that this represents can be illustrated by changing attitudes towards the mythical centaur, half man, half animal—even though neither Lucretius nor Scala believed in centaurs.[61] According to later classical and Christian morality, men who "obeyed their nature" like beasts represented the worst side of human nature, and so in Dante and his commentator Cristoforo Landino, Chiron the centaur represented a bellicose man brutalized by his ambition and lust to dominate, although not totally lacking in learning or reason.[62] By the time the centaur reappeared in Machiavelli's *Prince*, however, which was written some thirty years after Landino's *Commentary*, he had been transformed into a model for princes, as a result—we are told—of a new taste for "the primitive and the wild," inspired "largely by Lucretius," that reverted to ancient pre-Christian prototypes of power.[63] Scala's frieze and his fables

---

60 Lucretius 2: 40–43 (on mock battles); 5: 1297–1340 (on animals and fighting); 5: 1014, 1022–23, 1308–41(on civilization); discussed by Godwin, *Lucretius*, 36; Charles Saylor, "Man, Animal and the Bestial in Lucretius," *Classical Journal* 67 (1971–1972): 310–15; Segal, *Lucretius on Death and Anxiety*, 188–207 (referring on 211 to "contrasting tableaux of war and peace" that could be the inspiration for Scala's opposing panels of peace and war, business and leisure, rather than Aristotle, as I initially suggested).

61 Scala never refers to centaurs in his fables, nor did Lucretius believe they existed but read them instead as superimposed images of man and horse, encouraging the symbolic interpretation of the dual attributes of man's nature so familiar to Florentines, 4: 732, 739–42: "nulla fuit quoniam talis natura animalis; / verum ubi equi atque hominis casu convenit imago, / haerescit facile extemplo," cf. 5: 878–91.

62 Landino, *Commentary* (Florence, 1481), fol. h5r, ed. Procaccioli, 2, 627: "huomo bellicoso . . . benché sia efferato nell'ambitione et nella cupidità del signoreggiare, nientedimeno non è sanza alchuna doctrina et ragione et qualche iustitia et civile chostume"; cf. Rudolf Wittkower, "Transformations of Minerva in Renaissance Imagery," *JWCI* 2 (1938–1939): 200. On the Renaissance view of man typified by Alberti in *Della famiglia* 1: 168, see John Najemy, "The Republic's Two Bodies," in *Language and Images in Renaissance Italy*, ed. Alison Brown (Oxford, 1995), 255: "come uno carriuolo sul quale si muova l'anima."

63 Enzio Raimondi, "Il politico e il centauro," in id., *Politica e commedia dal Beroaldo al Machiavelli* (Bologna, 1972, repr. 1998), 138.

explain how Lucretius's primitivism helped to mediate this important change of attitude that was to emerge more clearly in Machiavelli in the following century.

During Lorenzo de' Medici's lifetime, Lucretian primitivism and religious skepticism remained understated and unfashionable. Contrasting with the hierarchical elitism and cosmic determinism favored by Lorenzo's neoplatonic "golden age" culture, it became a counterculture supported by Lorenzo's cousins, Lorenzo and Giovanni di Pierfrancesco de' Medici, who had their own reasons for being alienated from the political hegemony of the elder branch of the family. Like their father, they considered that they had been defrauded of their rightful inheritance by the elder branch during their years of tutelage as minors, and they later expressed their resentment in the form of cultural, as well as political, opposition.[64] After coming of age in 1485, Lorenzo di Pierfrancesco gradually gathered his own circle of scholars and artists around him that included Amerigo Vespucci, a business colleague and neighbor in Trebbio who dedicated his *Mundus novus* to him, and the Greek poet and soldier Michele Marullo, who came to Florence in 1489.[65] Marullo became one of the foremost scholars working on the text of *De rerum natura*, which he is said to have read every night before going to bed, reputedly dying by drowning in 1500 with Lucretius in his pocket. He probably developed his love of Lucretius in Rome and Naples in the 1480s, dedicating his Lucretian *Hymni naturales* to his exiled Neapolitan patron, Antonello da Sanseverino, prince of Salerno. But when he came to Florence, Lorenzo di Pierfrancesco, with his brother Giovanni, became his patron and dedicatee of his *Epigrams*, and Bartolomeo Scala became his friend and later his father-in-law.[66]

Before he died in 1497, Scala dedicated a long, unfinished poem, *On Trees*,

---

64 See Brown, "Pierfrancesco de' Medici," *JWCI* 42 (1979): 102–3, rev. in *The Medici in Florence*, 100–101; on his political opposition, ead., "The Revolution of 1494 in Florence and its Aftermath: A Reassessment," in *Italy in Crisis: 1494*, ed. Jane Everson and Diego Zancani (Oxford, 2000), 13–40, rev. in Alison Brown, *Medicean and Savonarolan Florence*, chap. 5; Sergio Bertelli, "Ancora su Lucrezio e Machiavelli," 777–78; Jonathan Nelson, "Filippino Lippi's *Allegory of Discord*: A Warning about Families and Politics," *Gazette des Beaux-Arts* 128 (1996): 244–48.

65 On Lorenzo and Giovanni di Pierfrancesco's patronage, see John Shearman, "The Collections of the Younger Branch of the Medici," *Burlington Magazine* 117 (1975): 14–27; Nicoletta Baldini, "In the Shadow of Lorenzo the Magnificent: The Role of Lorenzo and Giovanni di Pierfrancesco de' Medici," *In the light of Apollo: the Italian Renaissance and Greece*, ed. Mina Gregori (Athens, 2003), 277–82.

66 See Carol Kidwell, *Marullus: Soldier Poet of the Renaissance* (London, 1989), 145–85, 249; Bertelli, "Ancora su Lucrezio e Machiavelli," 776, note 5. On the *Hymni naturales*, and *Epigrammata*, see pp. 43 and 98–99 below.

to Lorenzo di Pierfrancesco as the son of his first employer and patron in Florence—completing the circle, as he put it, by returning in his extreme old age to the haven where his studies first began. As its title suggests, this is not his lost Lucretian poem, *De rebus naturalibus*, that Michele Verino was shown in the 1480s, but an agriculturalist poem influenced by Theophrastus.[67] Yet its account of man's emergence from a state of primitive nature to civilization remains heavily indebted to Lucretius and Epicurus. After an opening invocation to Bacchus and his patron, Lorenzo di Pierfrancesco (as Lucretius had invoked Venus and his patron, Memmius), the poem described the ever-changing Empedoclean conflict between opposing atoms, or "seeds of the world," hot fighting with cold and moist with dry, before Jupiter imposed his law and divided the world into two solstices and different seasons. Before then, men were cave dwellers, "mythically born from earth or trunks," slaying and devouring "whatever inhabits the earth, sky, and sea" and considering nothing unclean, for hunger meant death; without seeking harm, "we waged unremitting and continual war with wild animals," eating their flesh and their blood. Fire was provided by Vulcan or by lightning hurled down by Jupiter, and then it transformed life by the many different domestic and sacral uses to which fire and trees were put, including the provision of more and cheaper printed books. As in *De rerum natura*, however, technological progress brought its own penalties, including the plague and famine that ravaged Italy while Scala was writing, just as it had ravaged Athens—as Lucretius describes in Book 6. Fear of death is a predominant theme, based on the reality of these events, but Scala's description of how people were reduced by famine to "eating grasses" and even "devouring unclean food" before collapsing by the wayside serves to demonstrate (as in Lucretius and in Scala's fables) the rebrutalization that accompanied the growing sophistication of men's lives.[68]

---

67 *De arboribus*, ed. Brown, 426–45; Brown, *Scala*, 121. In the prolusion to his 1495–1496 lectures, Marcello Adriani referred to poems praising trees as a "novum genus laudis" (Florence, Bibl. Riccardiana, MS 811 [=R], fols. 10v–11r). On Theophrastus, see Scala's letter to Marco Giannarini in 1496: "ingenia quoque suum sequi caelum, non plantas modo, ut ait Theophrastus" (reflecting line 60 in the poem, "Namque ut non virtus caeli regionibus una est," *Writings*, 186, letter 224, 427, line 60); cf. Mauro Ambrosoli, *The Wild and the Sown: Botany and Agriculture in Western Europe, 1350–1850* (Cambridge, 1997), esp. 1–68. On *De rebus naturalibus*, note 26 above.

68 *De arboribus*, ed. Brown, 426, lines 12–15; 427–28, lines 69–86; 428, lines 105–12; 431, lines 229–40. On the hardship of these years, see Brown, "Revolution of 1494," at notes 69–73.

By the time he wrote this poem, its dedicatee, Lorenzo di Pierfrancesco, had actively worked with his brother to overthrow their cousins' regime, together with Marullo and Sanseverino, and were now part of the ruling elite, having renamed themselves "Popolano" instead of Medici. So Scala was thanking the man who probably helped to save his position as chancellor in 1494, if not his life. The poem was not only an appropriate gesture of thanks but also politically apposite, in showing the relevance of the Lucretian life *ante legem* to contemporary life in Florence. The brief flowering of Lucretius's philosophy that followed the revolution is the subject of the following chapter.

3

Republican Florence: The University Lectures of Marcello Adriani

The years 1494 to 1498 were a time not only of political innovation and economic hardship but also of cultural change in Florence. The French invasion helped to bring about the downfall of the Medici regime in November 1494. Although the old ruling elite initially took charge, the influence of Savonarola's sermons encouraged the establishment of a republican regime with a new legislative council, the Great Council, of over three thousand eligible members. This gave people of middling or artisan status more power, but by greatly increasing the number of votes needed to pass a law, it also introduced gerrymandering and factionalism into the government, exacerbating the divisions between the Savonarolans and their opponents.[1] The events of 1494 transformed the cultural scene as well. Gone were the certainties of the hierarchical neoplatonism of Lorenzo de' Medici's circle, to be replaced by the cultural austerity of the new regime. For the revolution saw the end of a generation of humanists who had formed part of Lorenzo's circle,

---

1 On the revolution and its impact, see Brown, "Revolution of 1494," also ead., "Uffici di onore e utile" (trans. into English as "Offices of Honour and Profit") and "Ideology and Faction in Savonarolan Florence," both in *Medicean and Savonarolan Florence,* chap. 6 and 8.

including Poliziano, who died about a month before the revolution, and Giovanni Pico della Mirandola, who died two weeks after it—leaving Bartolomeo Scala and Marsilio Ficino to represent the old guard.[2] They and Marcello Adriani, who replaced Poliziano as professor of poetry and oratory in Florence in October 1494, became the cultural spokesmen of the new era, together forming a counterpoise to the increasingly fervid sermons of Savonarola.

The revolution also brought back to Florence the exiled Lorenzo di Pierfrancesco and his brother, who reentered the city only three days after their young cousin Piero de' Medici fled on November 9. "The young Lorenzo," as contemporaries called him—to distinguish him from Lorenzo the Magnificent (although he was thirty-one at the time of the revolution, and Piero only twenty-two)—briefly entered the political scene and resumed his patronage of his former friends. His circle included Ficino, Marullo, the explorer-merchant Amerigo Vespucci, and the artists Botticelli and Michelangelo, as well as the chancellor Scala.[3] But far from supporting a counterculture, his patronage circle now represented the cultural avant-garde. Bartolomeo Scala, as we saw in his *Defense* of the new regime, quickly realized how relevant Lucretius's "fortuitous clash of invisible atoms" was to the chaos and unpredictability of the new situation, and in his long poem *On Trees* that he died writing for Lorenzo di Pierfrancesco in 1497, he similarly demonstrated the relevance of Lucretian primitivism to the hardship and famine of these years. It was exactly at this time, in December 1497, that Marullo's *Epigrams* and *Natural Hymns* were published in Florence in a single volume, which brought together the *Epigrams* dedicated to Lorenzo di Pierfrancesco and the *Hymns* dedicated to Antonello Sanseverino, prince of Salerno, Marullo's first patron and, like Lorenzo di Pierfrancesco, a rebel in helping to instigate the French invasion against their rulers.[4]

A month earlier, a friend and student of Marcello Adriani's, Roberto Ac-

---

2 Brown, "Revolution of 1494," 23–24, and Peter Godman, *From Poliziano to Machiavelli* (Princeton, 1998), esp. 78–79, 134–79.

3 Baldini, "In the Shadow," 278–79; ead., "Quasi Adonidos hortum. Il giovane Michelangelo al giardino mediceo delle sculture," in *Giovinezza di Michelangelo*, ed. Katherine Weil-Garris Brandt (Florence, 1999), 49–56; Kidwell, *Marullus*, 171, 233–34. On "the young Lorenzo," Brown, "Revolution of 1494," at notes 30 and 33.

4 *Hymni et Epigrammata* (Florence 1497); see Dennis Rhodes, *Gli Annali tipografici fiorentini del XV secolo* (Florence, 1988), 79 (no. 432); Mario Martelli, "Il 'Libro delle Epistole' di Angelo Poliziano," *Interpres* 1 (1978): 212–15. On the *Hymns*, see p. 99, note 31 below.

ciaiuoli, wrote to ask him if the university would be reopening in Florence (it had been temporarily transferred to Prato). Fearing its decline in the present straits, he went on to describe the desperate state Florence was in, "worn out by civil conflict, war, its citizens prostrate with famine and plague: what can we hope for? We live as we please . . . all we have left is you, as the only patron, benefactor, and defender of literary studies."[5] This letter confirms the instability depicted in Scala's poem, and it also explains the importance of Marcello Adriani's teaching at this time. Adriani came from an undistinguished Florentine family that had held some political offices but no longer belonged to the ruling group; his father was a lawyer who knew Scala, like Machiavelli's father, suggesting that the path of both men may have been "smoothed by the Scala connection."[6] What also bound Adriani to Scala in the years before he succeeded him as chancellor in 1498 was their shared interest in Lucretius for so aptly describing the primitivism of the post-1494 situation in Florence. The university was closed for most of 1495, and in his inaugural lecture for the following academic year, delivered in Prato towards the end of 1495, Adriani directly compared the self-interested free-for-all in Florence—in the early chaotic months of the new popular government—to Lucretius's description of primitive life *ante legem*. This was like the time, Adriani told his audience of students and their parents, "before the founding of cities, in that first newness of the world when, as Lucretius said:

> Men could not recognize the common good.
> They knew no binding customs, used no laws.
> Every man, wise in staying strong, surviving,
> Kept for himself the spoils that fortune offered."[7]

---

5 Roberto Acciaiuoli to Marcello Adriani, 4 November 1497, ed. Verde, *Studio* 4: 1261: "Nam hac tempestate seu temporum angustiis . . . infirma civitate et discordiis civilibus, bello, fame, civium strage, pesteque defatigata, quid boni sperare possumus? Ad libitum vivimus . . . Tantum nobis relinquitur ut te unum patronum, benefactorem, et defensorem suum literarum studia adclament." On Acciaiuoli, born in 1467, later a diplomat involved in the university's affairs, see Verde, *Studio* 3: 855; Guido Verucci in *DBI* 1 (Rome, 1960): 90–93.

6 Godman, *Poliziano*, 146–67. On Adriani, see also Verde, *Studio* 4: 1160–63, 1205–8, 1261–64, 1309–20, 1340–45.

7 R, fol. 8v: "Verisimile itaque est ante conditas urbes prima illa novitate mundi, quo tempore ut Lucretius ait, 'Nec commune bonum poterant spectare, neque ullis / moribus inter se scibant nec legibus uti. / Quod cuique obtulerat praedae fortuna, ferebat / sponte sua sibi quisque valere et vivere doctus," quoting Lucretius 5: 958–61 (trans. Esolen). Cf. Verde, *Studio* 4: 1205–8; Godman, *Poliziano*, 157–59.

Some of these lectures have been described and briefly summarized, but although an edition has been promised, they remain as yet unpublished. So it is not easy to follow the trail of Lucretius among the welter of citations from Greek and Roman authors in the lectures. Perhaps for this reason, nobody has discovered his almost continuous but undetected presence, who, "if not a leitmotif" (as I put it in the introduction), nevertheless makes his own persistent contribution to the argument of many of them. Together with the evidence of marginal comments in a manuscript of *De rerum natura* in Florence—several of which refer to "Marcellus's" reading of passages in Book I, while others are typical of Adriani's teaching methods[8]—these lectures provide us with the firm evidence we need to document Lucretius's influence on Adriani during his nearly twenty-five years spent teaching and working in the university and the chancery.[9]

Until recently, Adriani has been a largely neglected figure. Now, however, he and his lectures have been given an important place in Peter Godman's witty account of Florentine humanism between Poliziano and Machiavelli, where he is valued less for his novelty than for his nimble-footed conservatism in returning to the republican patriotism of Leonardo Bruni's era. He also appears briefly in Anthony Grafton's *Bring out Your Dead* for the practical examples he uses to explain natural history in his translation of Dioscorides.[10] But it is a third scholar, Armando Verde, who does most to explain the appeal of Adriani's secular lectures within the context of the religious, as well as the political, crisis, which was being fomented by Savonarola's parallel sermons at this time. In his definitive account of Florence's university up to 1500, which includes summaries of the lectures delivered in these years and references to Savonarola's sermons and other relevant writings, Verde explains how Adri-

---

8 Florence, Bibl. Laurenziana, MS 35, 32, fol. 3r: "clueo verbum a Κλυω pro celebro et illustro deducit Marcellus" (1: 119); fol. 12r (on the order of 1: 551–64) and 20v (on the lacuna between 1: 1013–14), both quoted in the appendix, p. 119 (note 20) below; cf. 7r (Lucretius's description of the right hands of bronze statues at gateways being worn away by frequent touching, 1: 316–18; cf. Cic. *Verr.* 4: 94). Other marginal comments in 35, 32 are described on p. 70 (note 7) below. On Adriani's fondness for topical exempla, see Godman, *Poliziano*, 178; Anthony Grafton, *Bring out Your Dead* (Cambridge, MA, 2001), 2–3.

9 Payments for his lectures from 1494 to 1503 are listed in Verde, *Studio* (Florence, 1973), 2: 476–77; 5 (Florence 1994): 315–436 passim; payments from 1503 to 1514 are listed in Bigazzi MS 109 (libro 6), in Florence, Bibl. Riccardiana, the reference to which I owe to Jonathan Davies. Peter Godman talks of a planned edition of his unpublished writings in *Poliziano*, 150, note 107.

10 Godman, *Poliziano*, 158–59, 186–87, 190, 266–67; Grafton, *Bring out Your Dead*, 2–10.

ani used his lectures to deliver "the most explicit formulation of a lay version of theology" in order to counter Savonarola's fundamentalism. According to Verde, they represented "an extraordinary reassertion of humanist studies," which rose up (quoting Adriani) "out of that ancient and misshapen site beneath which they had nearly putrified . . . almost out of untouched treasure chambers."[11]

None of these writers, however, has detected Lucretius among these almost putrified treasures, nor his importance—with the early Greek atomists—in providing the missing link between Adriani's apparently "backward-looking" republicanism and his forward-looking interest in natural science and history. Lucretius made his first appearance in Adriani's opening lecture after Poliziano's death, which he gave on October 24, 1494. Hurriedly prepared and delivered only two weeks before the revolution, Adriani chose the broad subject of poetry for his inaugural discourse, in which he defended the seriousness of poetry (in terms that Savonarola would approve) by arguing that it embraced philosophy as well as theology. With the Medici still—for two more weeks—in power, he was careful to pay tribute to his academic predecessors and to the Medici family as "the only protectors of letters in this city." For the same reason, although Lucretius was one of the earliest philosopher-poets to follow Empedocles and Parmenides in lucidly "unlocking the secrets of nature," Adriani was careful to voice his doubt about whether he should be praised—on account of "his worthless heresy about atoms"—any more than Epicurus, who believed the gods were indifferent to our affairs.[12] Nevertheless, that did not prevent him from using Lucretius to defend the "utility and pleasure" of poetry against critics like Plato (as well as Savonarola), by quoting at length from Lucretius's "most beautiful comparison to show the force of the most beautiful poetry of all":

---

11 Verde, *Studio* 4: 1310: "la più esplicita formulazione della teologia in versione laica"; 1311: "Questa straordinaria ripresa degli studi di umanità, che risorgevano 'ex antiquo illo et informi situ sub quo pene putruerant . . . quasi ex intactis tesauris,'" quoting R, fol. 18r; Godman, *Poliziano*, 163, note 179. Cf. Horace, *Epist.*, 2, 2, 116–18 ("situs informis").

12 R, fols. 1r–5v, a reference to Lucretius exceptionally discussed by Godman, *Poliziano*, 151–55, who cites Adriani's doubts about him at 154 (quoting fol. 2r: "vanam de athomis heresim"); cf. Verde, *Studio* 4: 1161–63. In my account of the lectures that follows, I cite R as the principal source for Adriani's prolusions, and L for comparison; these and other sources are discussed by Brian Richardson, "A Manuscript of Biagio Buonaccorsi," *Bibliothèque d' Humanisme et Renaissance* 36 (1974): 593–95. Unless otherwise stated, the translations of the lectures are my own.

> For as with children, when doctors try to coax them to take
> Foul wormwood, first they brush the rim of the cups
> All around with the sweet and golden juice of honey
> To fool unsuspecting childhood past the lips,
> So they drink down that bitter juice, tricked but not betrayed,
> Since they will all the sooner be restored to health,
> So I too [. . .] have desired
> To reveal my doctrine to you in sweet-throated song,
> And as though touching it with the Muses' delicious honey,
> In order that I might hold your mind by this device.[13]

Shortly after Adriani delivered this inaugural lecture, the university was closed. Pisa, where most of the teaching was based, had successfully rebelled against Florence and was now occupied by the French, and Florence itself was in no state to continue teaching the liberal arts curriculum. When it reopened in late 1495, teaching was transferred for two years to Prato, until the outbreak of plague there brought it back to Florence in 1497.[14] So it was in Prato, during this period of widespread dislocation and disorder, that Adriani delivered his second lecture after his appointment. Little wonder, then, that emphasis on fortune and on primitivism became fashionable among Florentine humanists (as it was in Naples at this time), who openly attributed these events to the power of Lucretian fortune.[15] The subject of Adriani's first lecture in Prato was not fortune, however, but rhetoric, which—as Verde and Godman have both pointed out—was used as an occasion to sing the praises of the newfound liberty in Florence, a city that for the past sixty years (that is, since the Medici took power in 1434) had scarcely been "free at all." During this period, rhetoric had been no more than a shadow, so the task confronting Adriani was to teach his students, cut off as they were from old books, the practical use of rhetoric for everything. Once again, he ranged widely among

---

13 Lucretius 1: 936–48 (I borrow from both Loeb and Esolen), quoted in R, fol. 3r ("Sed pulcherrime omnium Poetice vim Lucretius ostendit pulcherrima comparatione ad hanc rem usus"). This famous topos forms the title and the opening of Valentina Prosperi's *"Di soavi licor gli orli del vaso,"* 5ff.

14 Verde, *Studio* 5: 326, note 341; cf. Robert Black, "Higher Education in Florentine Tuscany," in *Florence and Italy,* ed. Peter Denley and Caroline Elam (London, 1988), 213.

15 See Santoro, *Fortuna, ragione e prudenza,* Alison Brown, "Rethinking the Renaissance in the Aftermath of Italy's Crisis," in *Italy in the Age of the Renaissance,* ed. John Najemy (Oxford, 2004), 246–50, and p. 32 above.

ancient sources to demonstrate the civilizing force of rhetoric, which, when supported by arms and law, was a means of achieving consensus among naturally unequal men. Lucretius made his first appearance in this lecture, together with Virgil, to show that, like nature, we cannot produce fruits without first preparing the ground and cultivating it, "for, as Lucretius says, 'the earth didn't produce lusty offspring without seasonal rain,'" and an active and vigorous mind is needed to overcome the incursions of wild beasts and enemies, "which, as Lucretius says, 'often used to make rest dangerous to the poor wretches [early men].'"[16]

To prepare the body, diet and gymnastics—by baring the body in the palestra—was what Quintilian called an honest form of exercise, but it was the cultivation of an active and vigorous mind that was Adriani's objective, to prepare his young students—who included the outstanding politician and writer Francesco Guicciardini—for the new political life that awaited them.[17] "First we will briefly describe what we think were the institutions of the life of new men," he began, before going on to quote the four lines from Lucretius that I have already cited, about early men lacking customs, laws, and a sense of the common good, and surviving by their own strength, helped by whatever booty happened to come their way ("brought to them by fortune," 5: 958–61). Adriani evidently found that Lucretius's primitive life *ante legem* aptly described the chaotic, egotistical life being lived in Florence, where each man—in Roberto Acciaiuoli's words—"lived for himself." Since this was also the life described in Scala's poem *On Trees*, it is tempting to see in Adriani's concluding reference to the many new types of praise that celebrated achievement by hard work—praise of horses, athletes, and even "Trees"— an allusion to his friend's poem and its realistic assessment of the gains and losses of civilization.[18] So this, perhaps, is an instance of a text giving reality

---

16 R, fols. 6r–11v, on 8r–v quoting Lucretius 1: 192–93 and 5: 981 ("ut Lucretius ait: 'uti sine certis imbribus anni laetificos nequeat tellus summittere flores,' 'infestam miseris faciebant saepe quietem'"), and also Virgil, *Georg.* 1: 192–99, and 2: 47–52. On this lecture, see Godman, *Poliziano*, 156–59; Verde, *Studio* 4: 1206–7.

17 R, fol. 8r: "a nudatione corporum in palestris"; Godman, *Poliziano*, 182, citing Guicciardini's letter to Alessio Lapaccini [autumn, 1499?] in which he asked for a copy of Adriani's inaugural lecture, "suarum enim rerum (ut discipulum decet) apprime sum studiosus," *Le Lettere*, ed. Pierre Jodogne (Rome, 1986), 3–4, cf. 6.

18 R, fol. 8v: "Describemus primum breviter qualia opinamus fuisse novorum hominum vitae instituta. Verisimile itaque est ante conditas urbes prima illa novitate mundi, quo tempore, ut Lucretius ait" (citing 5: 958–61); fol. 9v, referring to the "novum genus laudis"; and fol. 11r: "precipue vero

and concreteness to a confused moment in Florentine history. At any rate, it encouraged Savonarola, in response, to devote many of his Lenten sermons the following spring to ridiculing ancient philosophers, especially the atomists. "Listen, women. They say that this world was made of atoms, that is, those tiniest of particles that fly through the air," and he went on to ask the women to "laugh at the studies of these learned men."[19] So when Adriani delivered his inaugural lecture at the start of the next academic year, he carefully omitted any mention of Lucretius's name.

The subject of this lecture, delivered in November 1496, was grammar, another subject, like rhetoric, that belonged to the *trivium* and avoided the higher and more controversial realms of philosophy and religion in the *quadrivium*. Before launching on his theme, Adriani opened his lecture by expressing the hope that they would all soon be able to return to Florence, "after the storms that have shipwrecked our republic and tossed us asunder for the past two years, forcing us to throw overboard our studies—as we are still doing." What he went on to claim for grammar, however, was the status of a higher discipline, for by transmitting past thoughts to the future, he said, it belonged to the sphere of the mind and regulated not only poetry but also the quadrivial disciplines of music, philosophy, and astrology.[20] Lucretius was not mentioned by name throughout the lecture, and no one has noticed his presence, yet it was Lucretius who provided Adriani with both the opening imagery of his lecture and his important discussion of language that followed. It is not only the famous opening of Book 2 that must have influenced Adriani, but also a later passage in the same book describing how "after many great shipwrecks, the high sea tosses asunder transoms, ribs, yards, prow, masts, and oars, all swimming about and floating around the shores."[21] More relevant to the main theme of the lecture is Lucretius's account of the utili-

---

Arbores, quae ultime floreant et germinent, quarum nonnullae ab agricolis ob id sapientes appellate sunt."

19 Savonarola, *Prediche sopra Amos e Zaccaria*, no. 3 (19 February 1496), ed. Paolo Ghiglieri (Rome, 1971), 1: 79–81: "Udite donne. E' dicevano che questo mondo era stato fatto di atomi, idest di quelli minimi corpicini che volano per l'aria," "ora ridete, donne, delli studii di questi savi"; cf. Godman, *Poliziano*, 140.

20 R, fols. 12r–17v; Godman 159–62 at 161; Verde, *Studio* 4: 1261–64: "Post naufragia illa reipublicae, quibus abhinc biennium disiecti tantam fecimus et nos adhuc facimus studiorum nostrorum iacturam" (fol. 12r).

21 Lucretius 2: 1–2, 552–55: "Sed quasi naufragiis magnis multisque coortis / disiectare solet magnum mare transtra cavernas," etc.

tarian origin of language, which Adriani introduced by describing his task as a teacher of grammar being to perfect the way we humans use language to express our needs and emotions, just as animals do. Although he quoted from Virgil's *Georgics* to describe how men, like animals and birds, use different sounds for different purposes, changing their song according to their mood and the weather, the same point had been made by Lucretius as part of his extended account of the origin of language, which Adriani—like Scala before him, in his *Dialogue on Laws and Legal Judgments*—adopted to explain how language developed not from preexisting names, but from convenience (*utilitas*) and practice, replacing the gestures that children, like animals, use to express their needs before they can speak.[22]

By the beginning of the following academic year, in November 1497, the university was back in Florence, and Adriani celebrated its return with an inaugural lecture that, unusually, has two titles, called in one version "On Virgil's *Aeneid* and Aristophanes Containing the Utility of Humanist Studies" and in another *"Nil admirari"* ("Wonder at Nothing").[23] This is an important lecture, not only because of its probable influence on Machiavelli (as we shall see), but also because it is the one in which Adriani took on Savonarola with his "most explicit formulation of a lay version of theology," as Verde puts it. As Adriani explained, he had been forced to abandon his plan of lecturing on the *Aeneid* and Aristophanes because he had been attacked by those who thought his teaching was "useless and impious and harmful to the minds of young people on account of its false opinions about things," so he had decided, instead, "to talk to you today about the usefulness of your studies."[24]

---

22 R, fol. 14v: "Nonne et Maro etiam dixit alia voce corvos imbres, alia ventos vocare ... Nonne Cornix sicca pluviam vocat improba voce, quorum causam optime idem Poeta descripsit: 'Verum ubi Tempestas'" etc., quoting *Georg.* 1: 388, 417–18, but cf. Lucretius 5: 1084–86: "cornicum ut saecla vetusta Corvorumque greges ubi aquam dicuntur et imbris Poscere et interdum ventos aurasque vocare"; R, fol. 14v: "nam coeuntes in cetus homines utilitateque rerum cognita et usu singulis singulas appellationes distribuerunt . . . ceu infantes aut muti admovere illi manum semper cogerentur . . . ut digito quae sint presentia monstret"; cf. Lucretius 5: 1029–32: "et utilitas expressit nomina rerum, / non alia longe ratione atque ipsa videtur / protrahere ad gestum pueros infantia linguae, / cum facit ut digito quae sint praesentia monstrent." For Scala, see p. 30 above.

23 R, fols. 18r–26r (L, fols. 34r–45r), and R 767, fol. 97v; see Verde, *Studio* 4: 1309, who describes the lecture fully on 1309–18; cf. Godman, *Poliziano*, 162–67.

24 R, fols. 18v–19r: "inutile nos et impius et iuvenum animis noxium tractare opus credunt ob falsas rerum opiniones . . . et quoniam saepius sensimus damnari tanquam inutiles labores nos nostros . . . constituimus de utilitate eorum hodie apud vos dicere"; see Richardson, "A manuscript of Biagio Buonaccorsi," 594, and Verde, *Studio* 4: 1310–11 (cited in note 11 above); cf. 1278, describing

But although this was the theme he started out with, he in fact devoted the remainder of the lecture to the Lucretian task of eradicating our "wonder" or dread of the unknown by understanding the causes of things, with religion and the fear fostered by Savonarola's sermons his prime target.

This, however, was not immediately obvious from Adriani's *captatio benivolentiae*. Addressing an audience suffering the straitened circumstances of war and famine, he attempted to justify his liberal arts teachings by describing their "utility," which was the only word, he said, that would resonate in a town that reacted to everything by calculating its dividend or profit. His task was all the more difficult because there seemed "nothing new *(nova)* to say," and he did not want to repeat well-worn platitudes *(trita)* (here turning the well-known trope from Lucretius that Machiavelli later also employed).[25] The fathers and sons listening to Adriani might have been even more surprised if they had realized that Lucretius would be one of the "treasures" to be rescued from the "misshapen site" where they lay buried. For the lecture's underlying purpose, as its second title "Wonder at Nothing" suggests, was to abolish our fears of the unknown by explaining that there was not one but three "authors of events" in the world—Fortune and Nature as well as God—all needing to be understood if we were to lose our fear of them.

This title, *Nil admirari*, was in fact taken from a letter of Horace's: "'Marvel at nothing'"—to do so, "is perhaps the one and only thing . . . that can make a man happy and keep him so."[26] Horace, however, was influenced by Lucretius, as Adriani's later lectures on Horace demonstrate, and so was Virgil. So when in the course of the lecture Adriani paraphrased Virgil's famous praise of the poet—"They are indeed happy beyond measure who do not wonder at the majesty of nature because they know its causes"—we can guess that what follows comes from Lucretius and imitates his attempt to abolish fear through understanding nature. Adriani first addressed fortune and the need for mobility to adjust to new situations, which, he said, was

---

Savonarola's sermon on 13 February 1497 (on the devil's attempt to replace divine truth with "quell'altra verità dello intelletto, della logica, filosofia e retorica") as what Adriani might have been alluding to.

25 Lucretius 1: 926–28, already used by Valla and Poliziano in inaugural lectures as Godman shows (*Poliziano*, 40, notes 58 and 59), but *trita*, quoted in all their lectures, is only used by Lucretius, not by Quintilian or Cicero.

26 Horace, *Epist.* I: 6, 1: "Nil admirari prope res est . . . solaque quae possit facere et servare beatum."

something that Plato and other philosophers recognized in the saying: "not even God fights against necessity"; so, too, did God, in giving our minds mobility and freedom, in view of the fact that we often made decisions that went against the order of nature and even against the opportunities offered by fortune. Profiting from this freedom to speak without constraint to an audience that was equally free to accept or reject his opinion (a "polemical introduction" that Verde says would have been easily understood within the Savonarola context in which he was speaking), Adriani embarked on the theme of "wonder" and novelty that was central to his lecture.[27]

He introduced it by suggesting that it was man's ability to "wonder at everything amazing or unusual" that distinguished him most clearly from beasts. Our astonishment at entering the world was like that of "alpinists who descend into an elegant and magnificently built city," whether this was due to our mental "oblivion of things" in forgetting the life we had lived before, as he said Plato believed (here referring to his theory of metempsychosis), or whether it was because everything *was* in fact new—which was what Lucretius believed, although Adriani does not mention him (Lucretius thought that the absence of historical evidence earlier than "the Theban War and the ruin of Troy" was explained by the fact that the world was new and not eternal).[28] The influence of Lucretius is more obvious when—after paraphrasing Virgil's famous praise of the poet, "They are indeed happy beyond measure" (quoted above)—Adriani went on to explain that we are frightened only of novelties like comets and thunderstorms and not by the more familiar miracles of nature, such as the rising of the sun, the waxing and waning of the moon, rain, hail, frost, snow, and the ever-changing clouds, which instead give us pleasure.[29]

This fear, according to Adriani, stemmed from ignorance of the three "authors of events," which makes us project these fears as divinities that need

---

27 R, fols. 19r–v (L, fol. 36r): "Ut enim Plato et antiquiores omnes dixerunt: 'contra necessitatem nec deus repugnat'" (Simonides 3: 20), "Deus . . . sciens decreturos nos multa saepius quae contra naturae ordinem et Fortunae occasiones essent, mobiles ideo finxisse animos nostros"; cf. Verde, 1313: "questa polemica premessa facilmente comprensibile a coloro che stavano vivendo la fase discendente della curva savonaroliana."

28 R, fol. 20r (L, fol. 37r): "sive id ex oblivione rerum accidat in animis nostris, ut Plato voluit, seu quia illis omnia nova occurrant . . . quasi alpini homines descendisse in civitatem eleganter et magnifice aedificatam"; citing Plato, *Timaeus* A 23, *Laws* 682; cf. Lucretius 5: 324–31.

29 R, fol. 24r (L, fol. 42r): "Felices profecto nimium quibus ex cognitione causarum maiestatem naturae contingit non admirari"; paraphrasing Virgil, *Georg.* 2: 490–92, cf. 458; Lucretius 2: 1026–43.

placating. "We are very critical of the ancient Romans," he went on, "who, without any provocation, were so fearful of the power of the Caesars that they built temples to them all over the world and made sacrifices in order to placate them, thinking that if they were propitiated, everything would go well for themselves." So powerfully does this fear play on our minds that the Egyptians, who were less cultivated than the Romans, were impelled to honor vile animals in much the same way, by adoring crocodiles and dogs, "thinking there was something divine" in them.[30] Nor did he approve of the saying then on everyone's lips, that God was slow to punish in order to profit from the delay (by indulgences and people's propitiatory gifts), as though he were a pawnbroker or a hawker of penalties who became all the richer the longer he waited for repayment. Sixtus IV's controversial bull in 1476 granting indulgences to remit the sins of the dead in purgatory must have encouraged jokes like the one recorded by Giovanni Sabadino degli Arienti, in which thieves, sentenced to repay at the Last Judgment the cloak they had stolen from an abbot, intrepidly reply, "Mister, since you've given us such a long time for repayment, we'll take the rest of your goods"—and with that, took his mule, horses, clothes, and bags as well.[31] God was not like a pawnbroker, nor were we like such a person in repaying injustices, Adriani told his audience. He was more like a pharmacist, and just as the unqualified are not capable of dispensing medicine that only pharmacists know when and how much to give, so we are unqualified to dispense remedies in the field of divine affairs, which are unknown to us. Nor was God to be feared, since "it is his

---

30 R, fols. 20r–v (L, fols. 37r–v): "Deumque non tam ob magnitudinem imperii superstitiose colere et ob tarditatem suppliciorum impie de eo aliquid cogitare quam dare operam ut intelligamus non esse eum similem nobis." / "In quo maxime damnamus Romanos veteres qui Caesarum sine provocatione potentiam veriti, templa illis toto orbe constituerunt, sacrificiaque quibus eos placarent credentes si eos propitios habuissent omnia sibi secunda fore tantamque vim habet hic motus in animis nostris, ut hec eadem stolidiores Egyptios impulerit ad constituendos non dissimiles honores foedis animalibus adorandosque cocrodillos et canes, credentes inesse his animalibus divinum quidnam..."

31 R, fol. 25r (L, fol. 44v): "Non enim probamus illud quid in ore omnium est: lente irasci Deum ut tarditatem supplicii gravitate recompenset. Hii enim similem sibi Deum crediderunt feneratorem et institorem penarum, cui [L, qui R] quantum in penis eligendis temporis periret tantum pretia [L, presentia R] earum augerentur"; Giovanni Sabadino degli Arienti, *Le Porretane,* Novella 7, ed. Bruno Basile (Rome, 1981), 52–53; cf. Leonardo da Vinci's prophecy: "De' frati che spendendo parole ricevono di gran ricchezze e danno li paradiso," *Literary Works,* ed. Jean Paul Richter (New York, 1970), 2, 301 (and 302, "Del vendere il paradiso"). On Sixtus IV's bull, see Robert Shaffern, "Learned Discussions of Indulgences for the Dead in the Middle Ages," *Church History* 61 (1992): 380.

nature to bestow benefits for nothing," and if you should want to propitiate him, good behavior is more effective than incense.³²

This was an amazing rebuff to Savonarola. Not only did he instill great fear in the hearts of his followers, which was the bane of superstitious religion, according to Adriani; he also claimed to be, like a prophet, qualified to speak about divine affairs, which Adriani thought were unknowable. The fear aroused by Savonarola's sermons is well documented. Ser Niccolò Michelozzi's wife, for example, who heard his famous Lent sermon in San Lorenzo in 1492 threatening that God's avengeance would come "Quickly, quickly, and speedily, speedily" *("Cito, cito e velociter e velociter"),* then believed "that any day now, indeed, at any hour, the heavens and the earth are going to collapse." "She's so frightened, it's too much," Ser Pace Bambello told his friend Niccolò, urging him to write to his wife and comfort her as he best knew how to do.³³ And Niccolò's friend, the banker Filippo da Gagliano, also reported to him how frightened women were by the friars' sermons and yet irremovable from the churches and feet of the friars.³⁴ Savonarola's claim to be God's prophet is equally well documented and equally contentious: "He has made me say it and if He errs, I too err; but He cannot err, so neither do I in telling you what God says."³⁵ This must explain the vehemence of Adriani's 1497 lecture, which he ended by saying that his studies might seem useless to some people, who thought they should be spurned "because they are ancient and regarded as alien to our religion, and also because the high priests of the Christian religion taught more fully and certainly about all these things." Nevertheless, ancient writings did not lose their scent over time like perfume,

---

32 R, fols. 25r–v (L, fols. 44v–45r): "Sed non talis natura Deus quemadmodum, nec nos in iniuriis referendis illi similes . . . Pena autem Deus utitur quasi pharmaco quodam, cuius oportunitatem ipse novit et mensuram, utque medicinae imperiti colligere nequeunt . . . sic profecto divina nobis incognita sunt . . . potentiam Dei non esse timendam, natura enim illi est benefacere gratis beneficia dare, quem si velis [L, volueris R] propitiare, bonus esto [L, est R], satis eum coluit quisque imitatus est, quo enim iustior, sanctiorque eris eo minus thure indigebis."

33 Pace Bambello to Niccolò Michelozzi, 14 April 1492, BNF, GC, 29, 84, fol. 99: "[Nannina Giovanni] va alla predica a San Lorenzo a frate Girolamo che tucta via dice che 'cito, cito e velociter e velociter el fragello di dio ne viene' e a llei pare che ogni dì, anzi ogni hora, e s'abbi a disfare el cielo e la terra, e sta in tanta paura che è troppo. Scrivetele e confortatela come sapete."

34 As we saw in chap. 1 above.

35 Savonarola, *Prediche sopra Ruth e Michea,* ed. Vincenzo Romano (Rome, 1962), 1 (8 May 1496), 27: "e' me l'ha fatto dire Lui; e se Lui erra, erro ancora io. Ma Lui non può errare, adunque non erro ancora io a dirti quello che dice Dio"; cit. Alison Brown, "Savonarola, Machiavelli and Moses: A Changing Model," in *Florence and Italy,* ed. Denley and Elam, 61; repr. in *Medici in Florence,* 271.

and those who attacked them failed to realize what they lost by disowning them, since the ancients, far from being alien, were excellent witnesses in the defense of Christianity, reaching the truth "both by knowing [what they were learning] and by not knowing it, as Aristotle said"—presumably meaning that the ancients were teaching the same morality, but without knowing "the precise sense and manner" in which Christianity was to teach it.[36]

By arguing that it was contemporary religion that was superstitious and less moral than the apparently "alien" morality of the ancient philosophers, Adriani reversed the orthodox view of Christianity as civilized and paganism as alien. The propitiatory, or *do ut des,* view of religion, according to which "I give to you in order that you give to me," was traditional in Florence. In fact, Savonarola had been attacked the previous year by one traditionalist Florentine for not understanding the gift relationship between Florence and God, according to which God gave Florence prosperity in exchange for the charity and lavish church building that the city gave to God.[37] Adriani knew that Savonarola understood and played on this exchange relationship in promising the Florentines that they would become richer and more powerful if they accepted the reforms that he, as God's mouthpiece, urged on them, so Adriani's response was to subvert the relationship by using Lucretius to describe its psychological origins. According to Lucretius, we create figures of power as a projection of our own fantasies, hoping to become as powerful as they are by propitiating them with prayers and "stocking our cities with altars." But far from allaying our fears of the unknown, what we do instead is to place ourselves in thrall to these figures: "Unhappy human race, to grant such feats / To Gods, and then to add vindictiveness!"[38] This, of course, was exactly the hold that the Dominican friar was exercising on fearful Florentines by threatening God's vengeance on their sins, as Adriani well understood. His

---

36 R, fols. 25v–26r (L, fol. 45r), ed. Verde, *Studio* 4: 1318, referring to Horace, *Epist.* I: 2, 69–70 (on perfume not losing its scent): "scientes et non scientes, ut Aristoteles ait" (*Post Anal.* 71A–B, where Aristotle continues: "The strange thing would be, not if in some sense he knew what he was learning, but if he were to know it in that precise sense and manner in which he was learning it"; with thanks to Jill Kraye for help in identifying this reference).

37 By Francesco Altoviti in his *Defensione contro all'archa di Fra Girolamo* (Florence, Francesco di Dino, 1497?), ed. Gian Carlo Garfagnini, *Rinascimento* 31 (1991): 124–45; see Alison Brown, "Intellectual and Religious Currents in the Post-Savonarola Years," repr. in *Medicean and Savonarolan Florence,* chap. 12.

38 Lucretius 5: 1161–1240 at 1161–63: "et ararum compleverit urbis"; 1194–95: "O genus infelix humanum, talia divis / cum tribuit facta atque iras adiunxit acerbas!" (trans. Esolen, 191, 192).

lectures show how cleverly he used Lucretius's argument to attack the superstitious roots of Savonarola's fundamentalism.

The death of Savonarola at the stake the following year again made it possible for Adriani to refer to Lucretius by name. So in his opening lecture in 1498–1499, on the realism of ancient poets who showed how the good and bad are mixed in life, we find Lucretius quoted for calling love both generative (as in the famous opening lines of *De rerum natura* in praise of Venus) and base (in his lengthy account of the snares and delusions of "our Venus" in Book 4). He is also quoted for believing, as a "follower of Epicurus," that happiness consists in knowing the causes of things and in "scorning religion" (here Adriani cited the "famous" lines from Virgil), whereas other poets found happiness in obscene love.[39]

After the return of the elder branch of the Medici to Florence in 1512 and the elevation of Giovanni de' Medici to the papacy in 1513, Adriani laid more emphasis on Plato's stable and hierarchical universe in his lectures: he was, as Godman describes him, a nimble survivor, a "chameleon of cultural politics," laughing with Democritus at his own success in surviving unscathed when his assistant in the chancery, Machiavelli, lost his job.[40] The political context of Adriani's lectures in this later period was, of course, very different from that of post-1494 Florence. Nevertheless, what is striking about the lectures, even in this later period, is not their opportunism or seeming novelty, but their continuing interest in the aspects of Epicureanism that we have tracked in his earlier lectures. For despite the lectures' changing emphasis, Adriani's thinking continued to be dominated by three themes that I shall discuss in turn: primitivism, superstitious religion, and atomism, all interpreted within a naturalistic philosophical framework in which Fortune and Nature costar

---

39 R, fols. 26r–33r (cf. Verde, *Studio* 4: 1340–45; Godman, *Poliziano*, 171–79, 186–87) at fol. 28r: "contraria contrariis miscuisse simul aut vinxisse bonum malo"; fols. 30r–v: "cum distortis pravisque oculis in iudicando amantes sint. Quod Lucretius elegantissime pluribus versiculis prosecutus est" (Lucretius 4: 1141–70, later citing 1: 1–2); fol. 31v: "secuti Epicurum felicitatem metiantur scientia causarum omnium et dispectu relligionis, ut est notissimum illud [citing Virgil, *Georg.* 2: 490], nec desunt qui turpi amorem hanc ipsam felicitatem decernant."

40 Godman, *Poliziano*, 148, 194–99, 213. The topic of Adriani's 1512 lecture, Democritus's laughter and Heraclitus's grief, was already familiar from the fresco on the walls of Ficino's "academy"; Arthur Field, "The Platonic Academy of Florence," in *Marsilio Ficino: His Theology, His Philosophy, His Legacy*, ed. Michael Allen and Valery Rees (Leyden, 2001), 372–74; see his letter on the theme, *Lettere*, ed. Sebastiano Gentile, 1: 110–11.

with God as equal "authors" of everything that happens, with fortuitous chance and nature helping as well as hindering men's success, but never controlling their destiny if men can learn to react flexibly to their influence.

The theme of primitivism appears in Adriani's opening lecture for the academic year 1514–1515, in which he describes the twenty years since 1494 as a period so far removed from the "innocence of antiquity and the sanctity of our forefathers" that older men would scarcely recognize the region, nor would the fathers of his students recognize their own city, transformed as both were by the dissolute behavior and licentiousness of barbarian armies.[41] Once upon a time, Adriani told his audience, soldiers had fought with stakes, without laws, signs, oaths of allegiance, or military leaders; sickness was cured by experience, not by medicine; and nature was understood to consist only of fire, air, atoms, "and that infinite matter called *homoeomeria*" (as Anaxagoras had wrongly described it, according to Lucretius).[42] Later developments in art and philosophy—including discoveries like printing and the new worlds found and colonized by the Portuguese—transformed this early primitivism, yet it remained relevant as a model for imitation.[43] For everything was based on imitation, he argued, even Platonic ideas, which were not separate from, or "outside," the works they produced but were simply an earlier, or metaphysically prior, model for them. Thus in the early days, when fields lay neglected and uncultivated, the art of weaving was learned from spiders, ploughing was copied from rooting pigs, grafting from birds hiding seeds in trees, navigation from floating tree trunks, sailing from the flight of birds. As civilization developed, letters were copied from cranes in flight, houses from swallows, architecture from the human body, and both of our political models were copied from nature—republics from ants and monar-

---

41 R, fols. 96r–109r at fol. 96v (L, fols. 74r–88v at fol. 75r), summarized by Godman, *Poliziano*, 200–201: "Nos etiam intra vigesimum annum quo temporis spatio tot barbararum gentium armis et dolis pene omnes periimus alienorum morum contagia [R, collagio L] . . . ut nec senioribus omnis haec regio, nec patribus vestris eadem haec civitas videatur, tam longe ab antiquitatis innocentia et maiorum nostrorum sanctitate discessimus"; cf. Lucretius 1: 830, 845–46.

42 R, fols. 96v–97r (L, fol. 75v), quoted by Godman (*Poliziano*, 200–201, note 106), beginning: "Fuit quondam cum praeustis sudibus et ex corticibus arborum ocreis sine lege, sine signis, sine sacramento, sine duce miles pugnaret"; cf. Lucretius 1: 830ff.

43 R, fols. 97v–98r (L, fol. 76v): the Pillars of Hercules "finem illic orbis ipse constituit quo tantum progredi potuerat; supererat tamen quod nostra aetate a Lusitanis Regibus inveniendum et possidendum adhuc esset"; the reference to printing is quoted by Godman, *Poliziano*, 201, note 108.

chies from bees.⁴⁴ Although Godman explains Adriani's theory of mimesis as his bid for novelty as he attempted to combine "the disparate strands" of his many interests into an integrated whole, we can also see it as evidence of his continuing interest in Lucretian naturalism. There was tension in the university between the Platonizing philosophers Francesco Verino and Francesco da Diacceto (appointed to teach "philosophy" in Pisa in 1501 and "moral and Platonic philosophy" in 1503–1504) and the Lucretian philosopher Raffaele Franceschi, who taught moral philosophy and logic there for two years before being replaced by Verino in 1509.⁴⁵ So Adriani's lecture may reflect these "cultural antagonisms" in defending Lucretius in face of the current fashion for Plato.

This is even clearer in the oration he delivered on the death of Giuliano de' Medici two years later, in 1516.⁴⁶ Although praise of the Medici was, in this context, inevitable, what is striking—as John McManamon has described so well in the introduction to his edition of the oration—is the naturalistic imagery adopted by Adriani to praise the Medici within a framework of republicanism. Portraying the Medici as a source of illumination, Adriani explained

---

44 R, fols. 101v–102r (L, fols. 79v–81r): "forma in opere, idea extra opus, nec tantum extra sed ante opus est"; "Nulli colebant arva quondam agricolae, squalebat omnis ager, inculta omnia in eo erant: id solum ex terra homini aderat quod sponte sua conspersave imbre aut sole tepefacta comunis mater proferebat; docuit eos tandem sus, tam brutum animal, dum rictu suo arva subigit, radices herbarum querens proscindere arva, friatisque exemplo eius multa aratione glebis uberiorem annonam expectare. In hoc ipso studio insitionem aliam casus aliam docuerunt aves in arborum cavis semina abscondentes, eaque imitatione multam deinceps in alienis arboribus pomorum nos fecimus adoptionem. Tota est navigatio nobis a fluctantibus in aqua arborum truncis . . ."; ". . . litteras primum formaverunt in caelo volantes contemplati grues, et domos sibi aedificare non aliunde priusquam ab hyrundinibus didicerunt: et in architectura humani corporis modulos secuti eius artis primi auctores columnas earumque quantitates et partes constituerunt . . . Iam vero in civili illa disciplina quae omnium princeps et domina ceteras omnes in se complexa est, bone deus, quam felici exemplo et presenti imitatione a natura usi sumus, quae premonstrata nobis in formicis popularitate, in examine apum regiae potestatis imagine, temperandas contrahaendas in medium a duobus extremis alias nobis rerumpublicarum formas reliquit . . ." On imitation and the growth of civilization, Lucretius 5: esp. 1350–60, 1440–56; Vitruvius, *De architectura* 2: 1, esp. §1; 3: 1, §2.

45 Verde, *Studio* 2: 218–19: "forti antagonismi culturali" (cf. Bigazzi MS 109 [libro 6], fol. 2r: 11 March 1503–1504); id., "Dottorati e Firenze e a Pisa, 1505–1528," in *Xenia Medii Aevi Historiam Illustrantia oblata T. Kaeppeli* (Rome, 1978), 767, and "Il secondo periodo de Lo Studio Fiorentino (1504–1528)," in *L'Università e la sua storia*, ed. Paolo Renzi (Arezzo, 1998), 109 (an article that Jonathan Davies told me about and very kindly sent me a copy of). Cf. Godman, *Poliziano*, 201–2.

46 Edited, with an introduction, by John McManamon, "Marketing a Medici Regime: The Funeral Oration of Marcello Virgilio Adriani for Giuliano de' Medici (1516)," *Renaissance Quarterly* 44 (1991): 1–41.

their exile and return as phases of the sun and moon that were welcomed and mourned as they alternately provided light and warmth before disappearing to illuminate others.[47] Yet instead of drawing out the Platonic implications of this metaphor by comparing the Medici to the sun as the ultimate Good, above the control of the laws and the stars, as earlier eulogists had done, Adriani interpreted it through the lens of anthropological primitivism. From this perspective, the sun's changing phases were Nature's device to make its reappearances more appreciated "through its ritual of coming and going," and the Florentines in their changing attitude to the Medici were behaving like primitive peoples who reacted to the phases of the sun in the same way: from wanting to capture and control the sun when it first departed only to welcome it back on its return.[48]

Closely related to the theme of primitivism is Adriani's attack on superstitious religion, the second unacknowledged Lucretian theme that runs through his lectures. Far from a simple celebration of his success in surviving the return of the Medici unscathed (as Godman has suggested), Adriani's comparison of Democritus and Heraclitus in his first lecture after their return in 1512 in fact served a very different purpose. A clue is provided by the homely story that Adriani used to illustrate his argument: "Not many days ago," he told his audience, "a father, a working man [*e plebe homo*], cheerfully performed the burial of his dead son with his own hands, which his sad and grieving parish priest had refused to do." Surprised by the contrasting reactions of the cheerful father and the grieving priest, supported by duly pious local mourners, he was told by some unlearned soul—but who, as it turned out, showed ancient wisdom—that the priest was grieving because he was prohibited by religion and law from making money out of the burial, whereas the father was happy that his son was freed from life's perils and dangers.[49] "I began to think how wise and serious the laughter of that plebeian man was," Adriani continued, for he showed that there were no laws against piety

---

47 Ibid., 33, 35; cf. 16.

48 Ibid., 36–37; cf. 17. On Platonizing eulogies of the earlier Medici, see Alison Brown, "Platonism in Fifteenth-Century Florence," *Journal of Modern History* 58 (1986): 394–402, repr. in *Medici in Florence*, 227–34.

49 R, fol. 38r (L, fol. 89r): "Sepelliebat non multo ante hanc diem pater, e plebe homo, defunctum filium propriisque manibus ridens sepulturam curabat quam tristis et merens sacerdos parochus eius a se reiiciebat. Convenerant [enim ad eum *om*. L] tristes aliquot et merentes circumstabant [ad eum L] ut fit, vicini et amici plures officiosa pietate et relligione homini faventes."

and religion, reminding him of Democritus's laughter. This "homely image" also served to demonstrate how the great weight oppressing our minds can be moved by something quite small, like laughter in the face of death—in the same way, he suggested, that a heavy ship can be driven by the wind and steered by a simple rudder, or heavy bodies can be moved by small cogs and treadwheels.[50] These homely images of rudders and cogs in fact come from Lucretius, who uses them to describe how movement is caused. An image, he explains, is responsible for striking the mind and moving our will, which then moves the whole mass of the body, just as an airy wind drives a great ship, steered by a single rudder, or as cogs and treadwheels move a heavy machine.[51]

This, as Adriani admits, is a long detour from his theme of laughter and sadness, to which he returned by listing contrasting opening lines from poets, like "'O curas hominum,' 'O miseras hominum' . . . 'O fortunati,' 'Beatus ille vir' et 'Suave mari magno.'" Of these, it was to the famous lines of "the greatest of our poets" (unnamed), *Suave, mari magno*, that Adriani returned in his peroration: "O how sweet it is, when the winds are whipping the oceans, to watch another's struggles."[52] How much better it is, Adriani continued, to laugh and rejoice with Democritus than to grieve with Heraclitus over men's unhappiness and false values, worst of which is "praying to the gods as the authors of all good things and then despising them for being incapable of punishing us, and fearing them as judges yet swearing falsely by them as though they were nothing."[53] This was delivered more than a decade after Savonarola's death,

---

50 R, fols. 38r–v (L, fols. 89v–90r): "Coepi ego tunc mecum cogitare quam gravis et sapiens plebei hominis risus ille esset . . . ut est mens nostra in cogitatione sua velox et ad omnia preceps fieri in me sensi quod in subductione navium ex mari fit, aut maiorum lapidum et onerum subiectione non pigeat vos queso ex quotidianae rei imagine cogitationis nostrae motum intelligere," going on to describe how "plurium instrumentorum troclearum orbiculorumque versationibus . . . unum . . . vim affert et alterum ex altero motum accipit," etc.

51 Lucretius 4: 881–906: "animo nostro primum simulacra meandi accidere atque animum pulsare . . . inde voluntas fit," etc.; "quippe etenim ventus subtili corpore tenvis trudit agens magnam magno molimine navem et manus una regit . . . atque gubernaclum contorquet quolibet unum, multaque per trocleas et tympana pondere magno commovet atque levi sustollit machina nisu."

52 R, fol. 38v (L, fol. 90r) (citing Persius, *Sat.* 1: 1; Lucretius 2: 14 and 2: 2; Horace, *Sat.* 1: 1, 4; and *Epod* 2: 1); fol. 41v (L, fols. 94r–v): "Audite quae maximus nostrorum vatum cecinerit de voluptate sapientis," "Suave mari magno turbantibus aequiora ventis . . . qui cernere suave est" (Lucretius 2: 1–4), following a long passage invoking Democritus and urging him to "ingredere et accedere propius ad nos" (R, fols. 40r–41v; L, fols. 92v–94r).

53 R, fol. 42r (L, fol. 95r): "Et quod turpissimum est, precantes deos velut omnium bonorum auctores, despicientes deinde eos [*om.* L] velut ulcisci non valentes et timentes eos ut iudices peierantes, autem per eos veluti nulli sint"; cf. note 40 above.

under the newly restored Medici regime, and yet we can see how closely it follows the themes of Adriani's earlier lectures in using Lucretius to attack propitiatory religion.

It seems likely that Lucretius was, in a more general way, the source of Adriani's practice of illustrating his lectures and texts with vivid contemporary images to make his point—a practice that, as we shall see, he described in his later *Commentary* on Dioscorides as Lucretius's use of everyday and ordinary examples "to bring out into the open" clandestine theories about nature "that had until then been hidden in darkness."[54] So when we find him opening his first lecture on Horace's *Satires* with an account of the recent visit to Naples of the ambassador of Sultan Bajazet II, a man well received by Alfonso although "ignorant of our religion," we are alerted to the possibility that this story, too, may provide the vehicle for another "clandestine" or heterodox opinion—as indeed it does.[55] For among the many sights in Naples that amazed the ambassador was a fresco of the miracle of St. Benedict moving a heavy stone placed by a "bad devil" that no one else could shift. A bystander was again conveniently at hand to explain the fresco to him. And although the ambassador was delighted by its novelty, admiring the goodness of a god who was so kind to Christians, and the sanctity of a man so empowered by his religion that he could perform this miracle, he nevertheless wondered what non-Christians back home would make of it.[56] To the more intelligent of those "ignorant of the Christian religion," Adriani suggested, the stone would represent our minds crushed by the immovable weight or "mountain of misery" that lies on our hearts, which through ignorance makes us long to change places and travel, only to return home because we feel no better abroad, as "our poet, not always sound in mind," put it:

> If, when men sense a weight upon their minds
> A trouble deep within that wearies them,
> They could but recognize the source, and know

---

54 Discussed at note 66 below.

55 N, "Prima in sermones Horatii schola" (autograph); fols. 1r–10v, "relligionis nostre tamen ignarum hominem" (1r). According to *Una cronaca napoletana figurata del Quattrocento*, ed. Riccardo Filangieri (Naples, 1956), 108, 110, an ambassador of Bajazet visited Naples in November–December 1494, preceding a peace treaty between Alfonso II of Naples and Bajazet signed on 16 December.

56 Ibid., fols. 1v–2r: "laudavit hominis sanctitatem qui religionis nostrae signo tantum potuerit, admiratus est etiam Dei bonitatem qui tam benigne cum Christianis agat, tamque aperte eos de se moneat" (1v). The miracle is described in *Gregorii magni dialogi*, ed. Umberto Moricca (Rome, 1924), 2: 9, 96–97.

> Why such a huge misery masses in the heart,
> They'd never lead their lives as we see now—
> As men who never know what they want, who move
> From place to place to lay their burden down.

"Why is it," he went on to ask, now quoting Horace, "that no one is content with his lot?"[57]

"Our poet, not always sound in mind" was, of course, Lucretius, and it is his attack on superstition that explains the topical example chosen by Adriani as a device to introduce his theme. Closely associated, through Democritus, with this attack on superstition was the search for happiness by acknowledging the fickleness of fortune. This was also a clear response to the fluctuating fortunes of Florence during Adriani's years of teaching: three different political regimes, religious strife, and foreign invasions, which explain his emphasis on the need to adapt to change and accept life as a mixture of good and bad.[58] So his second lecture on Horace opened with another reference to Democritus's laughter at mankind's follies in the face of fortune. This, too, he illustrated with a contemporary example, the unexpected and disastrous storm that turned the French victory after the battle of Ravenna in 1512 into defeat and in turn helped to destroy the republican regime in Florence, or—as Adriani called it—"the shipwreck of your popular state."[59] And in his third lecture on Horace, the opening theme of men's inability to stick to the golden mean soon led him into a discussion of change and mobility in ancient theories of the universe: the ever-changing cycles of Empedoclean particles that were in

---

57 N, fols. 2r–v: "Raciocinatus etiam est . . . ut qui illic ingeniosiores sint, Christiane relligionis ignari, imaginem novae rei admirati credant signari lapide illo animos nostros . . . nullis opibus [etc.] exonerare te possis . . . Neque enim est quod minus intelligamus, neque quo magis decipiamur, quam incognito hoc nostri animi pondere, tantum non poetae nostri non semper bene sani illud enuntians," quoting Lucretius 3: 1053–59 (trans. Esolen), followed by three lines from Horace, Sat. I: 1, 1–3 (quoting the more famous lines, "caelum, non animum, mutant, qui trans mare currunt," Epist. I: 11, 26, later in the same lecture, 8r).

58 Cf. note 39 above. On the misery of these later years, see Iacopo di Piero Guicciardini's letter in 1523 to his nephew, quoted by Verde, "Il secondo periodo de Lo Studio Fiorentino," 105.

59 N, fols. 11r–v, "Secunda in Oratii sermones schola," beg. "Ridebat quondam, ut audistis, Democritus omnia quae quottidie male sani homines peccarent . . . Qualem [the French victory] Christianae salutis anni xiimo supra millesimum et quingentesimum anno ad Adriaticum mare sub Ravennae moenibus . . . gloriosam sibi, regi calamitosam, amicis inutilem, omnibus vero lamentabilem" // "satisque sit doluisse tunc naufragia popularitatis vestrae, et in dolore illo cognovisse quam turpiter et irrito vincendi studio propositaeque finis inutili eventu, fere omnes laboremus." The battle of Ravenna on 11 April 1512 was followed in May by the Swiss descent on Milan, their control being confirmed after the battle of Novara in 1513, which also established Maximilian Sforza as its puppet duke.

turn attracted to and then dispelled from the center of the universe, like the similarly restless "atom of Epicurus" that moved endlessly through an infinite void, "driven about [now quoting Lucretius] with frequent meetings and partings."[60]

Epicurean atomism is the third theme that represents continuity in Adriani's naturalist philosophy, even after the return of the Medici. Like the other themes, it formed part of his argument for responding to unpredictable change and conflict by understanding the world of nature and not fearing it. Acknowledging the practical bent of the Florentines, he began another lecture by accepting that his audience would be less interested in philosophy than in agriculture *(rem agrariam)*; but by working with and not against nature, he told them, they would at least be helped to achieve the tranquil life that Epicurus had recommended and be encouraged towards the lesser evil, if not towards the higher good. So those interested in investigating the crimes and misfortunes of others would turn instead to investigate the secrets of nature, the politically ambitious would turn from the republic to the mastery of dancing and gymnastics, and the bloodthirsty would turn from manslaughter to hunting and the slaughter of animals.[61] Gesturing in this way towards the new Florentine lifestyle of dancing and hunting as lesser evils in the present time, he nevertheless insisted that it was far more praiseworthy to reach to the heavens in their studies. And as "a sort of winetasting," he at once plunged into a discussion of Empedocles' theory of the conflictual elements, which moved endlessly between sympathy and antipathy, strophe and antistrophe, agreement and discord—a theory with which Lucretius ("he who constructed everything from the chance clash of atoms") only partly approved. Adriani did not intend to teach the heavens' influence on the plane-

---

60 N, fols. 13r–15r, which opens by quoting Horace, *Sat.* I, 2, 1–3, and goes to compare Tigellus's never-ceasing songs to Empedocles' unceasing "primordia rerum . . . sui animi impetus movere semper de caelo ad terram, de terra ad sydera mundi" and the "athomus Epicuri, cui nihil in medium ferebatur per infinitum inane iactata nullibi quiescere poterat, 'Conciliis et discidiis exercita crebris'" (Lucretius 2: 120, with "vide Lucretius in 2 <. . .>" in the margin in Adriani's autograph, fol. 14r). Cf. Horace, *Epist.*, 1, 12, 12–20, where he suggests moving to "loftier themes" like the theories of Democritus and Empedocles.

61 R, fols. 89r–95r (L, fols. 95v–103r), beg. "Admonuit nos"(possibly delivered in 1513–1514 or 1515–1516, since what Godman describes as the 1515 lecture was delivered in 1511, *Poliziano*, 199, cf. 196–97): "non esse scilicet contra naturam pugnandum sed . . . paulatim ad meliora aut quae minus turpia sint in eo genere transferri animum oportere, curiosos ab investigandis sceleribus et infortuniis aliorum ad eruscationem secretorum naturae . . . ambitiosos a republica ad imperia chorearum puerorumque in gymnasiis, feroces et caedis avidos ad venationem et carnificinam animalium."

[63]

tary system that was thought to control our lives, nor the topic of the temperaments adopted by "the great expert in nature," Galen, since nothing "could be farther from the truth and our religion than to deprive our minds of liberty and leave them subject to matter."[62]

This was clearly dangerous ground, but Adriani nevertheless admitted that it was a generally received opinion, confirmed by experience, that certain foods, birds, sacrifices, and incantations have the power to move our minds—like the amulet that he remembered his grandmother hanging around his neck when he had a quartan fever as a child, which he laughed at until he later read that Galen approved of it as a cure, being "very skilled in medicine but a bad writer about religion, affirming there were only natural causes of things."[63] Adriani's interest in the medical role of contraries looked forward to his *Commentary* on Dioscorides' *De materia medica*, which was first printed by the Giuntine Press in Florence in 1518 and dedicated, appropriately, to the Medicean pope, Leo X, who "practices medicine."[64] But although his interest in medicine seems to sanitize the less orthodox topics of his lectures, in fact it serves to highlight their unorthodoxy by reminding us not only that Galen was regarded as "a bad writer about religion," but also that the determinist theories of planetary influences were contrary to Christian religion—as, of course, were the atomist theories of Democritus, Epicurus, and Lucretius. Despite this, Adriani continued to discuss them in his lectures as well as in his *Commentary* on Dioscorides. It was in the surprising context of this *Commentary* that Adriani introduced the subject of the "new and clandestine" theory

---

62 R, fols. 89v–90r (L, fols. 96r–97r): "Verumtamen sunt et aliae huius studii plures et maiores laudes . . . ex immortali incorruptoque caelo conformationeque siderum eius et ex media natura, quarum brevem vobis hodies mensuram et quasi gustum (ut in vindemia fit) rendere est animus . . . Habet natura duas quasi basis . . . sympathiam Graeci alteram, alteram antipathiam appellaverunt . . . / et is qui fortuito concursu athomorum omnia construebat non nisi hoc consensu earum vitam fieri probavit" (cf. Lucretius 1, esp. 758–60), "Galenus vir naturae peritissimus . . . quandoquidem nihil magis a veritatem religioneque nostra abhorret quam privatis animis libertate sua obnoxios materiae eos relinquere."

63 R, fol. 90v (L, fol. 97v): "cum Galenum legissem virum quidem totius medicine peritissimum sed relligionis malum auctorem et extra naturales causas nihil affirmantem." See also his discussion of amulets in his 1497–1498 inaugural lecture, R, fol. 22r (L, fols. 39v–40r), and in his *Commentary* on Dioscorides (Florence, Giunti, 1524, which I cite in what follows), 4: 126 (De Tripolio herba), fol. 264r.

64 Godman, *Poliziano*, 212–34 at 233; Grafton, *Bring out Your Dead*, 2–10; and Jerry Stannard, "Diocorides and Renaissance Materia Medici," in *Herbs and Herbalism in the Middle Ages and Renaissance*, ed. Katherine Stannard and Richard Kay (Aldershot, 1991), 9–10; on the Galenic cure by contraries, Nancy Siraisi, *Medieval and Early Renaissance Medicine* (Chicago, 1990), 145.

of atomism, in order to explain why some plants have a bitter taste and others are sweet, according to "the Epicurean maxims that the Roman poet once taught his citizens in his most delightful poem about the nature of things, which was in turn based on the much earlier heresy of Abderitan Democritus."[65] The reason was that honey and milk were made of smooth and round atoms, whereas bitter wormwood and centaury were made from atoms that were hooked and angular (as Lucretius had explained), since every natural thing that met and adhered in the immense void consisted of different shapes. "And because the thing was new and clandestine, Lucretius [now named for the first time] used an everyday and simple analogy to bring into the light of day what had hitherto been hidden in the majesty and shadows of nature"; that is, he compared the creation of objects by atoms to the formation of words by letters in the alphabet, some letters formed to mean one thing, or one substance, some another, "and, as he said, by changing or adding a little or changing place, 'fire' *(ignis)* becomes 'wood' *(lignis)* and so on."[66]

The use of "everyday and simple" analogies to illustrate his argument was Adriani's own practice, as we have seen, suggesting that he, too, employed them to illuminate topics he regarded as clandestine. Not all his references to Lucretius in his Dioscorides *Commentary* were equally tendentious; for instance, the houseleek that thrives best on its own recalled Lucretius's happy man living in isolation from the troubles of others, the "sweetness" of whose situation, Adriani reminds us (in case we should miss the allusion to "Suave, mari magno"), lay not in enjoying another's troubles but in escaping them himself.[67] But we know that Lucretius remained a dangerous poet

---

65 Dioscorides, *De materia medica* 1: 20; "De musco," fol. 21v: "Qui ex Epicuri placitis rerum naturam suavissimo carmine cives suos Romanus poeta quondam docuit, et qui multo ante in eadem haeresi eadem primus instituerat Abderites Democritus."

66 Ibid., fol. 21v, "Et quoniam nova et clandestina res erat, quotidiano et humili a vocum nostrarum elementis et litterarum notis exemplo quod in maiestate et tenebris naturae adhuc occulitur in aperto a Lucretio ostendebatur, qui non aliter variari in natura formas diceret quam variatis in sermone nostro elementis, alias subinde atque alias significari et intelligi rerum substantias passim videmus; fierique, ut ille dicebat, mutatis paucis additisve aut non suo loco servatis ex lignis ignes et ex aliis alia"; Lucretius 1: 912–14; cf. 1: 197, 824–27; 2: 688–98, 1013–16; and on hooked atoms, 2: 398–407.

67 Dioscorides 4: 81, fol. 251r; cf. Lucretius 2: 1–4. Other references discuss Lucretius's names for plants, his praise of Athens, his account of man's dreams, the "slippery snake that casts off its vestment among the thorns," Dioscorides 1: 49 and 3: 43; 1: 126; 3: 149; 2: 17, fols.34r–v and fols. 174r, 62v, 215r, 88v; cf. Lucretius 2: 847, etc.; 6: 2–; 4: 1014–17, 1020–23; 4: 60–61. Cf. Dioscorides 4: 67, and 5: 100, fols. 284v, 328r, referring to Lucretius 5: 898–900, and 6: 906–9.

when Adriani again called him "the not always completely sane Roman poet" or failed to name him at all, as when discussing *tus* or frankincense. Dioscorides called it an atom, he tells us, because it was indivisible and not because it was like the atoms of Democritus or Epicurus, without explaining that it was Lucretius who had compared the difficulty of separating the scent from lumps of frankincense to that of "drawing the mind and spirit from the whole body without the dissolution of all."[68] In a book dedicated to a pope who had recently promulgated a decree declaring the immortality of the soul an official dogma of the Church, this would not perhaps have been appropriate.[69] Despite this, nearly all of Adriani's references to Lucretius did threaten Christian orthodoxy, especially the three themes that were leitmotifs in his university lectures.

In quoting Lucretius at the expense of the many other ancient philosophers in Adriani's canon, I am aware that I may seem to be exaggerating his influence. We all read texts with an eye trained on what we want to find, and I have done the same, like the two other readers of his lectures, Verde and Godman. Adriani himself had an immensely well-stocked repertoire of classical tags and homilies, enough to provide him with exempla for every occasion. His repeated listing of ancient philosophers reads like a mantra to defend his own teaching in a city that—as he so often said—was more devoted to money than to learning. Against pain and grief, he was able to produce "the school of the Stoics, the academy of Aristotle, the synthesis of Empedocles' discord and friendship, the silence of Pythagoras, the *homoeomeria* of Anaxagoras, the pleasure and the garden of Epicurus and the atom of Democritus flung into empty space, the patched cloak of Diogenes and the Academy, through which Socrates taught mortals how to find the explanation of all divine and human affairs."[70] But without pursuing the Epicurean

---

68 Dioscorides 1: 161, fol. 81r (cf. 1: 78, fol. 43v): "Nec qua ratione Democritus et Epicurei atomos suas dixerunt intelligendum id est"; see Lucretius 3: 327–34.

69 On the lively debate about immortality and the papal decree of 19 December 1513, see Paul Blum, "The Immortality of the Soul," in *Cambridge Companion to Renaissance Philosophy*, ed. Hankins, 217–23, and on the decree, Eric Constant, "A Reinterpretation of the Fifth Lateran Council Decree *Apostolici regiminis* (1513)," *Sixteenth Century Journal* 33 (2002): 353–79.

70 R, fols. 36v–37r (L, fol. 65r), ("Incredibile est," dated 1511 by Richardson, "A Manuscript of Biagio Buonaccorsi," 594): "et contra dolores nostri portus obstetricium quo Zenonis porticus crevit, patuit licium Aristotelis, Empedoclis discordi et amicitia coierunt, Pithagorae silentium auditum est, Anaxagorae omiomeria, floruit Epicuri voluptas et ortus Democriti athomus per inane iactata est, Diogenis sartum est pallium et Academia . . . gloriosa salubrisque fuit, per quam Socrates mortales docuit divinorum et humanorum omnium certam inveniet rationem."

trail through Adriani's almost continuous lectures on "Poetry and Oratory" in Florence, we would have missed the clues that lead us into genuinely new territory. For in imitating Lucretius's practice of using homely examples to discuss "new and clandestine" theories, Adriani points us, through his own exempla drawn from local events, to topics that he similarly regarded as new and clandestine—not only atomism, which he explains in Lucretius's instructive analogy of the alphabet, but also Lucretius's critique of superstitious religion. This weighs us down like the stone in the fresco of St. Benedict's miracle, which was removed—as he explained in another lecture—not by the grieving priest and mourners but by the cheerful plebeian, who cast off the stone by happily burying his son himself.

Adriani's long career teaching in the university influenced a generation of young Florentines. We know that Francesco Guicciardini was an enthusiastic member of his audience, and traces of Adriani's influence can be seen in his and his brothers' political and scientific writings.[71] It was undoubtedly Machiavelli, however, who was most influenced by him. Whether or not he was Adriani's student in the university before becoming his colleague in the chancery in 1498, he must have been familiar with Adriani's 1497 lecture *Wonder at Nothing* and, through him, with the manuscript of *De rerum natura*. Their relationship provides the introduction to understanding the important role played by Lucretius in Machiavelli's thinking, described in the chapter that follows.

---

71 See above, at note 17; also Francesco Guicciardini, "Delle condizioni d'Italia dopo la giornata di Ravenna" and "Sulle mutazioni seguite dopo la battaglia di Ravenna," in id., *Scritti politici e ricordi*, ed. Roberto Palmarocchi (Bari, 1933), 80: "Mutossi in uno subito la fortuna"; cf. Luigi Guicciardini, "Dialogo delle pecchie e ragnateli," BNF, MS Magl. 8, 1422, fols. 69r–108v, perhaps influenced by the 1514–15 lecture, see pp. 57–58 and note 44 above.

4

Machiavelli and the Influence of Lucretius

Lucretius has been undervalued as an influence on Machiavelli. Although Sergio Bertelli first wrote about Machiavelli's transcription of *De rerum natura* in the Vatican Library in 1961, scholars have been slow to recognize its importance for understanding Machiavelli's thinking. If the humanists who preceded him were cautious about citing Lucretius by name, Machiavelli was even more so—explicably, perhaps, after his loss of office on the Medici's return in 1512 and the Church's ban on both Epicurean and Averroist philosophy the following year, at the start of Machiavelli's writing career.[1] He never mentions Lucretius's name and rarely quotes him, so without knowing that he had copied the whole text in his own hand, it would be difficult to trace Lucretius's influence on his outlook or philosophy. Yet it is clear that the experience of copying and commenting on his poem influenced Ma-

---

1 His transcription of Lucretius is in Rome, Vatican Library, MS Rossi 884, together with Terence's *Andria;* see Sergio Bertelli, "Notarelle Machiavelliane" and "Ancora du Lucrezio e Machiavelli"; Paul Rahe, "In the Shadow of Lucretius" and *Against Throne and Altar;* also Gennaro Sasso, *Machiavelli e gli Antichi e altri saggi*.

chiavelli's rational and skeptical outlook in important ways. Machiavelli never wrote systematically about his understanding of philosophical issues, so perhaps we should not attempt to talk about his "outlook" as a coherent whole. On the contrary, his view of the cosmos and of man's nature as unchanging seems difficult to reconcile with the flexibility he demanded in the field of politics, where his ideas about republicanism, princely rule, and religion appear to be equally at odds. Yet one of his contemporaries did talk admiringly about Machiavelli's "philosophy" *(filosofia)*, by which he meant not what we would call philosophy today but rather the originality of Machiavelli's thinking in a broader context.[2] Part of this originality lay in his novel emphasis on the role of fortune in life and on the need for his natural hero, the man of prowess or *virtù*, to behave with moral flexibility in adapting to change—ideas familiar to us from the preceding chapters. So to track the influence of Lucretius and the Epicureans on Machiavelli, we should begin with his early years in the 1490s, when we know he was in touch with Adriani and probably with Bartolomeo Scala, too, as a friend of his father's. This was the time, he later wrote in the *Discourses,* when, as a young man, what one hears "spoken of well or badly" influences one for the rest of one's life.[3]

Adriani had been lecturing on poetry and oratory in Florence's university since the death of Poliziano in late September 1494, as we have seen, and it was in 1497 that he delivered his inaugural lecture, *Nil admirari* ("Wonder at Nothing"), in which he modeled himself on Lucretius in order to rid his young audience of their fear of the unknown. Scala had died earlier that year, in the middle of writing his long Lucretian poem *On Trees,* having published his official *Defense* the previous year, in which he had discussed fortune in terms of Lucretius's theory of creation by "the fortuitous clash of individual atoms."[4] So Lucretius was in the air. The year 1497 is also when it is assumed that Machiavelli transcribed his copy of *De rerum natura,* while he still had time on his hands before entering the chancery the following year. This is,

2 See Filippo Casavecchia to Machiavelli, congratulating him on the capture of Pisa on 17 June 1509, *Opere*, 1108, translated as "ideas" by James Atkinson and David Sices, *Machiavelli and His Friends*, 182. Allan Gilbert translates his literary writings in *The Chief Works and Others*.

3 *Discourses* 3: 46; *Opere*, 252; *Works* 1: 525, cited by Roberto Ridolfi, who suggests it probably reflects his own experience, in *The Life of Niccolò Machiavelli*, trans. Cecil Grayson (London, 1963), 4. On Bernardo Machiavelli as an interlocutor in Scala's *Dialogue on Laws*, Brown, introduction to Scala's *Essays and Dialogues*, xi–xii.

4 See pp. 32 and 39–40 above.

therefore, one of the earliest texts—apart from the books in his father's library[5]—that we can be certain he read, although we do not know whether he copied it for personal reasons, perhaps in order to follow Adriani's university lectures, or whether he was commissioned to do so by Adriani or by someone else. According to Sergio Bertelli, Machiavelli's transcription included some of the corrections in the first book of the manuscript of Lucretius associated with Adriani in the Biblioteca Laurenziana in Florence (MS Laur. 35, 32), suggesting that he may have been preparing a clean copy incorporating Adriani's annotations—or even that both men were working on a Florentine printed edition to compete with the Venice 1495 edition, in anticipation of the Florentine Giuntine edition of 1512.[6] The marginalia in both manuscripts reveal an interest in Lucretius's atomism, the manuscript associated with Adriani containing lengthy comments on the atom as the smallest mathematical point *(punctus)* that cannot be seen or divided and on the limit to the breakup of atoms (against what mathematicians say), without which we would die at thirty years instead of eighty, drawing the comment that "the flower of life is thirty-five, the rest old age."[7]

Apart from the possible influence of Adriani on Machiavelli's transcription of Lucretius, there are clear signs that Adriani's 1497 lecture *Nil admirari* was heard or read by Machiavelli in the words and phrases from it that reappear in Machiavelli's writings. One example comes from the preface to Book 1 of the *Discourses,* where Machiavelli talks of following a path untrodden *(trita)* by others in order to find "new ways and methods." This is an allusion most obviously borrowed from Lucretius ("I traverse pathless tracts . . . never yet trodden [*trita*] by any foot . . . to pluck new flowers"), but it also reflects earlier inaugural lectures, including Adriani's, who neatly turned the topos to make it reflect on the impossibility, in the current state of intellectual life

---

5 Bernardo Machiavelli's library is described by Catherine Atkinson in *Debts, Dowries, Donkeys* (Frankfurt, 2002), 137–48 and Appendix C; on its influence on Machiavelli, Carlo Ginzburg, "Machiavelli, l'eccezione e la regola: linee di una ricerca in corso," *Quaderni storici* 38 (2003): 195–213.

6 MS Laur. 35, 32; see Bertelli, "Notarelle Machiavelliane," 531, referring to "un tentativo di edizione critica del Lucrezio, ben presto interrotto"; cf. Reeve [I], 47 and 45, referring to MS Ross. 884 without clarifying its descent; it is not mentioned in Reeve [II] and not discussed in Reeve [III]. See the appendix below.

7 MS Laur. 35, 32, fols. 11v, 12r ("utputa homines ad 35, id enim est flos, reliquendum qua aetas senectus"); 12v, commenting on Lucretius 1: 532–55, 564 ("aevi . . . florem"), 604.

in Florence, of finding anything "new" to say without repeating platitudes *(trita)*.[8] Another passage in this lecture that seems to have influenced Machiavelli was Adriani's description of our "wonder" and astonishment at entering the world being like that of alpinists entering an elegant city, due either to our "oblivion of things," as Plato believed, or because the world *was* new, as Lucretius (though unnamed in the lecture) believed. In the controversial chapter *Discourses* 2: 5 ("that the variations of sects and languages, together with floods and plagues, wipe out our memory of events"), Machiavelli explained that our ignorance of the past was partly due to the "oblivion of things" created from natural disasters like floods, from which the only survivors were "uncouth mountain dwellers," which clearly echoes Adriani.[9] Although Machiavelli does not name Lucretius or attribute our oblivion of the past to the world being new (as Adriani had done), the opening of this chapter ("To those philosophers who have held that the world is eternal, I think one could reply that if such antiquity is correct, it is reasonable there should be a record of more than five thousand years") follows the line of Lucretius's thinking (that if the world was everlasting, why is there no historical evidence earlier than the Theban War and the ruin of Troy?—hence his belief that the world was new), and it may have been in Machiavelli's mind when pondering this question. If so, Lucretius and his hostility to religion may also help to explain why, in the same chapter, Machiavelli particularly attacked the role played by religious sects in destroying records of the past.[10]

More substantial influences on Machiavelli, however, are the two key topics of Adriani's lecture concerning fortune and the superstitious origins of religion. Both were very relevant in the context of Florence's precarious situation after 1494 and Savonarola's frightening sermons, and in his writings Machiavelli followed Adriani in the importance he attributed to fortune, as well as to the power of religion. They are also topical and controversial themes

---

8 Machiavelli, *Discourses* 1: pref., *Opere*, 76, *Works* 1: 190; Adriani, "Nil admirari," cited on p. 51 (note 25) above. Lucretius 1: 926–8 (cf. 4: 1, quoted by John Najemy, *Between Friends: Discourses of Power and Desire in the Machiavelli-Vettori Letters of 1513–1515* (Princeton, 1993), 337.

9 See p. 52, note 28 above ("oblivione rerum," "quasi alpini homines"), Machiavelli, *Discourses* 2: 5, *Opere*, 154–55, *Works* 1: 339–41: "uomini tutti montanari e rozzi . . . questo effetto della oblivione delle cose."

10 *Discourses* 2: 5; Lucretius 5: 324–31; Gennaro Sasso's interpretation is discussed on p. 77 below.

in Machiavelli scholarship, which interprets them either within a pagan, pre-Christian context or (more recently) as traditionally Christian.[11] To approach fortune and religion from the perspective of Adriani's lectures and Lucretius may throw new light on the problem of reconciling man's freedom to act within Machiavelli's circumscribed cosmos.

The problem, or "puzzle," is first presented in his 1506 *Ghiribizzi* (musings) and in his poem *On Fortune* to Giovan Battista Soderini. The *Ghiribizzi* uniquely reveal Machiavelli thinking out loud, as it were, about problems, weighing them up and having second thoughts about them, which he added in the margin of his draft letter, to provide what one writer has called "a harsh counterpoint, the beginning of a negation, the temptation—even more than the attempt—to overcome" the problem.[12] The problem in this case was the difficulty of formulating rules about political behavior (as he had been taught to do in the chancery) when he had just witnessed Pope Julius II's amazing success against the odds—and against all the rules—in winning over a hostile and rebel city (Perugia) through chance and in entering it unarmed (although in fact accompanied by his Swiss guards, as Machiavelli later acknowledged in *Discourses* 2: 27), suggesting that success was sometimes the result of chance or fortune and sometimes the result of preparation. If only we were free to change our natures and leap from top to top of fortune's wheel—as Machiavelli expressed it in his poem *On Fortune*—we would all be happy and successful, but since "this is denied by the occult force that rules us," not even the wise man, let alone ourselves, can change the disposition we are born with, leaving us helpless in the face of fortune. Because he expressed similar ideas in Chapter 25 of *The Prince* and in the *Discourses,* where he also acknowledged the role of prodigies and prophecies in predicting "great events," it has been argued that natural astrology played an important role in his philosophy, casting "a dark shadow on his attempt to safeguard free will."[13]

---

11 See Cary Nederman, "Amazing Grace: Fortune, God, and Free Will in Machiavelli's Thought," *Journal of the History of Ideas* 60 (1994): 617–38; on fortune, Santoro, *Fortuna, ragione e prudenza;* Thomas Flanagan, "The Concept of *Fortuna* in Machiavelli," in *The Political Calculus*, ed. Anthony Parel (Toronto, 1972), and Hanna Pitkin, *Fortune is a Woman: Gender and Politics in the Thought of Niccolò Machiavelli* (Berkeley, 1984).

12 *Ghiribizzi*, 13–21 September 1506; *Opere*, 1082–83; *Letters*, 134–36. I quote Gennaro Sasso, "Qualche osservazione sui *Ghiribizzi* al Soderino," in *Machiavelli e gli Antichi* 2: 3–56 at 52; cf. Mario Martelli, "I *Ghiribizzi* a Giovan Battista Soderini," *Rinascimento* 92 (1969): 147–80; Carlo Ginzburg, "Diventare Machiavelli: per una nuova lettura dei *Ghiribizzi* al Soderini," *Quaderni storici* 41 (2006): 151–64 (with thanks to Serena Ferente); Anthony Parel, *The Machiavellian Cosmos* (New Haven, 1992), 76–77.

However, there is an alternative solution to this puzzle about man's ability to act freely in Machiavelli's circumscribed cosmos. Two years before writing the *Ghiribizzi* to Soderini, Machiavelli sent a now lost letter to Bartolomeo Vespucci, a Florentine teacher of astrology at the University of Padua, in which he evidently entertained a more positive view of the individual's freedom to act. For in his reply to this missing letter, Vespucci wrote:

> Your opinion is absolutely right, since all the ancients agree that the wise man can himself change the influences of the stars. This should be understood not with respect to the stars, since nothing can change what is eternal, but rather with respect to the wise man himself, who, by changing his step this way and that, can change and alter himself.[14]

Machiavelli's opinion seems to have been that, although the wise man cannot change the course of the stars and the universe (as the adage had it), he can change his own actions and, in doing so, change himself. We should not be surprised, then, that in the *Ghiribizzi* Machiavelli added afterthoughts in the margins that form a counterpoint ("the beginning of a negation," as Sasso describes it) to the mainly negative drift of these musings:

> Each man must do what his mind [*animo*] prompts him to—and do it with daring [*audacia*], then try his luck, and, when fortune slackens off, regain the initiative by trying a different way of proceeding from his customary one.

This suggests that it may be possible to regain the initiative by trying a new way of proceeding—by doing what one's mind prompts one to do, and then "changing one's step this way and that," as Machiavelli's astrologer friend Bartolomeo Vespucci put it. Flexibility, or "mental mobility," was what Adri-

---

13 Anthony Parel, "Human Motions and Celestial Motions in Machiavelli's Historiography," in *Niccolò Machiavelli: politico, storico, letterato*, ed. Jean-Jacques Marchand (Rome, 1996), 382; cf. 363–64, notes 1 and 2; on fortune and on the adage quoted in the *Ghiribizzi*, "Vir sapiens dominabitur astris," id., *Machiavellian Cosmos*, 11, 12, 69–70. See Machiavelli, *Di fortuna*, lines 115–19; *Opere*, 978; *Works* 2: 747; *Discourses* 1: preface and chap. 39 and 56; and 2: preface and chap. 29; *Florentine Histories* 5: chap. 1.

14 "Aliter et aliter passum, ipsum immutando et alterando," my own translation, based on *Letters*, 103; Sasso, "Sui *Ghiribizzi*," 43 (and on Vespucci, 32–46).

ani had recommended in his 1497 inaugural lecture as a response to fortune's changes. It might be difficult, despite this lecture, to integrate Machiavelli's thoughts on flexibility into his overall philosophy but for one new piece of evidence: Machiavelli's marginal notes in his transcription of Lucretius. For there, marking several passages in Book 2 referring to the atomic swerve, Machiavelli clearly picked up Lucretius's association of the swerve with free will, suggesting that Lucretius may provide the missing link in our understanding of Machiavelli's philosophy.

The first sign of Machiavelli's interest in the atomic swerve is a hand in the margin pointing to line 82 of Book 2, on the mistake of not believing in the spontaneous movement and collision of atoms in the void.[15] This is followed by two marginal comments on passages concerning free will or (literally) "a free mind." The first, at lines 250–55, is on the atomic swerve that, by breaking the decrees of fate, enables us to enjoy free will. Without this free will wrested from the fates *("libera . . . fatis avulsa voluntas")* asks Lucretius (2: 256–60), how would living creatures all over the world be able to go where pleasure leads them, "swerving our motions not at fixed times and fixed places, but just where our mind [*mens*] has taken us?"[16] Here Machiavelli wrote in the margin: "from motion there is variety, and from it we have a free mind [liberam habere mentem]." After omitting line 258 (on proceeding where pleasure leads us), Machiavelli then replaced *motus . . . rigantur* with *homines reguntur,* at line 262 (an alternative reading offered in Pomponio Leto's emendations to the 1486 edition of Lucretius), suggesting that instead of the will conveying movement through the limbs, "men" are "ruled" by their will through their limbs. This leads to the second marginal comment at lines 284–97, which concerns our ability to resist external pressure to act against our will: "weight, blows, and the swerve [*clinamen*] are in the seeds," condensing Lucretius's argument that motions are caused by something other than

---

15 MS Rossi 884, cit., fol. 22r (at 2: 82: "Avius a vera longe ratione vagaris"). The marginalia are discussed more fully in the appendix below. They are in the same hand as the transcription, and (unlike the brief marginalia in later chapters) they are not replicated in the other versions that influenced his text, suggesting that they are Machiavelli's own or, if copied, represent his own personal interest in the topics commented on.

16 MS Rossi 884, fol. 25r: "motum varium esse et ex eo nos liberam habere mentem," marking Lucretius 2: 250–55 ("sed ubi ipsa tulit mens", 260). Free will is not a classical concept, Peter Stacey commented to me, and that for Seneca and the Stoics (as here for Lucretius), *arbitrio libero* means the mental freedom to act without restraint.

the external force of weights and blows, thanks to the freedom given to us by the swerve of the very first atoms.[17]

Other brief marginalia in Book 2 include, at line 112: "image of first beginnings of things" (on the minute particles that dance like the motes in a sunbeam); at line 142: "on the speed of motion"; and at a line inserted between 164 and 165 in Machiavelli's transcription ("For [the first beginnings] should not delay, held up by deliberation"), the comment: "nothing happens by deliberation."[18] The comments on free will are then followed by the marginal comment on lines 294–96: "nothing is more closely packed or more scattered than at its beginning," for (Lucretius continues in lines 296–303) nothing can increase or decrease the mass of matter or the sum total of things: not only are atoms permanent and unchanging, but so, too, is their motion, which is the same now as it used to be and will be in the future, everything being born under the same conditions and developing in the same way according to the laws or "pacts" of nature.[19] Lucretius's ensuing "teachings" are also noted by Machiavelli as marginal comments—on the variety of shapes of atoms, including atoms that tickle the senses and that have a finite number of differences and range of temperature, although those of a similar shape are infinite in number; on the earth as the Great Mother and creator of animals, humans, and the gods; and on the gods, who contribute nothing, moved neither by propitiation nor by wrath as they "enjoy a life of deepest peace" (lines 646–48, 651), which is summed up in the margin: "the gods don't care about the affairs of mortals."[20]

These marginal comments testify to the particular importance Lucretius

---

17 Ibid., fol. 25v: "in seminibus esse pondus plagas et clinamen," marking 2: 284–87. For Pomponio Leto's emendations in Utrecht, University Library, X col. 82 (Rariora), fol. c3v, see the appendix below.

18 Ibid., fol. 22v ("simulachrum principiorum"); fol. 23r ("de celeritate motus"); fol. 23v ("nil fieri consilio"); commenting on the line "Nam neque consilio debent tardata morari," noted as a lacuna by Pontano and in the Loeb edition (ed. Smith, 106) but included in MS Rossi 884 and added to MS Laur. 35, 25, to Munich, MS Clm. 816a, and to the printed (Venice, 1495) edition in Paris, BN Rés. M Yc 397.

19 MS Rossi 884, fol. 26r: "nil esse suo densius aut rarius principio," marking Lucretius 2: 294–96.

20 Ibid., fol. 26v ("variam esse figuram principiorum," at 2: 294–96); fol. 28r ("semina quae titillant sensum" added after two lines inserted between 425–26); fol. 29r ("mare ex quibus constet principiis," "in uno principio non posse esse plures formas, idest, infinitas," at 2: 471–72, 479–82); fol. 30r ("in eodem principio frigus, tepor & calor esse possunt," "principia cuiuslibet formae esse infinita," at 2: 516–18, 523–25); fol. 31r ("unum quoque ex vario principiorum genere constare," at 2: 585–88); fol. 31v ("de genitrice deorum," following 2: 598–99); and fol. 32r ("deos non curare mortalia," at 2: 646–48).

held for Machiavelli, concentrated as they are in Book 2 on the structure of the universe and focusing on the topics of free will, motion, matter, and the indifference of the gods to mortal affairs. Moreover, they all contribute key ideas to his philosophy that have hitherto seemed difficult to reconcile. First, an unchanging universe, in which "the things that are now, were before in the past, and will move in the same way in the future," as Lucretius wrote (2: 297–99), or, as Machiavelli put it (closely following Lucretius's rhythm), "And it is, and always has been, and always will be, that evil follows after good, good after evil," for "the world has always been in the same condition" (*The Golden Ass,* or *L'asino,* 5: 103–5; *Discourses* 2: preface, cf. 1: 39).[21] Then, a world "always in incessant motion" (*"semper in adsiduo motu,"* Lucretius 1: 995), or "always in motion" (*"sempre in moto,"* Machiavelli, *Discourses* 1: preface; *Asino* 5: 100–101). This world enjoyed a natural cycle of development governed by laws to preserve the species and "the sum total of things" (Lucretius 2: 302–3; 5: 923–24; Machiavelli, *Discourses* 1: 2); and within this life cycle there was the possibility of change and the exercise of free will through the swerve, in the passages already cited, which enable a man wise and energetic enough to "change his step" or, as Machiavelli put it in *The Prince,* Chapters 25 and 26, to exercise his free will *(libero arbitrio)* in the half of his life not controlled by fortune—or by God, who "does not want to do everything."[22]

Another major influence on Machiavelli came from the debates on the eternity of the world that were engaging scholars just at the time Machiavelli was writing the *Discourses,* particularly those held at the University of Pisa (whose provost, Francesco del Nero, was related to Machiavelli by marriage and employed his brother Totto as his assistant). The apparent discrepancy between Lucretius and Machiavelli concerns precisely the issue of the eternity of the world debated at Pisa: are both the world and the universe eternal, as Machiavelli is said to have believed, or is it only the universe that is eternal and not the worlds within the universe, as Lucretius held? We do not know what position the "Lucretian philosopher," Raffaelle Franceschi, upheld in the "arcane debates on the nature of the soul" in Pisa in 1517, which, he said, could not have been livelier if Pomponazzi (the famous Padua Averroist) had been there. He only reported that "we dared to take the side of Themistius

---

21 *Opere,* 967, 145, cf. 122, *Works* 2: 763, 1: 322, cf. 278; cf. *Discourses* 3: 1, 43; *Florentine Histories* 5: 1.
22 *Opere,* 145 and 967, 80–81; 295–97, *Works* 1: 322, and 2: 763; 1: 199, 89–94.

and Alexander of Aphrodisias against Averroes." Since Alexander of Aphrodisias could be assimilated to Lucretius, this might suggest that he was arguing as a Lucretian, although since he had been replaced as a teacher of moral philosophy and logic in 1509 by the Platonizing Francesco Verino, he may have been in no position to do so. Nor do we possess copies of Franceschi's and Nifo's later 1520 lectures that Machiavelli's brother Totto was requested to send to Florence. We only know that they were thought interesting enough to copy, and since Franceschi was known as a Lucretian both in Florence and Pisa, they may have discreetly reflected some Epicurean influence in favor of the mortality of the soul.[23]

Machiavelli, at least, would certainly have known about the lectures from the copies his brother sent to Francesco del Nero in 1520, and although delivered too late to have influenced the ambiguous opening to *Discourses* 2: 5, they could have reflected the earlier "arcane" debates on the soul at the time the *Discourses* was being written. Gennaro Sasso reads this chapter as a scholastic question or *quaestio* for debate, "on whether the world always existed," from which he concludes that Machiavelli was an Aristotelian-Averroist.[24] It is more likely that the chapter's ambiguity reflects Machiavelli's own open approach to the question, influenced by Adriani's 1497 lecture and Lucretius in the way suggested above, and possibly also by the later debates in Pisa. What concerned both Adriani and Machiavelli, with differing emphasis, was why almost all knowledge of antiquity (which Adriani called "an almost untouched treasure chamber") had been lost. This is the context in which Machiavelli pursued what seems to be the main point of the chapter, an attack on the role of all sects, including Christianity, in destroying evidence of the past. In 1513, just as Machiavelli was beginning his writing career, both the Epicureans and the Aristotelian-Averroists had been condemned as heretical by the Fifth Lateran Council for believing "in the mortality or in the unity of the soul and the

---

23 On the debate over the immortality of the soul, especially after Pietro Pomponazzi published his *Treatise* on it in 1516, see Paul Blum, "The Immortality of the Soul," 217–23, referring to Alexander of Aphrodisias on 213, 216–17. On Franceschi, see Verde, "Il secondo periodo de Lo Studio Fiorentino," 111–12, note 18 on 123–24, and pp. 101–102 below.

24 On Totto, Verde, "Il secondo periodo," 112, and note 12 on 122; Sasso, "De aeternitate mundi," in id., *Machiavelli e gli Antichi* I: 167–192; also 195 (on the *quaestio*), 172–73, 208, 215 (on the radicalism of Machiavelli's "relativizzazione" of sects and religions in this chapter, which, despite its "non pochi spunti lucreziani," shows a "netta, profonda, non componibile" difference between Machiavelli and the Epicureans).

eternity of the world."²⁵ To understand better where he stood on this issue, we need to turn to the equally contentious question of Machiavelli's attitude towards religion, which is the second of the topics discussed in Adriani's 1497 lecture *Nil admirari* that exercised an important influence on him.

Religion as superstition based on fear of punishment, *metus poenarum*, was the great theme of *De rerum natura* that Adriani had developed at length in the 1497 lecture, where he also attacked the idea of propitiatory religion that had God playing the role of pawnbroker.²⁶ "Fear of God" based on fear of punishment is also a central theme of Machiavelli's writings, where he consistently represents God as a judge to be feared or a "friend" to be placated and practically never as the providential creator of the universe.²⁷ All wise legislators claim their authority derives from God, Machiavelli wrote in *Discourses* 1: 11, "because otherwise their laws would not have been accepted"; for where "fear of God is lacking," a kingdom will fall unless religion is replaced by fear of a prince. "Fear is the greatest master there is," he told Francesco Vettori several times, for—he wrote in Chapter 17 of *The Prince*—it is "sustained by a dread of punishment that never leaves you."²⁸ In *Discourses* 1: 14 he explains how the Romans inculcated fear and superstition for political purposes through bloodcurdling ceremonies, oath taking, and the manipulative use of soothsayers and diviners, and how they interpreted "their auspices according to necessity"—by which he meant that their leaders were never deterred by adverse auguries from doing what they needed to do, while at the same time managing to manipulate the rituals to avoid showing any disrespect for religion.²⁹

Machiavelli's interest in the political value of religion to rulers was, of course, very different from Lucretius's wish to liberate men from its thrall through enlightened teaching—as Adriani had attempted to do in his lectures —and was much closer to Polybius and Livy than to Lucretius. As several

25 Giovanni Mansi, *Sacrorum conciliorum nova et amplissima collectio* (repr. Graz, 1961), 33: 842.
26 See chap. 3 above.
27 Sebastian de Grazia, *Machiavelli in Hell* (Princeton, 1989), 220–21 and 50–54 ("divine friendship," though missing any allusion to Lucretius and propitiation).
28 *Discourses* 1: 11, *Prince*, chap. 17 (*Opere*, 94, 282, *Works* 1: 225, 61–62); Vettori to Machiavelli, 5 August 1526 (*Opere*, 1238, *Letters*, 395); see also Emanuele Cutinelli-Rèndina, *Chiesa e Religione in Machiavelli* (Pisa-Rome, 1998), 165, note 275 (citing the influence of Lucretius as well as Averroes on Machiavelli); id., *Introduzione a Machiavelli* (Rome-Bari, 1999), 80, note 14.
29 John Najemy, "Papirius and the Chickens, or Machiavelli on the Necessity of Interpreting Religion," *Journal of the History of Ideas* 60 (1999): 674–78.

historians have noted, Machiavelli's attitude to religion presents two quite different faces, one valuing it as a form of political control, the other following Lucretius in describing religion anthropologically as the expression of the deeply rooted beliefs and fears of ordinary people.[30] Both are present in *The Golden Ass,* the long autobiographical poem that Machiavelli wrote around 1517, which neatly summarizes the two poles between which Machiavelli "oscillated" in his approach to religion. On one hand, it criticizes the idea of propitiatory religion (and with it, the legacy of Savonarola), since, "to believe that without effort on your part God fights for you, while you are idle and on your knees, has ruined many kingdoms and many states"; on the other, it appreciates the function served by ritual in keeping people happy and united—"there is assuredly need for prayers, and altogether mad is he who forbids people their ceremonies and devotion"—which, unlike Lucretius, Machiavelli saw as the basis of their respect for law and civilized behavior.[31] This latter view underlies a passage in the *Florentine Histories* (1: 5) describing the impact of the barbarian invasions of Italy, which, he writes, "overturned the laws, customs, way of life, religion, language, dress, and the very names of things"; for not only did old beliefs fight with "the miracles of the new," but Christianity itself was divided into different churches with different heresies, leaving people to die miserably, not knowing which God to turn to for help, "as all unhappy people are accustomed to do."[32] Religious disunity was symptomatic of political disunity and popular distress, both of which needed addressing in order to achieve the ordered society that Machiavelli strove for.

These two aspects of religion also help to explain Machiavelli's attitude to Christianity and the Church of his day. He attacked the papal court in *Discourses* 1: 12 for its impiety and immorality, and then went on, in *Discourses* 2: 2, to criticize the Christian ethos for glorifying "humble and contemplative men rather than active ones" and suffering evil passively instead of reacting to it boldly—as the Romans did in their bloody and magnificent wars. For the same reasons, he criticized the friars for teaching the people passivity in not

---

30 See Najemy, "Papirius and the Chickens," esp. 663, alluding to what Sasso calls the contrast or contradiction in Machiavelli's thought, perhaps better described by Cutinelli-Rèndina as "oscillazioni . . . tra due poli," in *Chiesa e Religione,* 212–14.

31 *L'Asino,* 5, lines 106–27, *Opere,* 967, *Works* 2: 763–64. The poem is discussed more fully on pp. 83–84 below.

32 Najemy, "Papirius and the Chickens," 666–67 (his translation).

speaking out against evil, which allowed their dishonest prelates and leaders to do whatever they wanted, unafraid of punishment that "they cannot see and do not believe"—while at the same time admiring their founders, St. Francis and St. Dominic, for reviving the idea of primitive Christianity "in the minds of the people," who saw it as their authentic culture.[33] The Dominican friar Girolamo Savonarola integrated both facets of ancient religion that fascinated Machiavelli: as a political force based on fear, and as the expression of the deeply rooted culture of ordinary people. He admired Savonarola for using religion to support political necessity in persuading the Florentines (who, Machiavelli adds, were far from stupid) that he "spoke with God" and in reading the Bible "judiciously" when it was necessary to break its commandments. But he criticized Savonarola for misusing his influence with the people, since instead of preaching boldness, he encouraged passivity by suggesting that they would be saved through fasting and through their prayers alone, "idle and on their knees," and, worse, he lost their respect through his hypocrisy over the law of appeal.[34]

There is little in the evidence of his friends' or his own writings to suggest that Machiavelli believed in Christian revelation, or even in the special authority accorded to religious states and holy men. Despite calling Christianity "our religion" that "teaches us the truth and the true way," he also treated it "relativistically" as a form of power, one of a succession of religions with a limited life cycle, just as Bartolomeo Scala had done when discussing religion in his *Dialogue on Laws* and his *Defense* of Savonarola.[35] We cannot, of course, know what Machiavelli's personal beliefs were, but given the tradition of skepticism in the chancery, we need to explore his reputation for nonconformity to see what light, if any, it throws on the role of religion more widely in his philosophy. We know, for example, that every year from 1500 until 1513 Niccolò and his brother Totto (who was a priest) paid the friars of S. Croce money to commemorate their father's death and pay off money owed for their great-uncle's bequest, but in May 1513, shortly after Niccolò's loss of

---

33 *Discourses* 3: 1; cf. 1: 55, on Germany, where "goodness and religion" were still prevalent; *Opere*, 196–97, 137; *Works* 1: 422, 307.

34 *Discourses* 1: 11; 1: 45; 3: 30 (*Opere*, 94–95, 127, 237; *Works* 1: 226, 288–89, 497); *Asino*, in note 31 above. Cf. Brown, "Savonarola, Machiavelli and Moses," 274–79.

35 *Discourses* 2: 2; and 5 (see note 24 above, quoting Sasso); on Scala, see pp. 29, 31–32 above.

office and brief imprisonment, payments for their father's bequest were terminated. The following year, it was reported by an ecclesiastical visitation to the family's patronal church of S. Andrea in Percussina that the church was very badly maintained, and "everything was rented out, according to Niccolò Machiavelli."[36] Although their father was apparently devout and belonged to a confraternity, there is no evidence that Niccolò was a member of a religious company. Indeed, he parodied such companies in his "Statutes for a Pleasure Company," and despite writing an "Exhortation to Penitence" (perhaps for someone else, it has been suggested), he said he never made a practice of listening to sermons himself.[37] Other evidence about Machiavelli's religion is retrospective and not totally reliable, such as his famous dream about preferring to be with the damned in hell than with the saved in heaven, or his reported deathbed confession to friar Andrea Alamanni, which, even if it happened, might—like the baptism of his children, evidently arranged by his wife and family—reflect the wishes of others as much as his own.[38]

In the opinion of his friends, Machiavelli was certainly not typically devout. Francesco Vettori told Machiavelli in November 1513 that he attended mass at the church near where he lived in Rome "since I am religious, as you know . . . I do not do as you do, who sometimes do not bother."[39] When the Wool Guild appointed Machiavelli to select a Lenten preacher for Florence in 1521, Francesco Guicciardini likened it to appointing Pachierotto (a well-known homosexual in Florence) to choose a wife for a friend, adding that, if Machiavelli at his age started thinking about his soul, it would be attributed

---

36 ASF, Corporazioni religiose soppresse 92, no. 69, fol. 99 left-right; cf. ASF, Notarile antecos. 6234, fols. 153r–v; Atkinson, *Debts, Dowries, Donkeys*, 166, §7; on the visitation, Florence, Archivio arcivescovile, Visite pastorali 004.1 (26 October 1514), fol. 69r, information kindly given to me by Gene Brucker, to be published in his article "Niccolò Machiavelli: His Lineage and the Tuscan Church" (in *I Tatti Studies*, forthcoming).

37 Letter to Francesco Vettori, 19 December 1513 (*Opere*, 1162; *Letters*, 267). On his "Capitoli" and "Exhortation" (*Opere*, 930–34; *Works* 2: 865–68; 1: 170–74), see Emanuele Cutinelli-Rèndina, "Riscrittura e mimesi: il caso dell' Esortazione alla penitenza," in *Cultura e scrittura di Machiavelli: atti del convegno di Firenze-Pisa . . . 1997* (Rome, 1998), 413–21; id., *Chiesa e religione in Machiavelli*, 279–84.

38 Gennaro Sasso, "Il 'celebrato sogno' di Machiavelli," in id., *Machiavelli e gli antichi* 3: 211–20, 269–94; Giuliano Procacci, "Frate Andrea Alamanni confessore del Machiavelli?" in id., *Machiavelli nella cultura europea dell'età moderna* (Rome-Bari, 1995), 423–31; Biagio Buonaccorsi to Machiavelli, 17 November 1503, cf. Agostino Vespucci to the same, 20–29 October 1500: "tametsi non baptizes" (*Opere*, 1058, 1023, *Letters*, 91, 32).

39 23 November 1513, *Opere*, 1158, *Letters*, 261.

to senility, not goodness, "since you have always lived in a contrary belief."[40] Moreover, his last testaments of 1511 and 1522 were drawn up in the chancery and in the Mercanzia, not in the church, and neither made any provision for his soul.[41] Further evidence of the "contrariness" of Machiavelli's religious beliefs is his posthumous role in the dialogue "On Free Will," written by a close friend, Luigi Guicciardini, who told his brother Francesco in 1533 that (the now deceased) Machiavelli represented "someone who finds it difficult to believe the things that should be believed, not just those to laugh about." Luigi seems to have been aware of the originality of Machiavelli's thought in using him to challenge Luigi's own efforts in the dialogue to reconcile Christian free will and astrology, though without grasping "the inner unity" of Machiavelli's thought.[42]

This brings us to the heart of the question about the mortality of the soul, for if Machiavelli really did not believe in the soul, it could imply that he supported Lucretius and the Epicureans in the debate about whether the world or the universe was eternal. He revealingly deleted the word *soul (anima)* from his draft preface to the *Discourses,* and in a letter written to Vettori in April 1527 he famously declared that he loved his country more than his own soul, just as he praised the Florentines who fought against the papacy in 1375–1378 for valuing their country more than their souls.[43] Nor did the soul play any part in Machiavelli's physiology, where imagination *(fantasia)* replaces the soul or "spirit" *(anima)* in its relationship with the mind or intelligence *(animo)*. Despite the emphasis placed recently on the role of imagination in Machiavelli's later plays in creating the self, or "self-fashioning," in his letters it describes a process of critical psychological and political analysis that distinguishes the "effectual truth" of a situation from appearance, much as Lucretius distinguished the reality of a man, "the thing itself," when his mask was ripped away through adversity. This process is closely connected with the metaphor of the theater, which for Machiavelli, as for Lucretius, served to represent the distance that separated appearances and reality; although Ma-

---

40 17 May 1521, cf. Machiavelli to Guicciardini on the same day (*Opere,* 1202, 1203 4, *Letters,* 335, 336).

41 They do, however, make the customary payments to the Duomo and New Sacristy, *Opere* ("Italia," 1813), cxxxiii–cxliv; see p. 109, note 61, below.

42 Felix Gilbert, "Machiavelli in an Unknown Contemporary Dialogue," *JWCI* 1 (1938): 163–65.

43 Parel, *Machiavellian Cosmos,* 27–28; Machiavelli to Vettori, 16 April 1527; *Florentine Histories* 3: 7 (*Opere,* 1250, 696, *Letters,* 416, *Works* 3: 1150).

chiavelli sometimes employed it as a device for political manipulation or deception, he used it as well to convey the Lucretian idea that life itself is a spectacle like the theater, to be viewed as a spectator with the same imagination or *fantasia* with which we view theatrical representations.[44]

We see the beginning of this process of critical analysis in the early 1506 letter to Giovan Battista Soderini and its culmination in the letter Machiavelli wrote, a year before he died, to Francesco Guicciardini. This last letter he wrote with his head full of *ghiribizzi* that would seem "either rash or ridiculous," but in fact his musings produced a final, consistent statement of the political philosophy that he had outlined twenty years earlier, in which the valiant Giovanni delle Bande Nere (son of Giovanni di Pierfrancesco de' Medici) appears as the hero with exactly the qualities needed to outstep the fates.[45] And between these two letters Machiavelli resorted to another imaginative writing, his poem *The Golden Ass*. Its opening chapter describes a young man who could not stop running, a malady that returned to him when he saw opening before him the wide Via Larga (where the Medici had their palace). Shouting, "Not even Christ can stop me here!" he continued to run for the rest of his life—or (in Machiavelli's own case) until 1513, when his loss of office induced the midlife, Dantesque crisis described in the remainder of this unfinished poem (which describes his encounter with a handmaiden of Circe and one of her victims, the heroic upstanding boar). As Sasso has written, the young man must be Machiavelli himself, whom a chancery colleague described in 1502 as "so eager for riding, wandering, and roaming about," and whose roaming was only stopped by his fall from office, leading to his disillusioned years of exile and unemployment in the country.[46]

In the poem, Machiavelli combined the issue of the individual's independence with criticism of traditional Christianity in order to defend the naturalistic right of all living creatures to act freely. In doing so, he not only

---

44 Lucretius 3: 58: "eripitur persona, manet res." On imagination or *fantasia* in Machiavelli, see Najemy, *Between Friends*, 185–97, especially 190, note 23, citing Lucretius on images (4: 51–52; cf. 2: 112, where Machiavelli picked out *simulachrum principiorum* in the margin of his transcription). On Lucretius and the theater, see pp. 8–9 above.

45 Machiavelli to Francesco Guicciardini, 15 March 1526 (*Opere*, 1229–30, *Letters*, 380–83).

46 Gennaro Sasso, "L'*Asino* di Niccolò Machiavelli: una satira antidantesca. Considerazioni e appunti," *Annali dell'Istituto Italiano per gli studi storici* 12 (1991–1994): 457–552 at 464 (citing Agostino Vespucci's letter of 14 October 1502, *Letters*, 50); on the poem as a political satire, see Gian Mario Anselmi and Paolo Fazion, *Machiavelli, L'Asino e le Bestie* (Bologna, 1982), discussed by Giorgio Inglese, "Proposte per l'*Asino*," *La Cultura* 23 (1985): 236.

overturned the traditional Christian terminology of providence and grace, and even the power of Christ, but also the idea of propitiatory religion represented by Savonarola.[47] Underlying its religious unorthodoxy is a more pervasive theme, however; that is, the virtue of leading a life of Lucretian naturalism, which links the topic of primitivism to Lucretius's critique of life through the metaphor of the theater. It is the boar in Chapter 8 that demonstrated the free will enjoyed by all living creatures (as Lucretius put it) by rearing up on its hind legs and contemptuously refusing the young man's offer to return it to human life: "I don't want to, and I refuse to, live with you." The similarity of this episode to Machiavelli's real-life advice to his son Guido shortly before Machiavelli died—to let their mad mule free to "go wherever it likes to regain its own way of life"—suggests it represents his own personally held views about freedom.[48] And since the boar then went on to ask the man to "direct your imagination [*fantasia*] to me before you leave, so I can rid you of your self-love" (in believing that only human life has value), Machiavelli succeeds in blending Lucretius's naturalism with his moral criticism of human life. For, as the boar proposes, it is through the use of his imagination or fantasy that the wise man can distance himself sufficiently to view life critically, as if he were a spectator at a theatrical show. These two themes suggest the poem should be interpreted less as political satire than as a statement of his own deeply felt philosophy.

Like the centaur Chiron in *The Prince,* who is said to reflect a Lucretian "taste for the primitive and savage," animals in *The Golden Ass* are closer to nature than man is; they are more philanthropic to each other and better equipped for survival than man, who (following another familiar Lucretian theme) is alone born nude and helpless, his life beginning in tears.[49] There is also "a precise echo" of Lucretius in Machiavelli's account of the origin of society in the *Discourses* I: 2, which describes how early men passed their lives "wandering about like wild beasts," or "scattered like beasts" as Machiavelli

---

47 *Golden Ass* 1: 84; 3: 115–25; 5: 106–27; 8: 16–18 (*Opere,* 956, 962, 967, 973, *Works* 2: 752, 758, 763–64, 770); discussed by Sasso, "L'Asino," 459, 467–68, 471–72.

48 *Golden Ass* 8, line 28: "Viver con voi io non voglio e rifiuto" (discussed by Rahe, *Against Throne and Altar,* p. 35); Machiavelli to his son Guido, 2 April 1527 (*Opere,* 973, 1248–49, *Works* 2: 770, *Letters,* 413). The poem continues with lines 31–34: "Ma se rivolgi a me la fantasia . . . farò che 'n tale error mai più non stia."

49 Raimondi, "Il politico e il centauro"; *Golden Ass* 8, lines 46ff.; for Lucretian themes, 8, lines 118, 121, 124 (*Opere,* 974, *Works* 2: 770–72); cf. Lucretius 5: 222–26.

put it, in contrast to Polybius, who supposed the existence of some rudimentary form of society.[50] Machiavelli's utilitarian account of the origin of justice (which developed from laws made to prevent injuries inflicted on others from being done to themselves) also derives from Lucretius and Epicurus, whose maxims stated that natural justice is an expression of expediency—animals and tribes incapable of making agreements not to inflict nor suffer harm lack either justice or injustice, since justice consists in making mutual agreements and is nothing in itself.[51] In this context, Machiavelli did not follow Epicurus in describing economic prosperity as a motive for seeking security, but he did define it as an essential condition for a happy way of life later in the *Discourses*—provided it did not encourage ambition and a Sisyphean desire for power that he disliked as much as the Epicureans.[52]

This chapter began by tracing the influence of Lucretius on Machiavelli through the marginalia in his autograph transcription of *De rerum natura* and through borrowings from Adriani's 1497 lecture *Nil admirari*. In themselves, the notes and borrowings would amount to no more than fragmentary textual comments unless supported by other evidence. Interpreted within the context of Machiavelli's life and later writings, however, they emerge as the cornerstones of a coherent and original philosophy that integrates his political views with his scientific atomism and religious naturalism. Although Machiavelli accepted the important role played by astrology in our lives, following the view of many ancient philosophers and contemporaries, he was novel in allowing unexpected room in this deterministic universe for the swerve of chance that enabled a bold and clever person to exercise his free will, whether he was a political leader like Scipio, a young Medici prince, an imagi-

---

50 Sasso, "I detrattori di Roma," 469; *Discourses* 1: 2: "vissono . . . dispersi a similitudine delle bestie" (*Opere*, 79, *Works* 1: 197); Lucretius 5: 931: "volgivago vitam tractabant more ferrarum" (cf. Polybius, *Hist.*, 6. 5. 5–6).

51 *Discourses* 1: 2 (*Opere*, 79–80, *Works* 1: 197); Lucretius 5: 1019–20, 1120–22; Diog. Laert., *Lives*, 10, 143, trans. Traversari, fol. 138r, maxim 32 (in Loeb, no. 31, quoted on p. 29 above): "Queque animantes eo federe iungi non possunt ut nequid ledant mutuo neque ledantur . . . ius nullum aut iniuria est. Eadem est in gentibus ratio quae aut nolunt aut nequeunt ita federari ut neque ledant neque ledantur"; maxim 33: "Iustitia nihil per sese esset, verum in contractibus mutuis quibuslicet locis id foedus initur ut non laedamus neque laedamur."

52 Machiavelli, *Discourses* 2: 2 (*Opere*, 150, *Works* 1: 332–33); Diog. Laert., *Lives*, 10, 143, trans. Traversari (maxim 14), fol. 137r. In Luigi Guicciardini's "Del libero arbitrio" (fol. 67v), "Machiavelli" argues that man's only objective is to "uscire della povertà"; see Gilbert, "Machiavelli in an Unknown Contemporary Dialogue," 164. On Sisyphus, see Ezio Raimondi, "Il sasso del politico," in *Politica e commedia*, 37–43.

native teacher like Machiavelli himself, or even the upstanding boar in *The Golden Ass*. When he wrote *The Prince* in 1513–1515, it was Italy's position at the bottom of the cycle before its upturn that provided Pope Leo X's nephew, Lorenzo de' Medici, with the opportunity to exercise the "free will" left to him by fortune or by God, "who does not want to do everything."[53] When a republic was at the bottom of the cycle, it was "the good man" who had the opportunity to teach others what to do, as the wheel of fortune turned upwards, through his knowledge of the lessons of history; for despite appearances to the contrary (sometimes one's own declining life cycle made the past seem better than the present; sometimes it was the downturn of the country one lived in that made the past genuinely better than the present), "the world has always gone on in the same way."[54] And a decade later, in 1526, it was a similarly low moment in his country's cycle (as the Germans began their descent on Rome) that provided the valiant Giovanni de' Medici, "delle Bande Nere," with the opportunity to fight for his country. He was a man, Machiavelli told Francesco Guicciardini, who everyone was saying was "brave and impetuous, has great ideas, and is a taker of bold decisions," qualities that precisely define him as Machiavelli's man of *virtù*.[55] And even the boar in *The Golden Ass* showed its innate free will by rearing up on its hind legs and refusing to exchange its life with that of a human.[56]

This free will was not a supernatural gift bestowed by God's grace, but instead it was a natural characteristic, shared by animals and humans—by "living creatures all over the world," as Lucretius put it (2: 256) in the passage highlighted by Machiavelli—in a universe that allowed for the play of free will within its regulated cycles of development. For although other Greek philosophers, like Plato and Aristotle, accepted that humans exercised free will through their reason, it was novel to argue, like Lucretius, that this free will was enjoyed by animals as well—and, moreover, to attribute it to the swerve of atoms within a materialistic world.[57] In this scheme of things, God and providence had no special role to play, nor did religion or Platonic ide-

---

53 On the opportunity, see Hugo Jaeckel, "What is Machiavelli Exhorting in His *Exhortatio*? The Extraordinaries," in *Niccolò Machiavelli*, ed. Marchand, 59–84.

54 *Discourses*, preface to Book 2 and 2: 30; cf. 3: 30 and *Florentine Histories* 4: 1 (*Opere*, 146, 191, 236, 715, *Works* 1: 324, 412, 495–96, 3: 1187).

55 Machiavelli to Guicciardini, 15 March 1526 (*Opere*, 1229–30, *Letters*, 382–83).

56 See note 48 above.

57 I owe this comparison to James Hankins.

alism contribute to the civic and patriotic morality of Machiavelli's "good man," who would be judged not in a final court of appeal or a Last Judgment, but only by his success in providing for security and the common good.[58] Like Lucretius, Machiavelli was skeptical about political ambition and superstitious religion, believing instead in a morality based on the shared interests of animals and humans. Neither immoral nor religious, he thought religion was based on fear and should be used in the service of politics and not as their master.

58 *The Prince* 18, and on the common good, *Discourses* 2: 2 (*Opere*, 284, 148, *Works* 1: 66–67, 329).

5

Lucretian Networks in the Late Fifteenth and Early Sixteenth Centuries

The preceding chapters have traced the influence of Lucretius on three humanists employed in the chancery and in the university in Florence, who developed their mutual interest in *De rerum natura* relatively unimpeded by religious constraints. There were other humanists, like Ficino and Poliziano, whose interest took a different direction, and there were others again who reflected a wider cultural interest in Lucretius by owning copies of the poem in their libraries or by commissioning paintings on Lucretian themes. Not all these patrons necessarily read the Latin poem itself, but they would have been helped to get a gist of its contents by the way the early manuscripts of the text were written, with numerous red *capitoli* (or chapter headings) guiding the reader through each book.[1] Moreover, in this highly vocal society where ideas were exchanged in shops and in piazzas as well as in

---

[1] This is a little-commented-on characteristic; e.g., MS Laur. 35: 26 and 35: 27 (with titles in red throughout); cf. 35: 25, 35: 28, and 35: 32 (titles only in bk. 1; spaces left thereafter), and 35: 31(titles in the text and copied at the end). Earlier printed editions (e.g., Venice: de Ragazonibus, 1495) print the titles at the end of each book, then they disappear altogether.

public auditoria, some of its themes percolated into society at large to give substance to its post-1494 experience and to the images of the New World evoked by public storytellers on street corners. In October 1493, a poem or ballad was printed in Florence describing Columbus's discovery of the West Indies only a year earlier. It was written in Italian in a form for recitation in public (based on Columbus's own Latin letter describing his voyage, which had first been printed in April 1493), with pictures to enable the narrator "to cut a long story short." Its author, Giuliano Dati, was in fact a Florentine priest working in Rome, who ended by invoking God to "make ready for his blessed kingdom the people there," in the same spirit in which some Florentines greeted the discoveries in Africa in 1486; but his account of the great wealth that awaited explorers, spurred by fortune who "gives great returns for little outlay," would also have had wide appeal to the mercantile interests of Florentines like Amerigo Vespucci, the neighbor and business partner of Lorenzo di Pierfrancesco de' Medici.[2]

Amerigo Vespucci was a nephew of the learned scholar Giorgio Antonio Vespucci, who owned a manuscript of Ptolemy's *Geography* and tutored Lorenzo di Pierfrancesco as well as his nephew before entering the convent of San Marco in 1497. Amerigo himself was a merchant banker, and after working for Lorenzo di Pierfrancesco's branch of the Medici bank until 1491, he went to work in Seville, and it was from Spain that he set out on his first voyage to South America in May 1499, writing to Lorenzo di Pierfrancesco in July 1500 to describe his experiences there and the limited profits of his voyage. In the letter that got translated and printed in Latin (in 1502) as *Mundus novus*, he described to Lorenzo this "new world" that he had found, since "none of our fathers would have known about it, and it will be totally new to everyone who hears about it."[3] Among the novelties of the native inhabitants that he commented on—including their nude, beautiful, and "most libidinous" *(libidinosissime)* women—was the fact that they had no churches and

---

2 *Columbus in Italy: An Italian Versification of the Letter on the Discovery of the New World* (London, 1991), edited and with an introduction by Martin Davies (7–21, esp. 14), quoting from stanzas 67 and 16 (40, 35).

3 *Mundus novus* (Rome, 1502?), fol. a1r, repr. in *Prime Relazioni di Navigatori italiani sulla scoperta de'America*, ed. Luigi Firpo (Turin, 1965), 85: "invenimus quasque novum mundum appellare licet, quando apud maiores nostros nulla de ipsis fuerit habita cognitio et audientibus omnibus sit novissima res." On Amerigo, ibid., 81–82, also Angelo Maria Bandini, *Vita di Amerigo Vespucci*, ed. Gustavo Uzielli (Florence, 1898), and *Firenze e la scoperta dell'America*, ed. Gentile, 193–95 (no. 96).

no laws, nor were they idolatrous. "What more can I say? They live according to nature and can be called Epicureans rather than Stoics" (an opinion that he repeated in his second letter, in which he commented that the natives were not Muslims, nor Jews, and worse than Gentiles in making no sacrifices and having no churches: "their life I judge to be Epicurean, lived in communal dwellings built strongly of trees and covered with palm leaves").[4] So we know that among Lorenzo di Pierfrancesco's circle, these discoveries were interpreted within the conceptual framework of Lucretius, reflecting not only his primitivism but also his belief that the world was new—*mundus novus*—and not eternal.

The discoveries coincided with apocalyptic fears generated by the French invasions and the half-millennium in 1500, which were encouraged by storytellers and pamphlets telling of dire events to come.[5] In one of his many scientific notes, Leonardo da Vinci referred to the bestial cannibalism of men "on the islands of others" who, in contrast to animals, eat their own kind, and in his prophecies he dreamt of "new destructions in the sky," with the world and its hemispheres turned upside down, East becoming West and North becoming South.[6] The French invasions themselves caused panic and fear by overthrowing political regimes and slaughtering people as the armies descended on Naples. In Florence, the overthrow of the Medici regime also brought political instability as rival groups vied for power, creating the free-for-all that in 1495 Adriani had compared to Lucretius's primitive life *ante legem*.

Even before the revolution, however, there were divisions within the ruling elite in Florence that were reflected in the city's cultural circles. The differences between Lorenzo il Magnifico and his second cousins, Lorenzo and Giovanni di Pierfrancesco, helped to influence the campaign waged against

---

4 *Mundus novus*, fol. a2v, ed. Firpo, 88: "Preterea nullum habent templum et nullam tenent legem, neque sunt ydolatre. Quid ultra dicamus? Vivunt secondum naturam et epycuri potius dici possunt quam Stoici"; cf. *Lettera delle isole nuovamente trovate* (fol. a4r, ed. Firpo, 101): "la loro vita giudico essere Epicurea, le loro habitationi sono in comunita, & le loro case . . . fabricate con grandissimi arbori & coperte di foglie di palme." Firpo refers to the letters being based on authentic material, "se non totalmente attendibili a causa di qualche . . . intervento editoriale" (82).

5 See Ottavia Niccoli, *Prophecy and People in Renaissance Italy* (1987, trans. Princeton, 1990), esp. chap. 1–2.

6 *Literary Works*, ed. Richter, 2: 104 (no. 844, where the editor quotes Vespucci's second letter, describing cannibalism on the Canary Isles), 293 (no. 1293), and the "profetie" on 295, 296, and 299 (1295), 303 (1297), etc.

Marullo and his patrons by Angelo Poliziano as the regime's apologist—which he continued after Lorenzo's death in 1492 as propagandist for Piero di Lorenzo's regime.[7] The conflict then widened to include former leading Mediceans like Bernardo Rucellai and Domenico Martelli, who were incensed by the power exercised by Piero's unpopular secretaries, the Dovizi brothers from Bibbiena. Following the exile of Piero and his secretaries in 1494, these former leading Mediceans and their sons formed a group determined to prevent Piero's return, bonded by a shared interest not only in ancient republican ideology (which they discussed in the Rucellai Gardens, the Orti Oricellari), but also—as we shall see—in Lucretius. Interested in Lucretius for perhaps different reasons were the Compagnacci, a group of young men who opposed the puritanism of Savonarola and his followers with an ostentatious display of good living as Epicureans or *godenti*. Opposed to both these groups were the supporters of Piero, especially Poliziano. The death of Poliziano in 1494 left only Ficino (and later his successor, Francesco da Diacceto) to support the hierarchical neoplatonism that had upheld the Medici regime—as it would do again, under Piero Soderini's regime and, especially after 1512–1513, under the aegis of Lorenzo il Magnifico's son Giovanni as Pope Leo X.[8] Before his death, Poliziano had tried to win the support of Giovanni Pontano, secretary of the king of Naples, to act as a counterweight to the Francophile sympathies of Marullo and his supporters.[9] Pontano, like Marullo and Poliziano himself, was also a distinguished textual critic of *De rerum natura*, so it is interesting to see emerging from the triangular political struggles of these years the three contrasting approaches of some of Lucretius's leading editors at this time.

This is the context in which I examine the wider response to Lucretius outside the chancery circles that have been my focus up to now. As we saw, Ficino had been one of the earliest humanists to quote and write a commentary on *De rerum natura*, showing his enthusiasm for Lucretius in letters to his

---

7 See Martelli, "Il *Libro delle Epistole*," esp. 189 and 193 ("evidente scopo di propaganda politica"), 204, 212–15, 219; cf. Godman, *Poliziano*, 125; and more generally, Alison Brown, "Lorenzo and Public Opinion in Florence: The Problem of Opposition," in *Lorenzo il Magnifico e il suo mondo*, ed. Gian Carlo Garfagnini (Florence, 1994), 61–85 (in Brown, *Medicean and Savonarolan Florence*, chap. 4); also ead., "Ideology and Faction in Savonarolan Florence," ibid., chap. 8.

8 See Humfrey Butters, "Piero Soderini and the Golden Age," *Italian Studies* 33 (1978): 56–71; Janet Cox-Rearick, *Dynasty and Destiny in Medici Art* (Princeton, 1984), 65–86.

9 Martelli, "Il *Libro delle Epistole*," 205–17.

friends and in the treatise *On Pleasure* that he wrote in the later 1450s. Soon after this, he devoted himself to studying Plato and the Hermetic texts that Cosimo de' Medici asked him to translate in the 1460s, possibly after suffering some sort of spiritual crisis. It was not until after he became a priest with the cure of souls in 1473, however, that he openly disowned the "Aristippean and partly Lucretian rather than Platonic" letters circulating in his name, and much later (in 1492) he claimed to have burnt his youthful commentary on Lucretius.[10] Ficino, in turn, was responsible for turning Poliziano against Lucretius, or—as Poliziano later put it—for teaching him to reject the errors of Epicurus, as well as "the impious theories of Lucretius, who had lost his reason."[11] Yet despite this public disavowal of both these writers, Ficino and Poliziano remained more strongly influenced by them than they liked to suggest.

In his *Platonic Theology* (written between 1469 and 1474 and printed in 1482), Ficino devoted much of his argument in favor of the immortality of the soul to attacking Lucretius, in order to make it "impregnable to the Lucretian attack on religion."[12] To confront a materialist with the difficult argument for the existence of an immaterial soul, Ficino relied heavily on scholastic arguments drawn from Aquinas, as well as from Aristotle's *De anima* and Plato, as Hankins demonstrates, but occasionally he used contemporary analogies drawn from his own experience. He responded, for instance, to Lucretius's argument for the creation of the world by chance with the recent example he saw in Florence of a small cabinet made by a German craftsman, in which "statues of different animals were all connected to, and kept in bal-

---

10 Ficino to Poliziano (before September 1474?), *Opera omnia* (repr. Turin) 1: 648, cited by Sebastiano Gentile, "Poliziano, Ficino, Andronico Callisto e la traduzione del 'Carmide' platonico," in *Agnolo Poliziano, poeta, scrittore, filologo*, ed. Vincenzo Fera and Mario Martelli (Florence, 1998), 376–77; see p. 20, note 5 above.

11 In a poem to Bartolomeo Fonzio, ed. Ida Maier, *Ange Politien: La formation d'un poète humaniste (1469–1480)* (Geneva, 1966), 75, at lines 173–74: "(Hic [Ficino] docet) . . . Impia non sani turbet modo dicta Lucreti, Imminet erratis, nunc, Epicure, tuis."

12 As James Hankins argues in two papers that he generously allowed me to see before publication: "Monstrous Melancholy: Ficino and the Physiological Causes of Atheism," in *Laus Platonici Philosophi: Marsilio Ficino and His Influence*, ed. Stephen Clucas et al. (Leiden, forthcoming), now published in Italian as "Malinconia mostruosa: Ficino e le cause fisiologiche dell'atesimo," *Rinascimento* n.s. 47 (2007): 1–23, and "Ficino's Theology and the Critique of Lucretius" (to be published in the proceedings of the conference *Platonic Theology: Ancient, Medieval and Renaissance* held at the Villa I Tatti and the Istituto Nazionale di Studi sul Rinascimento, Florence, 26–27 April 2007), where he offers a clear analysis of Lucretius's arguments against immortality and of Ficino's responses.

ance by, a single ball." Although all moving in different ways and times, they were nevertheless controlled by the movement of one ball—or, by analogy, by God, "the universal center" from whom everything else depends; so "let us hear no more from Lucretius the Epicurean, who wants the world to come about and be borne along by chance."[13] He bolstered his argument for the immortality of the soul by referring to a discussion held in the country villa of Giovanni Cavalcanti, whose conclusion in favor of the soul being divine was then supported at a dinner party in Florence attended by the Venetian ambassador Bernardo Bembo, various Peripatetic philosophers, and the Florentine humanists Naldo Naldi, Bartolomeo Fonzio, and Giovan Battista Buoninsegni: "so this is not only my view," he concluded.[14] His response to Lucretius's argument that religion was invented for political or scientific reasons, to enforce obedience or explain frightening natural phenomena, was similarly pragmatic and personal. Far from being invented by laws to coerce people, religion flourished throughout the world before there were cities and households, he wrote, and far from being invented for the simple, God was adored by clever and wise men, as well as by simpletons; even Epicurus and Lucretius, who were "impious beyond others," were occasionally "compelled by nature to assent to sundry religious observances, as their books testify." As Plato said, however, people were more religious in childhood and old age, and in their youth they "largely put religion behind them"; "if they engage in studies or participate in conversations" about the causes of things *(rerum causae)*, he went on, "they begin to want to assert almost nothing unless they themselves perceive its rational principle." This statement suggests he was referring to his own youthful Lucretian moment, before his mind "had been purged" and the principles of divine things finally perceived.[15] His interest in Lucretian *voluptas* also goes back to these early years, and it, too, helped to influence one of his later writings, his 1469 *Commentary on Plato's Convivium on Love* (translated into Italian as *Il libro dell'amore*), which provided a safer academic context for his quotations from *De rerum natura* on the act of love ("before the chill sets in," already cited in his treatise *On Pleasure*) and on how to escape from its madness. And although he renounced his early interest in Lucretius, his engagement with "obstreperous" Epicurean arguments in the

13 *Platonic Theology* 2: 13, 5, ed. Hankins, trans. Allen; 1 (Cambridge, MA, 2001): 200–201.
14 Ibid., 6: 2, 1–8, in 1: 122–27.
15 Ibid., 14: 10, 1–3, in vol. 4: 300–303, citing Plato, *Laws*, 10. 888. A–D.

Platonic Theology represents, as Hankins has put it, a constant "dialogue with contemporary Lucretians."[16]

Angelo Poliziano faced the same problem as Ficino in being a scholar in clerical orders. He owned a heavily annotated copy of Lucretius that was inherited by the library of San Marco when he died in 1494 as recompense for unreturned books.[17] Its marginalia demonstrate Poliziano's advanced "critical methodology" and include two notes referring to a manuscript of Pomponio Leto, probably the one that Poliziano borrowed from Pomponio in 1487 and returned only in 1491.[18] So we know he continued to read the "impious" Lucretius after claiming that he had renounced both him and Epicurus. We also know from the evidence of his lectures and writings that he was himself more influenced by Lucretius than he would have liked to admit. His university prolusion *Nutricia*, delivered in 1486 and printed in 1491, was a brief literary history offered as a gift to his nurse Poetry, defined as "a kind of cosmic force at the origin of human civilization." This at once betrays the influence of *De rerum natura*, especially its reference to "the recent world" (line 34), and to man's mental acuity (36) that enables him to understand the "secret causes of things" and to emerge from the obscurity of a bestial life lived without laws and morality (45–47): "not seeking the common good, but each measuring his own advantage, strong and living for himself."[19] Despite these clear borrowings from Lucretius, Poliziano nevertheless "overturns" him by ascribing the "secret causes of things" not to the fortuitous meeting of atoms but to creation by a single *artifex* ruling the land, seas, and stars according to his will (37–39); it is this "ethereal parent," not evolution, that brought

---

16 Ficino, *Commentarium*, Oratio Septima, chap. 5, 6, and 11, in his *Opera* 2: 354–57, quoting Lucretius 4: 1059–60 and 1047–51; 1052–56 with 1107–14; and 1063–66 (cf. chap. 2 above, and Prosperi, *Di soavi liquor*, 160–64); Hankins, "Monstrous Melancholy," and Ficino, *Platonic Theology* 2: 8.1; 5: 14.5; and esp. 8: 2.4, 4.12–19, 10.5: "Neque obstrepat his nostris auribus Epicureus aliquis," in vols. 1: 144–44, and 2: 96–97, 274–75, 308–21, 340–41.

17 Florence, MS Laur. 35, 29 (listed as L5 in the appendix below), fol. 1r: "pro compenso librorum qui aseruerunt commodari Domino Angelo Politiano in eius morte amissi sunt."

18 Ubaldo Pizzani, "Angelo Poliziano e i primordi della filologia lucreziana," in *Poliziano nel suo tempo*, ed. Luisa Secchi Tarugi (Florence, 1996), 349: "una metodologia critica che anticipa di secoli la sofisticata critica testuale dei nostri tempi"; Sergio Bertelli, "Un codice lucreziano dall'officina di Pomponio Leto," *La parola del passato* 20 (1965): 28–38; Reeve [I], 39–40.

19 *Nutricia*, ed. Giuseppina Boccuto (Perugia, 1990), at 18–19, discussed by Ubaldo Pizzani, "La poetica di Poliziano nei 'Nutricia' fra neoplatonismo e suggestioni lucreziane," in *Studi sulla tradizione classica per Mariella Cagnetta*, ed. Luciano Canfora (Bari, 1999), 414–17, citing Lucretius 1: 72, 74; 5: 907, 932, 953–61.

about civilization by reactivating our sluggish minds through the divine spark given to its offspring Poetry (67–70).[20] Like Ficino, Poliziano moved in a neoplatonic world influenced by Pythagorean, Hermetic, and Platonic philosophers who could more easily be reconciled with the Christianity both men professed and with the culture of the Medicean circles within which they moved. Yet they were both ambivalent towards Lucretius—Ficino because of his early devotion to him as a young man, Poliziano also because of his admiration for the poetry and the intellectualism of "the learned Lucretius," who wrote "sublimely about the arcane causes of the world and the elements of things" despite his madness (487–90).

The same was true of their friend Bartolomeo Fonzio, who transcribed and commented on a copy of Lucretius for his patron, Francesco Sassetti.[21] Fonzio was one of the humanists who participated in the dinner party held for the Venetian ambassador at which the immortality of the soul was discussed, and—as we saw in Chapter 1—it was he who later reflected on whether, "as ministers of God," it was right for him, Ficino, and Poliziano to publish what they had written when they were still laymen. Fonzio taught poetry and rhetoric in Florence University (and later, after becoming a parish priest in 1492, holy scripture, too). We know the topics that interested him in Lucretius from his marginal notes on *De rerum natura* (perhaps made "to facilitate Sassetti's own study of his books," de la Mare suggests). They include comments on "superstition" (at 3: 980–81, where Lucretius declares "There is no Tantalus, as the story goes"); on stories of the underworld being untrue (at 3: 1011–13: "Cerberus and the Furies . . . Tartarus . . . these neither exist anywhere nor in truth can exist"); "how well put and how true!" at the lines in 3: 1045–60, marked in red (on our life being all but dead though we still live, and on the mountain of misery that lies on our hearts, ignorant of what we want); and in Book 4 a series of comments on love, following Ficino in his *Commentary*, including "a most elegant description of love and sexual love" (at 4: 1030: "De rebus veneriis"), "remedies against love" (at 4: 1063–82: by scar-

---

20 Ibid., 18–19, discussed by Pizzani, "La poetica di Poliziano," 415–18.

21 On Fonzio (his preferred name, otherwise "Della Fonte," 1446–1513), a prolific humanist who also taught in Rome and worked as a publisher as well as a librarian, see Raffaella Zaccaria in *DBI* 36 (Rome, 1988, s. Della Fonte), and Albinia de la Mare, "The Library of Francesco Sassetti (1421–90)," in *Cultural Aspects of the Italian Renaissance*, ed. Cecil Clough (Manchester, 1976), 160–61, 165–66, 178 (no. 13). His *De poetice* (1485–1486) refers briefly to Lucretius "in philosophicis rebus valde elegans and sublimis," ed. Charles Trinkaus, *Studies in the Renaissance* 13 (1966): 40–122 at 115.

ing away what feeds love and not retaining "the collected liquid"), "an excellent comparison" (at 4: 1097–1104: how Venus mocks lovers with images, as a thirsty man dreams of water), and the succinct conclusion: "love is to be avoided" (at 4: 1146–49: "to avoid being lured into the snares of love is not so difficult as getting out when caught in the toils"); and finally a comment "on the first kind of man and how wild and uncultured he was" (at 5: 925–75).[22] More light is thrown on his comments on early man and superstitious religion by his brief account of the birth and essence of religion, recently discovered in a folder of unfinished writings that he ordered to be "thrown on the fire and burnt after my death, to prevent them being read or copied."[23] Dated July 24, 1498, this autograph note anticipated by some years the letter expressing his worry about publishing what he had written as a layman, providing us with early evidence of his later concerns. His outline describes religion not as a providential revelation but as a historical development, according to which man moved from self-interested materialism and the worship of elemental forces, of evil spirits, or of powerful and beneficent men, to the recognition (first by the Hebrews) of a single motor of the universe and thence to belief in a divine God and an immortal soul. Like Ficino's and Poliziano's naturalistic accounts of religion, it makes no overt reference to Lucretius, whom they had all read and responded to. Without knowing this, it would be difficult to appreciate the influence of Lucretius on their naturalism or the element of danger that his Epicureanism presented well before ecclesiastical censorship made reading him all the more perilous.

There is less evidence of how other Florentines read their Lucretius, such as the wealthy merchant Sigismondo della Stufa,[24] or Francesco Sassetti, Fonzio's patron, who was the general manager of the Medici bank from 1463 until his death in 1490. Although Aby Warburg discussed Sassetti's tomb and his unusual insignia of a centaur (which was also represented on his book-

---

22 Florence, MS Laur. 35, 28, fols. 62v–63v, 85r–87r, 108v–109r (cf. p. 30 above); Ficino, *Commentarium*, Oratio 7, chap. 5 ("Quam facile amore irretiamur"), chap. 6 ("Quo modo effectu vulgaris amoris"), chap. 11 ("Curatio amoris") (cf. note 16 above).

23 Ed. Alessandro Daneloni, "Genesi ed essenza della religione in uno scritto inedito dell'umanista Bartolomeo Fonzio," *Rinascimento* 45 (2005): 117–34 at 122: "die xxiiii Julii 1498. Questo involto di mie scripture imperfecte dopo la mia morte gittatele nel fuocho et ardetele, ché non sieno lecte né copiate, sotto la execratione de la mia anima in chi contra facessi."

24 A *De rerum natura* is listed in Sigismondo's *schrittoio* in the 1495 inventory of his possessions, ed. James Lindow, *The Renaissance Palace in Florence: Magnificence and Splendour in Fifteenth-Century Italy* (Aldershot, 2007), 210.

plate, as well as in one of his illuminated manuscripts) without mentioning Lucretius, it is possible—in view of the comment on early man in his copy of Lucretius—that the centaur conveys the same taste "for the primitive and savage" that Raimondi found in Machiavelli's Chiron.[25] Other younger Florentines interested in Lucretius include the scholar Pietro Crinito, who was a friend of Bartolomeo Scala and of the Lucretian textual scholars Marullo, Pontano, and Pomponio Leto. Crinito wrote a life of Lucretius in his *De poetis latinis,* and he also quoted him in his miscellany of philological studies, *De honesta disciplina*—as a philologist criticizing the impudence of those who dared to change readings through their ignorance, like Marullo, as well as quoting anecdotes drawn from Lucretius.[26] We know from *De honesta disciplina* that he also participated in the early literary gatherings held in the Orti Oricellari, the gardens where Bernardo Rucellai retreated from political life from 1502 to 1506.

Bernardo Rucellai is the most interesting and inscrutable of the alienated *ottimati* in this period of Florentine history. As Lorenzo il Magnifico's brother-in-law, and the "representative citizen" chosen from the inner circle of family and scholars to attend the dinner for the Venetian ambassador in 1490, he seemed a pillar of the establishment.[27] Yet, as Francesco Guicciardini describes in his perceptive summing-up of Bernardo's character, he was, despite his intelligence, learning, and eloquence, a restless man "who could never accept and be happy with any regime that governed the city." After Lorenzo's death, Bernardo attempted to restrain the young Piero and then openly defied Piero's authority by marrying his daughter to a member of the Strozzi family, while his son Cosimo became an open supporter of Lorenzo and Giovanni di Pierfrancesco de' Medici, like them, being exiled from Florence after the feared coup in April 1494.[28] Equally unhappy with the popular regime of Savonarola and Piero Soderini's appointment as life head of state in 1502, Bernardo retreated to his villa in the suburbs of Florence, where he

---

25 Warburg, *Renewal of Pagan Antiquity,* 244–45; de la Mare, "The Library," 180, describing MS Laur. 47, 35; cf. pp. 101 (note 35) and 84 above.

26 Pietro Crinito, *De honesta disciplina,* ed. Carlo Angeleri (Rome, 1955), see pp. 120–121 below. On his life, see Angeleri's introduction, 6–18; Roberto Ricciardi in *DBI* 36 cit. (s. Del Riccio Baldi); John Masson, *Lucretius: Epicurean and Poet* II (complementary volume, London, 1909), 195; his letters to Scala in October 1496 are in Scala, *Writings,* 394–95.

27 See Felix Gilbert, "Bernardo Rucellai and the Orti Oricellari," *JWCI* 12 (1949): 101–31, citing Piero de' Medici's letter to his father, 10 May 1490: "et non uscire di parente e letterato, togliemmo Bernardo Rucellai" (106, note 2).

28 Guicciardini, *Storie fiorentine,* ed. Roberto Palmarocchi (Bari, 1931), 283–84: "fu di una natura

hosted literary discussions in his gardens, the Orti Oricellari. We know more about the later discussions held in the gardens after the Medici's return to Florence in 1512, thanks to Machiavelli's participation in them under the aegis of Bernardo's grandson Cosimo (to whom Machiavelli dedicated his *Discourses on the Decades of Livy*), but the earlier meetings from 1502 to 1506 are equally interesting. Members during these years included Pietro Crinito, who refers to these early meetings in his *De honesta disciplina,* as well as the young Piero Martelli, owner—as we shall see—of an important edition of Lucretius. Bernardo himself had adopted a Lucretian view of the power of fortune in his *De bello italico,* written after meeting Pontano in Naples in 1495,[29] but there is no evidence that he shared the same interest in Lucretius as Lorenzo di Pierfrancesco and his protégé Michele Marullo, with whom his son Cosimo helped to plot the revolution in the spring of 1494.

The peripatetic Greek soldier and poet Michele Marullo, although not apparently a member of the Orti Oricellari gatherings, nor—as we saw—admired by Crinito, was nevertheless at the center of Lucretian studies in Florence. An exile himself from his birthplace, Constantinople, he fought for the exiled Neapolitan prince of Salerno, Antonello Sanseverino, during the 1494 invasion, collaborating with Cosimo Rucellai and Lorenzo di Pierfrancesco in France before the invasion to help to bring it about. He later put down social roots in Florence by marrying Bartolomeo Scala's daughter while continuing to combine his Lucretian studies with a military career.[30] Shortly after his marriage and the death of his father-in-law in July 1497, Marullo published a Florentine edition combining his four books of *Epigrams,* all now dedicated to Lorenzo di Pierfrancesco, with his *Hymni naturales* dedicated to Salerno. Despite the influence of Plato and Orphism on the initial books of the *Hymns,* invoking gods and the Demiurge Jupiter, the last book is Lucretian in affirming the autonomy of a material world governed by ether, which al-

---

che . . . non potette mai stare contento e quieto a alcuno governo che avessi la città"; cf. 84–85; Gilbert, "Bernardo Rucellai," p. 107; and Brown, "Revolution of 1494," note 25.

29 Gilbert, "Bernardo Rucellai," 107, 110, note 2; Santoro, *Fortuna, ragione e prudenza,* 135–77.

30 See p. 39 above; Kidwell, *Marullus,* 120, 145–46, 158, 201, 220, 233, etc. In Naples, in the mid-1470s, Marullo became a friend of the exiled Zanobi Acciaiuoli, who was his first host in Florence eleven years later (ibid., 65) and, as Lorenzo di Pierfrancesco's cousin, possibly the person who introduced him to Lorenzo.

lows for change and endless regeneration.³¹ He died in 1500 before completing his planned commentary on Lucretius, leaving his notes to be used by his "great friend," Pier Candido, in the first Florentine edition of *De rerum natura* printed by Giunti in 1512, which was based on his emendations as well as on Pontano's.³² One of the manuscripts of Lucretius with emendations influenced by Marullo was owned by the grandsons of Lorenzo di Pierfrancesco in 1526, a year after their father's death. It could possibly have belonged to their great-grandfather Pierfrancesco (at the time that Scala was working for him as his secretary in the 1450s–1460s), but it is perhaps more likely to have been acquired by their grandfather Lorenzo as a friend and patron of Marullo's, to be inherited by his son and later by his grandsons.³³ Interestingly, when the marquis of Mantua, Francesco Gonzaga, sought a copy of Lucretius in 1501, Lorenzo di Pierfrancesco claimed to be unable to find Poliziano's Lucretius (which was in the library of San Marco) and sent him instead the version "emended by Marullo, who is praised by men of learning."³⁴

Marullo's emendations were known to other Florentines who formed part of this Lucretian network. One of them was Piero di Braccio Martelli, member of another leading family who became alienated from the elder Medici, like Lorenzo and Giovanni di Pierfrancesco, the Rucellai, and a branch of the Soderini family. Braccio Martelli had been a close friend of Lorenzo il Magnifico's, but both he and his son deserted the family after Lorenzo's death. In December 1500, at a time when the government seemed

---

31 On the *Hymni*, see Valentina Prosperi, *Di soave liquor*, 139–40; Fosca Mariani Zini, "L'inquiétude des mondes: Marulle lecteur de Platon et de Lucrèce," in *Le Timée de Platon: Contributions à l'historie de se réception*, ed. Ada Neschke-Hentschke (Paris, 2000), 201–33, especially 231; Giuseppina Boccuto, "Riprese Lucreziane nel Marullo e nel Poliziano," in *Rapporti e scambi tra umanesimo italiano ed umanesimo europeo*, ed. Luisa Tarugi (Milan, 2001), 705–16; and Yasmin Haskell, "Religion and Enlightenment in the neo-Latin Reception of Lucretius," in *Companion to Lucretius*, 186–89.

32 Described more fully by Hugh Munro, *De rerum natura* (Cambridge, 1886), 6–11; see the appendix below.

33 MS Laur. 35, 25 (L1 in the appendix below). According to Albinia de la Mare, it was copied by the scribe of "the Ottoboni Livy" who also copied the *Cosmography* of Ptolemy owned by Lorenzo di Pierfrancesco ("New Research on Humanistic Scribes in Florence," in *Miniatura fiorentina del Rinascimento, 1440–1525: Un primo censimento*, ed. Annarosa Garzelli [Florence, 1985], 1: 549, no. 96). On the brothers, see Gaetano Pieraccini, *La Stirpe de' Medici di Cafaggiolo* 1 (Florence, 1924): 413, 447–48; and on their grandfather, see pp. 39, 43 above.

34 Cited by Stephen Campbell, "Giorgione's *Tempest*, Studiolo Culture and the Renaissance Lucretius," *Renaissance Quarterly* 56 (2003): 326 and note 82: "il quale dalli docti homini è comendato."

immobilized in the face of Piero de' Medici's threatened return by force (helped by Cesare Borgia and—it was rumored—by France, as well as by the pope), a group of leading citizens decided to take action. Getting together with Bernardo Rucellai and Lorenzo di Pierfrancesco, Benedetto di Tanai de' Nerli held a supper party to which he invited members of "noble families hostile to the Medici" (including Piero Martelli, as well as Tommaso di Pagolantonio Soderini, Cosimo di Bernardo Rucellai, and Cosimo's brother).[35] It was evidently the first of a planned series of suppers for twenty-five to thirty citizens, "especially young and hot-tempered men," who were asked to take up arms to defend their own districts from Piero's threatened assault, but the government soon put an end to them because it was thought that they were intended not to protect the city against Piero but to stage a coup d'état.[36]

It is notable that several of these diners were also readers of Lucretius. Apart from Lorenzo di Pierfrancesco and Cosimo Rucellai, Piero Martelli "and his friends" owned a much-annotated copy of the Venice 1495 edition of Lucretius, now in Paris (VP, as I call it in the appendix below). Together with its note of ownership, "Petri Martelli liber & amicorum" (and at the end "Caroli Martelli liber"), there are other scattered names on its opening pages, including those of Crinito and Pontano, suggesting that Piero was perhaps studying *De rerum natura* at the university or involved in revising the text through his literary friendships—especially with Marullo. For the text contains emendations in at least three hands, one of which may be that of Marullo himself, with references in them to readings of another leading Lucretian scholar, Pomponio Leto.[37]

Piero attended the meetings at the Orti Oricellari, where he would have

---

35 Bartolomeo Cerretani, *Ricordi*, ed. Giuliana Berti (Florence 1993), 13; id., *Storia fiorentina*, ed. Giuliana Berti (Florence, 1994), 280: "più persone di case nobili e nimici della casa de' Medici"; Piero Parenti, *Storia fiorentina*, ed. Andrea Matucci (Florence, 2005), 2: 407, with warm thanks to Jill Burke for these references to Martelli and to Tommaso Soderini cited below.

36 Parenti, *Storia fiorentina* 2: 407: "massime giovani e uomini a cui ribollissi el sangue"; Cerretani, *Storia fiorentina*, 280: "la signoria . . . vietò il fare tali cene perché questi homini erano tenuti nimici del vivere publico, e che non per opporssi a Medici ma per mutare stato facevano tali raunate."

37 On Piero's career and later reconciliation with the elder Medici, see Verde, *Studio* 3: 1, 799; Francesco Guicciardini, *Storie fiorentine*, 324; and his letters in ASF MAP 105, 255; 145, 269; 145, 301 and 308. He was also a member of the Orti Oricellari; see Gilbert, "Bernardo Rucellai," 117.

known Pietro Crinito, as well as the Rucellai, of course. He was also a friend of Tommaso di Pagolantonio Soderini, one of the hot-spirited young men, like himself, who was allotted the task of defending his district at the supper party in December 1500. Tommaso's father, too, had fallen out with the elder Medici after Lorenzo il Magnifico's death, and both he and Bernardo Rucellai married their children to Filippo Strozzi's children in defiance of Piero de' Medici's wishes.[38] A year after the death of Lorenzo di Pierfrancesco de' Medici, Tommaso similarly defied social etiquette by betrothing one of his young daughters to Pierfrancesco, Lorenzo's son, by simply going to a notary without preliminary discussions within the elite. Although he was said by Guicciardini to have been a member of the Compagnacci in order to protect his family in case his father got into trouble as a committed Savonarolan, in fact his uncle's memoirs reveal that in April 1498, Tommaso, like his father, had had to hide, "because he was deeply hated by these compagnacci."[39] Nevertheless, in 1504 Tommaso accepted a dedication that was "equally compromising" (as Sergio Bertelli puts it): that is, the dedication of a *Paraphrase of Lucretius* by a man who was unequivocally homosexual, Raffaello Franceschi, and in addition, six years later, the dedication of the first Florentine edition of *De rerum natura* by its editor Pier Candido.[40]

As we have seen, Raffaello Franceschi was a teacher of moral philosophy and logic at the University of Pisa. In his dedication, he told Tommaso that he had dug out his introduction to Lucretius at the request of his friends, who urged him to translate it into Italian to make it easier for those wanting to understand the poet; the *Paraphrase* was printed in Latin, however, with a prophylactic appendix "On the immortality of the soul" (strongly influenced by Ficino), which seemingly repudiated "the harmful opinion of the Epicure-

---

38 Cerretani, *Ricordi*, 13; Parenti, *Storia fiorentina* 2: 407; Guicciardini, *Storie fiorentine*, 84–85; and Gilbert, "Bernardo Rucellai," 117; Rita Comanducci, "Impegno politico," 155, 164.

39 See Sergio Bertelli, "Embrioni di partiti alle soglie dell' età moderna," in *Per Federigo Chabod (1901–1960)* (Perugia, 1980–1981), 32, quoting Giovanvittorio Soderini's *Ricordi*, fol. 69v (21 April 1498), and Guicciardini, *Storie fiorentine*, 146–47. On his daughter's marriage, ibid., 272; and on Tommaso, Verde, *Studio* 3: 1, 1255.

40 Bertelli, "Embrioni di partiti," 32, referring to Raphaelis Franci Florentini, *In Lucretium Paraphrasis cum appendice de animi immortalitate* (Bologna, 1504); BNF, Postillati 101. See also Lucretius, *De rerum natura* (Florence, 1512 = G), fol. a4r: "Tibique non in poetica solum atque oratoria, in quibus tantopere excellis, sed in reliquis quoque omnibus disciplinis exculto, cuius amplissima optimo, doctissimoque cuique semper patuit domus").

ans."[41] Despite this, Franceschi had the reputation of being a committed Lucretian as well as a homosexual. For he was known as "our Lucretian philosopher" in Pisa, and when he died there in 1524, to the grief of many black-clad mourners, one friend reported the news that Franceschi had been received at the gates of Tartarus by Pluto with great joy, being greeted by Epicurus, Lucretius, and other philosophers with the words, "You've come at last!"[42] These links between an older generation of scholars and patrons like Scala, Lorenzo di Pierfrancesco, and Bernardo Rucellai, and the disaffected younger generation of their sons and friends, constitute what we can begin to call a "Lucretian network" in Florence by the early years of the sixteenth century. They may also provide us with the first connection in Florence between Lucretius and libertinism.

Although Tommaso Soderini may not have been a member of the Compagnacci as Guicciardini believed, there was clearly a connection between alienated young Florentines like Tommaso and Piero Martelli and the armed youths in the company disparagingly called the Compagnacci. Both consisted of aristocrats (nicknamed the *disperati*, or desperados) who were under the guidance of Lorenzo and Giovanni di Pierfrancesco and were opposed to both the exiled Medici and the Savonarolans; but because the Compagnacci were armed and consisted of some three hundred young men headed by Doffo di Agnolo Spini, they were a force to be reckoned with.[43] They particularly disliked Savonarola and held provocative supper parties during Carnival

---

41 *Paraphrasis*, fol. 3v: "[Raphael Francus Thomae Soderino]: Verum diutius ab amicis rogatus sum ut ipsam qualiscunque futura sit in vulgarem, aiunt enim his qui Lucretium intelligendum adibunt non fore incommodam"; fols. 27r–35v: "Opere praecium facturi videmur si nocuam et becillam Epicureorum de anima sententiam repudiaverimus." The edition also includes a letter to Franceschi from Giovan Pietro Machiavelli, "Florentinus canonum auditor" (fols. 1v–2r), evidently Niccolò Machiavelli's cousin (see Machiavelli, *Letters*, 207, 492). See now Valentina Prosperi, "Lucretius in the Italian Renaissance," 215.

42 Verde, "Il secondo periodo de Lo Studio Fiorentino," 118 and 128, note 35, citing the letter of Giovan Battista Pelotti to Francesco del Nero, 2 September 1524: "'venisti tandem' . . . Multi qui Pisis modo se habent induunt se vestimentis nigris propter eius obitum, sic tristantur etiam de nece tali et de perditione prefatae animae." On his presumed homosexuality, ibid., 117–18; on his lectures, see chap. 4 above.

43 On the Compagnacci, see Michael Rocke, *Forbidden Friendships*, 222; Guidubaldo Guidi, *Lotte, Pensiero e Istituzioni politiche nella Repubblica fiorentina dal 1494 al 1512* (Florence, 1992), 1: 374, defining them as "laici che . . . si atteggiano a gaudenti (contra l'austerità savonaroliana) e studiano Lucrezio"; Bertelli, "Embrioni di partiti," 22; cf. Parenti, *Storia fiorentina* 2: 153–54, 313–14, 316; Guicciardini, *Storie fiorentine*, 146–47.

time in defiance of his prohibition on good living, secure that their leader was protected by Giovanni di Pierfrancesco. In 1498, the supper was organized, we are told, by "the navigator and hedonist" *(navighatore et ghoditore)* Doffo Spini, who "always lived amid company and pleasure" and nominated ser Francesco di ser Barone as its secretary, "a man ready for everything and especially pleasure." It took place in a large room with a raised stage, where Doffo dined splendidly with twenty youths dressed in a special livery of white stockings, cloaks, and hats all edged with black velvet, and when they had finished, the tables were removed and the dancing began, with music and great festivity.[44] Although this was not necessarily a network of libertines, or *godenti*, the fact that Doffo and ser Francesco were both known homosexuals does suggest a link between these supper-partying friends and the libertinism with which Lucretius was later associated.

The theme of love and pleasure was, of course, fed by *De rerum natura*'s opening invocation to Venus, goddess of love, and by its detailed discussion of sexual love in Book 4. A topos discussed by all sixteenth-century poets, it formed a subterranean current in the earlier years of the Epicurean revival, from the hedonism of early thirteenth–fourteenth century Florence to the cautiously expressed interest of humanists like Alberti, Ficino, and Fonzio, who as clerics could safely adopt Lucretius's critique of romantic love without risk of chastisement.[45] It was not one of the themes developed by the chancery and university humanists interested in Lucretius, but it did provide inspiration to Renaissance artists in the later fifteenth century, who restored sensuality to the pagan goddess of love and fertility. Botticelli's *Primavera* has long been associated with the opening lines of *De rerum natura* invoking Venus, the goddess who in springtime strikes "into all hearts . . . your lure of love," later in the poem described as arriving with "Spring," followed by Zephyr and Flora close behind, "strewing their way with brilliant colors and scents."[46] Whether it was commissioned by Lorenzo il Magnifico for the

---

44 Cerretani, *Storie fiorentine*, 241–44.

45 The topos in the sixteenth century is fully discussed by Prosperi, *Di soavi licor,* chap. 2, now summarized in English in "Lucretius in the Italian Renaissance," 216–25. On later libertinism in Venice, see Edward Muir, *The Culture Wars of the Late Renaissance: Skeptics, Libertines and Opera* (Cambridge, MA, 2007), 63–107.

46 Lucretius 1: 2–19; 5: 737–40; see Aby Warburg, "Sandro Botticelli's *Birth of Venus* and *Spring*," in *The Renewal of Pagan Antiquity*, 129–30, 420–21, and more recently (in the wake of Ernst Gombrich, "Botticelli's Mythologies," 1945, repr. in *Symbolic Images: Studies in the Art of the Renaissance* [London,

wedding of the young Lorenzo di Pierfrancesco de' Medici to Semiramide d'Appiano in 1482 or by Lorenzo di Pierfrancesco himself, in 1482 or later, it seems likely that Poliziano helped to suggest its subject matter, which shows the influence of several classical poets, including Lucretius, as well as the influence of Poliziano's own poems, the *Stanze* and *Rusticus*.[47] Lorenzo di Pierfrancesco, as we have seen, was the patron and friend of Michele Marullo, and since *Primavera* was inventoried in his palace in Via Larga in 1499, it seems likely to have reflected his personal interest in Lucretius, among other poets. The same is not true of Botticelli's other great painting on the theme of love, *The Birth of Venus*, which is "highly unlikely" to have been owned or commissioned by Lorenzo di Pierfrancesco since it was acquired at a later date. In describing the pagan sensuality of the goddess of love, however, it, too, must have been influenced by Lucretius's Hymn to Venus, like Botticelli's *Mars and Venus*, which reflects the twin themes of sexual pleasure and peace, as Mars reclines, "his shapely neck thrown back."[48] After 1482, Lorenzo di Pierfrancesco replaced Lorenzo il Magnifico as a patron of Botticelli, and he was then perhaps responsible for commissioning Botticelli's later illustrations to the *Divine Comedy*, which portray centaurs and the metamorphosis of men into animals with new and startling naturalism: they combine, as Bredekamp puts it, "the elegant epicurism of the 1480s with the critical asceticism of the 1490s."[49]

The transition from the golden years of Laurentian Florence to the aus-

---

1978], 2: 37–64) Horst Bredekamp, *Sandro Botticelli: La Primavera* (Frankfurt am Main, 1988), 62–63 (and the following note); Ronald Lightbown, *Botticelli: Life and Work* (New York, 1989), 120–45, esp. 137–38, 143; and Charles Dempsey, *The Portrayal of Love: Botticelli's "Primavera" and the Humanist Culture at the Time of Lorenzo the Magnificent* (Princeton, 1992), 30–36, 50–51.

47 See Warburg, above, and Dempsey at 24, citing Ovid, Horace, and Seneca as well as Lucretius, Poliziano's *Stanze* 1: 68–70, and *Rusticus* (1483). Bredekamp now proposes a later date, "around 1485," for its composition, in "The Medici, Sixtus IV and Savonarola: Conflicting Strands in Botticelli's Life and Work," in *Sandro Botticelli: The Drawings for Dante's Divine Comedy* (London, 2000), 296, 346, note 24.

48 Lucretius 1: 31–40; Lightbown, *Botticelli*, 164–70; see now Prosperi, "Lucretius in the Italian Renaissance," 219–21. Lorenzo di Pierfrancesco did own *Pallas and the Centaur*, however, which was in the town palace with *Primavera* in 1499, Dempsey, *Portrayal of Love*, 20–24; Lightbown, *Botticelli*, 146, 152–62 (and on his possible portrait of Marullo, 259–60 and plate 104).

49 Bredekamp, "The Medici, Sixtus IV and Savonarola," 296; see especially Dante, *Inf.*, cantos 12 and 25, 61–63: "Poi s'appiccar . . . né l'un né l'altro già parea quel ch'era"; Ovid, *Met*. 4: 377–79: "sic ubi complexu coierunt membra tenaci . . . neutrumque utrumque videtur"; *Sandro Botticelli: The Drawings*, 64–68, 104–7.

terity of the 1490s was reflected by artists other than Botticelli. Piero di Cosimo is one artist whose paintings have long been associated with Lucretius's account of evolution. The two *Hunt* panels in the Metropolitan Museum in New York and the *Forest Fire* panels in the Ashmolean Museum in Oxford follow Lucretius's account of evolution particularly closely: in the *Hunt* panels we are shown men and animals slaughtering for self-defense and being slaughtered before both are eventually domesticated, and in the *Forest Fire* panels we see the fear implied by the discovery of fire and the advance of civilization. The *Vulcan* paintings (in the Wadsworth Athenaeum and the National Gallery of Canada), as well as the *Prometheus* and *Epimethus cassone* panels in Munich and Strasburg, and *The Discovery of Honey* and *The Misfortunes of Silenus* (in the Art Museum, Worcester, and Fogg Art Museum), also reveal Piero di Cosimo's fascination with primordial existence, while *The Battle of the Lapiths and Centaurs* in the National Gallery in London narrows the gap between humans and animals by depicting the dying centaur cradled in the arms of his lover with moving pathos.[50] We may not want to associate Piero's paintings too closely with his simple and vegetarian lifestyle, which Vasari described as "more bestial than human" (in not pruning his garden and eating only hard-boiled eggs, cooked fifty at a time), but it is difficult to interpret them without referring to the wider cultural context that we have been exploring.[51] They were produced for patrons like the Vespucci (related to Lorenzo di Pierfrancesco's close friends and neighbors, Giorgio Antonio and his nephew Amerigo, the merchant-explorer) and the staunchly republican Francesco del Pugliese in the period when Lucretian primitivism was the theme of Adriani's university lectures and Scala's long poem *On Trees*.

Another painter who reveals a similar interest in primitivism is Filippino Lippi, who was a pupil of Botticelli's and exhibited the same invention and "strange fancies" as Piero di Cosimo, as we can see from his *Wounded Centaur*

---

50 See Erwin Panofsky, "The Early History of Man in Two Cycles of Paintings by Piero di Cosimo," in id., *Studies in Iconology* (1939, repr. New York, 1960), 33–68, esp. 58. They are all illustrated in Sharon Fermor, *Piero di Cosimo: Fiction, Invention and Fantasia* (London, 1993), pls. 16–23, 28–33; cf. Brown, "Lucretius and the Epicureans," figs. 7–10. The subject of the *Battle of the Centaurs* was suggested by Lucian as a daring experiment; Lucian, *Satirical Sketches*, trans. Paul Turner (Bloomington, 1990), 31.

51 Sharon Fermor reacts against both Vasari and Panofsky in being unwilling to acknowledge a personal or ideological influence on the paintings, in *Piero di Cosimo*, 77–81, 195; Giorgio Vasari, *Le vite de' più eccellenti pittori, scultori e architettori*, ed. Rosanna Bettarini and Paola Barocchi (Verona, 1976), 4: 61–62, 69.

in Christ Church, Oxford. For although the ostensible subject of the painting is the centaur's wound, caused by Cupid's arrow, the almost incidental and obscure detail of his young family in a cave in the distant hillside points to its probable meaning, that "love with his arrows can stimulate even a half animal to establish a family, the basis of civilization."[52] Like Piero di Cosimo's *Battle of the Lapiths and Centaurs,* this domestic scene may have been inspired by Lucian, but it also reflects Lucretius's account of civilization, in which it was the sight of their offspring that first helped to soften the human race.

Leonardo da Vinci's interest in Lucretius is less specific but can be seen in his grotesque paintings of faces that—like his fables—also narrow the gap between humans and animals, as well as in his detailed studies of plants, animals, and storms. Leonardo's studies of motion, drawn by watching atoms of dust in the circular rays of the sun, have been said to show signs of "Epicurean atomism" but derived from Isidore of Seville rather than from Lucretius.[53] Yet Lucretius is far more evocative in describing how "the sun's rays . . . pour their light through a dark room," enabling us to see "many minute particles mingling in many ways throughout the void in the light itself of the rays." This is even more true of his extraordinary description of nature's forces, more than a hundred lines describing how "the vortex of wind enwraps itself in clouds . . . vomiting forth a prodigious violence of whirlwind and storm," which could have provided a powerful source of images for Leonardo's equally dramatic drawings of whirlwinds and storms, especially his *Hurricane over Horsemen and Trees.*[54] We do not know whether Leonardo read Lucretius, but he was a friend of Piero Martelli (owner, as we have seen, of a heavily annotated Lucretius), and it was in Piero's house that he started work on collecting the material for his *Book on Painting* in March 1509.[55] Like

---

52 Jonathan Nelson in Patrizia Zambrano and Jonathan Nelson, *Filippino Lippi: Catalogo completo* (Milan, 2001), 592–93 (no. 50) and fig. 344 (cf. Brown, "Lucretius and the Epicureans," figs. 11–12); Hugh Lloyd-Jones, "Filippino Lippi's *Wounded Centaur,*" *JWCI* 32 (1969): 390; and Antonio Giuliano, "La famiglia dei centauri: ricerca su un tema iconografico," in *Studi di storia dell'arte in onore di Valerio Mariani* (Naples, 1971), 123–24 and 129, note 8.

53 Martin Kemp, *Leonardo da Vinci: The Marvellous Works of Nature and Man* (London, 1981), 304, referring to Isidore's *Etymologiae* 13: ii.i.

54 Lucretius 2: 114–20, and on storms, 6: 423–534, at 443, 446–47; cf. Martin Kemp, *Leonardo da Vinci* (Catalogue of the Hayward Gallery exhibition, London, 1989), nos. 47, 63–66 (*The Vortex* and *The Forces of Destruction*), 12, 27, 28, 38, 42–44 (plants and animals); 33, 34 (faces). Campbell now suggests Lucretius as a source for Giorgione's *Tempest;* see note 34 above.

55 Ed. Richter, *Literary Works* I: 112 (no. 4: "Cominciato in Firenze in casa Piero di Braccio Martelli addì 22 di marzo 1508," i.e., 1509). I am indebted to Jill Burke for this reference.

Lucretius, Leonardo wanted to penetrate the natural laws underlying the phenomena that men attributed to the gods, studying storms in great detail in order to explain them scientifically.

Leonardo's fables and "prophecies" reflect the same anthropomorphism and deep interest in nature as his paintings. They also illustrate many of the "clusters of ideas" associated with Florentine primitivism that were encouraged by the discoveries of new worlds and political change, as well as by the apocalyptic ideas that circulated towards the end of the century. Like Scala describing men driven to eat unclean food in his poem *On Trees,* Leonardo described as bestial the cannibalism of men "on the islands of others": "does not nature produce enough simple [vegetarian] things for you to satisfy yourself?" We know that he was compared by a contemporary to "the Guzzarati, who don't feed on anything that contains blood and will not permit each other to harm any animate thing," so perhaps the new primitivism entailed an element of vegetarianism that was shared by Piero di Cosimo as well as by Leonardo da Vinci.[56] He also talked about trees anthropomorphically, describing nuts, olives, acorns, and chestnuts as their offspring, who were "snatched by cruel thrashings from the very arms of their mothers and flung on the ground, crushed," and how the walnut trees that had done their best would be the most beaten—a notion that again recalls Scala's poem *On Trees,* which describes the walnut tree in his garden close to the road as prey to "boys who attacked the pregnant mother and her fetus and happily ran off with the nuts they had shaken down."[57] Leonardo also reflects Lucretius's view of the soul being born, growing, and dying with the body, which he described as separate but complementary to each other, using the unexpected analogy of an organ whose sound is created by air, but "without the organic instruments of that body, it can neither act nor feel anything."[58]

There are, of course, multiple sources for many of these ideas, since humanists borrowed promiscuously from a wide range of available sources, and

---

56 Andrea Corsali to Giuliano de' Medici, cited by Kemp, *Leonardo da Vinci,* 94: "like our Leonardo da Vinci," and note 6 above.

57 *Literary Works,* ed. Richter, "On the cruelty of man," and on grafted trees, which delight in their stepchildren more than in their own, 302, 308 (nos. 1296 and 1310); cf. Scala, *De arboribus,* ed. Brown, 428–36, lines 86 ("noster bruto est de sanguine sanguis," 232 ("quaecumque immunda vorantur"), and 440–41 ("Et pueri gravidam matrem foetumque lacessunt Decussasque nuces laeti rapiuntque feruntque").

58 *Literary Works* 2: 238 (nos. 1141–43); cf. 297 (no. 1295), "De' libri che insegnano precetti": "I corpi sanz'anima ci daranno con lor sententie precietti utili al ben morire."

so did artists and sculptors like the Pollaiuoli brothers, Bertoldo and Michelangelo, who well before the 1490s adopted some of the themes of primitivism in battle scenes of nude men and centaurs.[59] Afterwards, primitivism became a literary and artistic topos that could have developed independently of the Lucretian revival, in response to contemporary events and classical influences. And although I have suggested that the gist of Lucretius's poem could have been familiar to a wider public through ballads and the exchange of ideas in shops and piazzas, helped by its summary titles as reading guides, the new reformist environment put it under increasing suspicion by the early sixteenth century. In 1516, shortly after Bartolomeo Fonzio became worried about publishing his early writings, the Florentine synod prohibited Lucretius being read in schools, and despite the success of the "dissimulatory code"— as Valentina Prosperi calls the self-censorship that ensured the poem's continued circulation and even kept it off the *Index of Prohibited Books*—too much quotation from Lucretius, even in learned circles, could still invoke the strong arm of the Inquisition.[60] This, of course, makes the trail all the more difficult to pursue, even in the fifteenth century, when—as we have seen—many humanists were already concealing Lucretius's presence and burning early evidence of the influence he had exercised on them.

Despite this, by concentrating on three humanists who we know read *De rerum natura* and were influenced by specific themes relevant to their interests—superstitious religion, evolutionary primitivism, and atomism—it has been possible to map the route of Lucretius's recovery as it evolved from an interest in moral issues to a scientific interest in atomism and theories of the universe. If his influence on young and politically alienated Florentines is more speculative, there is enough evidence to suggest the importance of *De rerum natura* as a thread linking the social and political networks to which they belonged. It represented a counterculture to the neoplatonizing golden age ideology that Lorenzo il Magnifico had favored, and even after the revival of this ideology under Piero Soderini and the restored Medici regime, Adriani and Machiavelli kept Lucretius's philosophy alive to transform later Renaissance thinking. They and Scala clearly shared Lucretius's skeptical out-

---

59 See Alison Wright, *The Pollaiuolo Brothers: The Arts of Florence and Rome* (London, 2005), 176–81, fig. 137, 98–102, figs. 72, 73; Michael Hirst and Jill Dunkerton, *The Young Michelangelo* (London 1994), 16, pl. 8; and David Summers, *Michelangelo and the Language of Art* (Princeton, 1981), 242.

60 Prosperi, "Lucretius in the Italian Renaissance," 214–16.

look on life and his religious naturalism, if not his views on death. Whereas Adriani was evidently a practicing Christian, drawing up his testament in the Florentine Badia and leaving fifty florins to be spent "for the remedy of his soul," Scala and Machiavelli both drew up their wills in the Florentine chancery (and the Mercanzia) and made no provision for their souls.[61] Though not perhaps unbelievers, they were not typically devout, and like Lucretius, they interpreted religion in anthropological and functional terms, as something practiced by all peoples and used by rulers for political purposes. They also shared Lucretius's evolutionary primitivism and, influenced by his atomism, increasingly emphasized the importance of fortune in life, as well as life's novelty. It cannot be entirely coincidental that three years after Adriani had referred to the possibility of the world being new and astonishing—in his Lucretian lecture *Nil admirari*—Amerigo Vespucci described to Lorenzo di Pierfrancesco (and his Lucretian circle) the extraordinary novelty of the West Indies and Brazil as an Epicurean *New World*. Underlying these ideas was Lucretius's revolution in depicting nature as an immense and dynamic "physical machine" *(machina mundi)*. Although there were other routes to a materialistic account of the world by the seventeenth century, Lucretius's rejection of teleology provided "an explanatory ideal" that exercised, we have recently been told, an important influence on modern science.[62] The first steps in this process had been taken, as we have seen, in fifteenth–early sixteenth century Florence. By admitting random chance and natural forces into the rigidly hierarchical universe of Ptolemaic Christianity, humanists there were already liberating themselves from an ancient Christian world chronology to emerge as "early modern thinkers."[63]

    61 Adriani's will (dated 1519) is in ASF, Notarile antecosimiano 21073, fol. 98r–v; Scala's (dated 1484) is edited in his *Writings*, 480–81; whereas Adriani and Machiavelli mention their burial and statutory payments to the Duomo and New Sacristy, Scala fails to mention either; cf. pp. 35 and 82 above.
    62 See Johnson and Wilson, "Lucretius and the History of Science," esp. 132, 134, 147; Jenkyns, *Virgil's Experience*, 211–93, esp. 214, 221. On the *machina mundi*, Lucretius 5: 96.
    63 Michael Allen, "Life as a Dead Platonist," in *Marsilio Ficino*, ed. Allen and Rees, 177.

Appendix

Select Bibliography

Index

Appendix:
Notes on Machiavelli's Transcription of MS Vat. Rossi 884

Vatican Library, MS Rossi 884 (which I call R in the list of texts below) was first described by Sergio Bertelli and Franco Gaeta in their article "Noterelle Machiavelliane: un codice di Lucrezio e di Terenzio" (*Rivista storica italiana* 73 [1961]: 544–55). The manuscript contains two texts. The first, which is described by Bertelli, is Lucretius's *De rerum natura* (1r–133v in modern arabic foliation, numbered by the copyist with signatures, a1r–o3v, on the bottom right corner); the second, described by Gaeta, is Terence's *Eununchus* (134r–153v, numbered o4r–q3v). Its attribution to Niccolò Machiavelli is based on the subscription at the end of *De rerum natura*, "Finis. Nicolaus Maclavellus scripsit foeliciter" (fol. 133v), which Bertelli—after comparing it with Machiavelli's autograph letters—said was "clearly in Niccolò Machiavelli's hand"; although Roberto Ridolfi initially disputed this attribution in *La Bibliofilia* 65 (1963) and 68 (1966), he retracted his objections two years later in "Erratacorrige Machiavelliano" (ibid., 70, 1968), and the transcription is now accepted as Machiavelli's autograph. Bound at the beginning of the volume (fol. Ia) on very thin paper are the last lines of Machiavelli's letter to Riccardo Becchi dated March 9, 1498 ("perhaps for a comparison of the two scripts, the autograph letter and the codex," Bertelli suggested, 545). Both Bertelli and Gaeta consider that the manuscript may have been copied for Adriani by Machiavelli as his aman-

APPENDIX

uensis or as his university student, although Gaeta also wonders if the Terence might not have been copied a little later for personal reasons (551, 554; see also Bertelli, "Ancora su Lucrezio e Machiavelli," *Rivista storica italiana* 76 [1964]: 774–75).

One of the features of Machiavelli's transcription is its pagination by signatures on the bottom recto, which—among all the early printed editions that I have consulted (Brescia? 1471, Verona 1486, Venice 1495 [=V95], Venice 1500 [Aldine and Avanzi =Ald], and Florence 1512 [Giunti =G])—corresponds only to the opening page (alone) of the Venice 1500 Aldine-Avanzi edition. This may, therefore, have been the edition he began to transcribe, which no longer corresponded to his own pagination after the opening page, but more probably it is a simple coincidence, since R is not identical with Ald despite sharing many readings with it. It does not, for instance, include 2: 1169, the line that according to Reeve [1], 43, cf. [II], 135, Avanzi was the first to restore (it is also lacking in the Giuntine edition). It is possible, but perhaps unlikely, that the signatures refer to a lost edition or to a planned Florentine edition of Lucretius based on Adriani's own textual emendations to antedate the Giuntine edition of 1512. Machiavelli's father had prepared an index of towns and places in Livy's *Decades* in 1476 for the printer Donnus Nicolaus Germanus, and Niccolò himself had his first *Decennale* printed in Florence in 1506, so he would have been familiar with the world of printing. So, too, was Adriani, and although he did not begin work on his edition of Dioscorides for another decade, the Giuntine press that published it began printing in the year that Machiavelli is thought to have transcribed his Lucretius, 1497.[1]

The question of what exemplar Machiavelli used for his transcription remains unresolved. Bertelli ruled out all the Roman manuscripts as well as all the printed editions between 1473 and 1500, and he noted that Machiavelli follows the corrections of MS Laur. 35, 32 (L7) up to 1: 1038, where the extensive emendations and marginal notes associated with Marcello Adriani (discussed in Chapters 3 and 4 above) come to an end, suggesting that any projected critical edition was quickly terminated ("Notarelle Machiavelliane," 551). Michael Reeve carried the discussion a little further in suggesting that Ross. 884

---

[1] See Bernardo Machiavelli's *Libro di ricordi*, ed. Cesare Olschki (Florence, 1954), discussed by Atkinson in *Debts, Dowries, Donkeys*, 142–44, 167–68; on Machiavelli's *Decennale*, Brian Richardson, *Printing, Writers and Readers in Renaissance Italy* (Cambridge, 1999), 84–85; Godman, *Poliziano*, 207–12.

APPENDIX

(R) "shows signs of transcription" from the 1495 Venice edition (V95), quoting four instances where it agrees with the uncorrected printed text: "Not much, but it will do." Another example is *torpedine* at 3: 994, where R follows V95 and Ald instead of the corrections *turpedine* in the copy of the Venice edition in Paris (VP) and *cuppedine* in the copy in London (VL), whereas a few lines later at 3: 1011 he deserts V95 and Ald for the corrected reading of *egestas*, not *egenus*.[2] Since there are many other instances where R does not agree with V95 or with Ald, the question of Machiavelli's exemplar remains open.[3] On the basis of the texts Reeve lists as involved in "the great complexity" of the Florentine tradition to which R belongs (Reeve [I], 44), it is clear that Machiavelli's manuscript mainly (though not consistently) follows the tradition in Florence associated with Marullus's earlier, but not his final, emendations rather than those associated with Poliziano and Pontano. Without taking these traditions into account, it is misleading to speculate—as Gennaro Sasso does—on the significance of Machiavelli's variants, such as a question mark added at 5: 328, without noticing that here Machiavelli is following VP, or his writing *partes* for *partim* at 5: 1143, which similarly follows VP's emendation. Sasso fails to notice another emendation in 5: 328, where Machiavelli writes *fata* for *facta* (like L1 before correction), as well as the emendations in 2: 262 discussed in Chapter 4 above, which appear as an alternative version in Pomponio Leto's emendations in U.[4]

These traditions form two separate groups among the manuscripts and incunabula of Lucretius that I have looked at (those listed in Reeve [I], 44, with the exception of Major Abbey's and the Ambrosiana manuscripts; I have looked at only selected passages in M and VM2 described below, and similarly in VH and U). They consist of three manuscripts in the Laurentian Library in Florence and one in the Staatsbibliotek in Munich; the 1486 Verona edition emended by Pomponio Leto in the University Library in Utrecht; five annotated copies of the Venice 1495 edition (V95) in Cambridge (Massachusetts),

---

[2] Both cited by Hugh Munro, *De rerum natura* (Cambridge, 1886), 4, as examples of Avanzi's readings.

[3] Reeve does not discuss Ross. 884 in his most recent "sequel," Reeve [III], "Lucretius from the 1460s to the 17th Century: Seven Questions of Attribution," *Aevum* 80 (2006): 171. I quote from Reeve [I], 45, and note 6.

[4] Sasso, "De aeternitate mundi," 211, note 49, and "I Detrattori di Roma," both in *Machiavelli e gli Antichi*, 1: 211, note 49, and 477; cf. p. 74 above, and note 19 below.

London, Munich (two copies), and Paris; the Venice Aldine-Avanzi edition of 1500; and the 1512 Giunti edition in London. I identify them as follows:

> **Ald** = printed in Venice in December 1500 by Aldo Manuzio, with a dedication to Alberto Pio, prince of Carpi, and one by its editor Girolamo Avanzi to Valerio Superchio of Pesaro (dated March 1, 1499/1500).[5]
>
> **G** = printed in Florence in March 1512 by Filippo di Giunta, London, British Library, 11375. aa. 20, which has marginalia referring to codex *a* and codex *p,* as well as to the "Puccii codice"; its editor Pier Candido says in his preface that he collated the ancient exemplars in Florence with those of "the outstanding scholars Pontanus and Marullus," the latter his great friend, whose textual criticisms he had closely followed.[6]
>
> **L1** = Florence, Biblioteca Laurenziana, MS 35, 25 (A in Merrill), which belonged in 1526 to the grandchildren of Lorenzo di Pierfrancesco Medici (149r: "Liber Laurentii ac Iuliani Petri Francisci De Medicis MDXXVI"). It is dated 1450–1460 by Albinia de la Mare and its writing compared to that of the Ottoboni Livy.[7] Its note of ownership is wrongly described by Gordon (*Bibliography,* 289, Appendix I, no. 32) as referring to "Lorenzo the Magnificent and his brother."
>
> **L5** = Florence, ibid., MS 35, 29 (E in Merrill), which belonged to Poliziano, who seems to have copied fol. IIIv (with excerpts from Eusebius, Ovid, etc.) and written most of the marginalia.[8]

---

5 See Samuel Ives, "The Exemplar of Two Renaissance Editors of Lucretius," *Rare Books: Notes on the History of Old Books and Manuscripts* 2 (April 1942): 4, a copy of which I owe to the kindness of Martin Davies; cf. Reeve [II], 120, note 25, and now Reeve [III], 171–74; Gordon, *A Bibliography of Lucretius* (London, 1962 = "Gordon"), 52, no. 4; *Aldo Manuzio tipografo, 1494–1515. Catalogo,* ed. Luciana Bigliazzi et al. (Florence, 1994), 38; Munro, 4.

6 Preface to Tommaso Soderini, fols. a2r–v: "vetustis, quae in nostra urbe . . . nacti sumus, collatis exemplaribus praestantissimorumque aetatis nostrae vatum Pontani, Marullique . . . Marullus sane amicus olim noster iucundissimus, cuius in hoc opere censuram potissimum secuti sumus"; Gordon, 52–53; Munro, 5–11.

7 William Merrill, "The Italian MSS of Lucretius," University of California Publications in Classical Philology (four parts, 1926–1929), 9 (1926), pt. 12, 28; Albinia de la Mare, "New Research on Humanistic Scribes," 549, no. 96. I am very grateful to Xavier Binnebeke for sending me information from de la Mare's notes, which he is currently using for an updated edition of "New Research."

8 Gordon, 287, no. 5; on the influence on Poliziano of Pomponio Leto's manuscript, which he borrowed and finally returned in 1491, Bertelli, "Un codice Lucreziano," 28–38, and Reeve [II], 144–45; cf. Pizzani, "Angelo Poliziano e i primordi della filologia lucreziana," 343–55, especially 350, 351, 353.

APPENDIX

L7 = Florence, ibid., MS 35, 32 (F in Merrill), with marginalia referring to "Marcello" (Adriani), as well as marginalia identified as *"l"* and *"m."*[9]

M = Munich, Bayerische Staatsbibliothek, MS Clm. 816, with marginalia in the same hand as those in L1 above.[10]

R = Rome (Vatican City), Vatican Library, MS Rossi 884, transcribed by Niccolò Machiavelli.[11]

U = Utrecht, Universiteitsbibliotheek, X fol. 82 (Rariora), the Verona edition of Lucretius (Paulus Fridenperger), 1486, emended by Pomponio Leto.[12]

V95 = printed in Venice on September 4, 1495, by Theodorus de Ragazonibus.[13]

VH = Venice 95 edition in the Houghton Library, Harvard University, Cambridge, MA, Inc. 5271 (24.2), with emendations made in 1499. The volume is discussed by Michael Reeve in Reeve [III], querying H. C. Hoskier's introductory note describing it as Avanzi's copy, with corrections used for Ald, and also reading what Samuel Ives suggested was a reference to the annotator's home in Florence as simply "in my suburban home" *(in edibus meis suburbanis).*[14]

VL = Venice 95 edition in London, British Library, IA 23564, printed as above (a1v blank), with Giovanni Pontano's emendations. It is prefaced by a manuscript letter (on four unnumbered folios, now edited by Giuseppe Solaro) from Girolamo Borgia, Pontano's secretary, dated July 7, 1502, "under the supervision of Pontano" *(sub Pontano cursim legente et emendante),* which describes his long work of transcribing Pontano's emendations *(in transcribendis emendationibus multum laboravi),* without whose

---

9 Gordon, no. 6.

10 Reeve [I], 45 (he has now—correctly, in my opinion—retracted his suggestion that this hand "bears a marked resemblance to Politian's"; see Reeve [III], 169; Munro, 11; Goddard, "Epicureanism and the Poetry of Lucretius," 102; Gordon, *Bibliography,* 291 (Appendix I, no. 43).

11 Gordon, 287 (Appendix I, no. 10).

12 Gordon, 50–51. It is referred to in Michael Reeve, "Lucretius in the Middle Ages," 211, note 34, with its location on line. I have used it principally for comparison with Leto's emendations cited in VP.

13 Gordon, 51–52.

14 Reeve [III], 171–74; Ives, "Exemplar," 4. I agree with Reeve's reading of "sub," not "fl" as in Ives.

help and long labors on Lucretius for more than twenty years he would have been unable make sense of the text.[15]

VM1 = Venice 95 edition in Munich, Bayerische Staatsbibliotek, ESIg/A lat. a. 316: "Emendationes ex Pontani codice testante ipsum ingenio has exprompsisse" (a1v). Provenance: [Pier Vettori].[16]

VM2 = Venice 95 edition (second copy) in Munich, ibid., ESIg/A lat. a. 317: "contuli cum duobus codicibus, altero Ioviani Pontani, altero vero Marulli . . . impressis quidem . . . quos commodum accepi ab Andrea Cambano patritio florentino MDXX, Idibus Martiis. Petrus Victorius." Provenance: Pier Vettori, with his marginalia.[17]

VP = Venice 95 edition in Paris, Bibliothèque Nationale, Rés. M YC 397, V95, which has marginalia in at least three hands, one of them, possibly Marullo's, closely following manuscript M, with some references to "Pomp" (Pomponio Leto). Its title page (a1r) has a manuscript note of ownership referring to "Petri Martelli liber & amicorum" (repeated on the last folio, q1or ". . . Semper ego auditor", and below "Caroli Martelli liber"). Reeve has now returned to it with a fuller description, reading the references on the top margin of the opening page (a2r, partly cropped) as "vitam require a Crinito Pe." (referring to Pietro Crinito's life of Lucretius, see Solaro, *Lucrezio,* note 14 above, 16–17) and "Nullast fatendumst certast et talia sic legendum more veterum teste Pontano" (in two hands); he also refers to a copy of Ald sold by Christie's in 1995, which mentions two copies emended by Marullus, one of them—"apud Pe. M"—possibly referring to VP, owned by Piero Martelli.[18]

---

15 "Quod nisi Pontani nostri labor diligentissimus hunc e tenebris extulisset, vix ullus sensus elici posset. Attamen ipse suo ingenio vigilantique studio (nam supra viginti annos cum Lucretio consuetudinem habuit) effecit uti magna ex parte intelligi possit" (IVr), ed. Giuseppe Solaro, *Lucrezio: Biografie umanistiche* (Bari, 2000), 33, 36. Cf. Masson, *Lucretius,* 3–4, 7; Reeve [I], 33.

16 *Bayerische Staatsbibliothek Inkunabelkatalog 3* (Weisbaden, 1993): 550; Munro, 11.

17 Ibid.; Munro (citing Vettori's colophon), 11.

18 It is described by Masson in "Lucretius," 194–95, who says it contains "a very complete copy of the readings of Marullus"; Reeve [I], 46, [II], 147 (listing references to "Pomp"), and now [III], 169–71 at 170.

APPENDIX

The first of the two groups of texts I have consulted adopts the emendations of Giovanni Pontano and sometimes Poliziano (L5): that is, the Venice 1495 edition in London (VL) and the first of two copies of the same edition in Munich (VM1), which follows VL closely without being identical with it. The second group adopts the emendations of Michele Marullo: that is, L1, M, and VP. The second Venice 1495 incunabulum in Munich (VM2) contains readings from both groups, sometimes cited together as alternative readings.[19] The Giunti edition (G) refers to alternative readings in codex *a*, which seems indisputably to be VL, while codex *p* I have not been able to identify, usually closer to the second group (although not at 2: 425–26, referred to below). The dense marginalia in L7 (the manuscript associated with Marcello Adriani) only go up to Book 1, line 1038. They provide a variety of alternative readings distinguished as *l* and *m* without necessarily stating a preference: in one instance, when discussing whether to insert the lines 565 to 576 in Book 1 after line 550 or not, we are told that "it seems to Marcello not to matter much how it is read"; on another, we are told that "Marcello" assumed a lacuna between 1: 1013–14, which Munro and later editors mistook for a brilliant example of Marullus's "critical acumen" instead of Marcello Adriani's.[20]

On the basis of a close collation of Book 1 and a more selective collation of passages in the later books, it appears that Machiavelli most frequently followed L1 and L7 (up to 1: 1038, and *l* rather than *m*), and VP's first or second but not its final corrections (and *p* more frequently than *a*).[21] Although, as Reeve suggests, Machiavelli does adopt uncorrected readings in the Venice 1495 edition (V95), as well as those of its annotators, he also has readings that follow neither V95 nor its annotators.[22] To give some examples of his eclecti-

---

19 E.g., at 1: 954 it replaces *nec sic* (V95) with *necne sit* in the left margin (like VL and VM1), writing *haec (sic)* in the right, like VP, L1, and R; at 1: 957 it corrects *paceat* (V95) to *pateat vel* over the text (like VL and VM1) and writes *patefiat* (like VP, R, G, etc.) in the margin; at 2: 262 it adds in the right margin *sensus* before *hinc* (like VL and VM1) and in the left *motus* (like VP and L1—and R, before R then replaces *motus* with *homines* and *rigantur* with *reguntur*, as in U, fol. c3v). Munro assumes that the corrections in VM2 that do not correspond to those of Pontano in VM1 are Marullo's (12).

20 L7, 12r: "sunt qui legant post id carmen [citing 1: 550] [lines 565 to 576]. Verum Marcello parum riferre videtur quomodo legatur"; 20v: "Credit Marcellus deesse hic aliqua carmina"; Munro, 9 and 10 (again misreading "Marullo" for "Marcello"); Reeve [I], 47; cf. chap. 3, note 8, and chap. 4, note 7, above.

21 As, for example, at 1: 720 (*freto/fretu*), 754 (*talia/mollia*), 933 (*pando/pango*), 978 (*emissum/missum*), etc.

22 In Book 1, for example, he follows V95 at 136 (*animus*), 149 (*cuius hinc*), 196 (*multi*), 220 (*disciu-*

cism: Machiavelli in R follows Pomponio Leto ("Pomp" in VP, which I compare to Leto's corrections in U) at 1: 66 (*Graius*, "al *Graius*" in U), 205 *(nilo)*, 573 *(fundamentis, fundamenti* uncorrected in U), 1058 *(sursum,* s<*ursum*> sup. lin., and *rursum* in marg. in U), 1059 *(in terramque),* and at 2: 85 *(per cita,* VP's first correction, "licet *per cita,*" in U); at 1: 144 R has *praepandere* like Pomp. in U, not *perpandere* like "Pomp" in VP, and at 2: 262 R replaces *motus . . . rigantur* with *homines reguntur,* which is added as an alternative reading in U, but not in VP; however, R does not follow Pomponio Leto in VP and U at 1: 200 *(pontum,* not *ponti),* 249 *(discidio,* not *dissidio,* "al *dissidio,*" in U), 566 *(constant,* not *constent),* 585 *(crescendi,* not *crescendis).* He follows Pontano (and Poliziano, not Marullo and VP) at 1: 634 *(quas,* not *quae)* and again at 681 *(alio, m* in L7, not *alia, l);* he also follows Pontano at 5: 1192 ("*glando* in Pontani libro," according to VL and VM1, although they and all my other texts apart from Machiavelli have *grando,* which encouraged Munro (12) to say that Pontano "must have used some printed edition now unknown"), but Machiavelli failed to follow him at 2: 168 *(rentur,* not *credunt),* 631 *(freti,* not *laeti),* nor at 5: 602–5, four lines that "in Pontani libro desunt," according to VL and VM1. Machiavelli also makes the same correction as Pier Vettori in VM1 (but not in VL) by changing *sedulo quae* (VP's correction to V95) to *saecla, novo.*

The list of Machiavelli's borrowings from Marullus is much longer: for example, at 1: 240 *(nexu),* 271 *(pontum),* 748 *(quicquam),* 885 *(herbas);* at 2: 325 *(ibi:* here following L1 and M, not VP), 356 *(linguit),* 439 *(confunduntque),* 919 *(sint),* 929 *(quum);* at 3: 321 *(dictis)* and 853 *(nec);* at 4: 471 *(mittam);* at 5: 690 *(caeli)* and 889 *(occipit);* at 6: 1007 *(utque).* But he nevertheless failed to follow him at 1: 122 *(perveniant,* with VP, not *permanent;* and not Poliziano's "important emendation" *permaneant),*[23] 487 *(credere,* with VP, not *forsitan,* which "In Marulli . . . est legere," according to VP (see Reeve [III], 170), 580 *(pereant,* not *cluant);* at 2: 369 *(balatum,* not "Marullus *balantum*" according to VP); and at 6: 360, where intriguingly he has *ventique colores,* which is not Marullo's correction in VP (Reeve [I], 46), nor Pontano's, but the text of L1 and L5 before correction. Criticizing the ignorant emendations and additions made to manuscripts of Lucretius, Pietro Crinito picked out two readings that point their finger at Machiavelli and Marullo; the first one (writing *quam gravior* in place

---

dium patere), 309 *(dispargitur),* and 316 *(hahena),* but he stands alone at 134 *(ut videamus),* 170 *(nascitur),* 177 *(fluxerunt),* 193 *(nequeat partus . . . tellus),* 296 *(factibus),* 298–99 *(qui porro . . . nares);* see Reeve [I], 45.

23 According to Pizzani, "Angelo Poliziano," 350–51.

of *quamde gravis* at 1: 640) I have so far found only in Machiavelli (R), which suggests that Crinito may have been familiar with his transcription, while the other, Marullo's misguided attempt to change *pars . . . multesima* at 6: 651, evidently refers to the reading in both R and VP, *"pars . . . multa extima."*[24] Machiavelli also followed L1 and VP (Marullo) in not adding the line "Illecebrisque tuis omnis natura animantum" at 1: 15–16, which is Poliziano's correction (in L5), added to VL and VM1 from Pontano and then adopted by Candido "ex vetusta exemplaria" in the Giuntine edition.[25]

More strikingly, Machiavelli follows Marullo in nearly all the passages associated with him from the second tradition (L1, M, VP) that are absent from the first tradition associated with Pontano and from most of the later printed editions.[26] Two of these have already been referred to in Chapter 4, above, when discussing Machiavelli's marginal comments on Book 2. The first is on folio 23v, where Machiavelli comments on the line "Nam neque consilio debent tardata morari," which is noted as a lacuna by Pontano and the Loeb editor; it is included in Book 2 between lines 164 and 165 in R, Ald, and G; added in L1, M, and VP; and omitted from L5, L7, VL, and VM1 (G comments: "hic versiculus non legitur in *p* nec in *a* et in margine codicis *a* scriptum est deest"). The second is on folio 28r, where Machiavelli comments on two lines in Book 2 inserted between lines 425 and 426—"At quae lenis et est iocundo predita sensu Haec aliquo sine seminio graviore creata est"—which are included in the same texts (in G between lines 325–26) and again omitted from L5, L7, VL, and VM1 (G: "in *a* et in *p* non leguntur hi versiculi"). Machiavelli, like Ald and G, also follows L1, M, and VP in completing lines 1068–75 in Book 1 that VL and VM1 omit; according to Poliziano (L5, fol. 24r) they were *"fragmenticium"* in Pomponio's book and hence were, he thought, new additions, *"adduntur novicia"* (quoted by Reeve [I], 40; [II], 145); in fact, L5's additions closely follow U and differ from R, VP, etc.

Other additions in Book 2 include the lines 492–94, in Loeb, R (following VP's first but not his second correction to line 492), and G; added to L5 (by Poliziano?); and in U, M, L1, and VP, but omitted from VL and VM1 (cf. Reeve [I], 135). They also include a line between 528 and 529 ("quod quoniam docui

---

24 Crinito, *De honesta disciplina* bk. 15, chap. 4, 311–12, the second reading being followed "a eius . . . sectatoribus . . . pro verissimis."

25 Munro, 8.

26 Three of them are referred to by Reeve [II], 135, simply as omissions from "most" of the Italian manuscripts, but they are present in VP, L1, as well as R.

APPENDIX

nunc suaviloquis age paucis"), which is also in Ald and G, and is added to L1, M, and VP but omitted from L5, L7, U, VL, and VM1 (G: "in *a* and *p* non legitur versiculus ille"), and a line between 680 and 681 ("Et tantum cupido contingere dente parato"), which is included in R and G (but not Ald); added to L1, M, and VP (where it replaces "Religione animum turpi contingere parato" present in L5, L7, U, and V95); and retained in VL and VM1 with the comment *"defectus"* and *"fragmentum"*; both lines are omitted in later printed editions. In Book 3, Machiavelli includes a line between 97 and 98 ("quamvis multa quidem sapientum turba putarunt") and 595 and 596 (cf. Reeve [II], 135); a line between 614 and 615 ("Gauderet praelonga senex aut cornua cervus"); eight lines between 818 and 819 ("At neque ut docui . . . ianua menti") that recur in Book 5; and a line between 820–21 ("scilicet a vera longe ratione remotum"), all of which are added to L1 and VP, and all, except for the last, printed in G but omitted from VM1, VL, L7, and (excepting lines 595–96) from U, as well as from later printed editions. In Book 4, Machiavelli adds in the margin two lines between 128 and 129 ("Quorum quantula pars sit imago dicere nemo est Qui possit neque eam rationem reddere dictis") that are also added to L1 and VP and included in G but are omitted from VL, VM1, L5, and U (G: "deerat hi duo versiculi in *a*"), and he includes line 512, added to L1, VP, and U, but not to VL and VM1 (cf. Reeve [II], 135).

Without discussing other textual alterations—such as changes in the order of lines—it appears Machiavelli closely follows the tradition that adopts Marullo's corrections in preference to Pontano's; that is, the manuscript L1 (and M, which closely follows it) and the emended printed edition, VP, all of which are associated with Marullo. As we saw in Chapter 5, L1 belonged to the grandchildren of Lorenzo di Pierfrancesco Medici in 1526, suggesting it may have been inherited from their father and grandfather, a close friend and patron of Marullo's, while the emended printed edition followed by Machiavelli (VP) belonged to the member of a family of former Mediceans, the Martelli, who—like Lorenzo di Pierfrancesco Medici and his brother—had become alienated by 1494 and were won back only after the Medicis' return in 1512. Despite this, Machiavelli's transcription (R) is identical to none of the texts discussed above. It not only adopts readings from Pomponio Leto as well as from Pontano, but it also includes uncorrected readings from the 1495 Venice edition (V95) and a few unique to itself. So the source of Machiavelli's Lucretius remains a tantalizing but elusive quarry for future research.

Select Bibliography

Acidini Luchinat, Cristina. "Di Bertoldo e d'altri artisti." In *La Casa del Cancelliere: Documenti e Studi sul Palazzo di Bartolomeo Scala a Firenze*, edited by Anna Bellinazzi, 91–120. Florence, 1998.

Atkinson, Catherine. *Debts, Dowries, Donkeys: The Diary of Niccolò Machiavelli's Father, Messer Bernardo, in Quattrocento Florence*. Frankfurt, 2002.

Baldini, Nicoletta. "In the Shadow of Lorenzo the Magnificent: The Role of Lorenzo and Giovanni di Pierfrancesco de' Medici." In *In the Light of Apollo: The Italian Renaissance and Greece*, edited by Mina Gregori, 277–82. Athens, 2003.

Bertelli, Sergio. "Ancora su Lucrezio e Machiavelli." *Rivista storica italiana* 76 (1964): 774–92.

———. "Notarelle Machiavelliane: un codice di Lucrezio e di Terenzio." Ibid., 73 (1961): 544–53.

Blum, Paul. "The Immortality of the Soul." In *Cambridge Companion to Renaissance Philosophy*, edited by Hankins, below, 211–33.

Brown, Alison. *Bartholomeo Scala, Chancellor of Florence, 1430–1497*. Princeton, 1979. Italian translation by Lovanio Rossi and Franca Salvetti Cossi. Florence, 1990.

———. "Ideology and Faction in Savonarolan Florence." In *The World of Savonarola: Italian Elites and Perceptions of Crisis*, edited by Stella Fletcher and Christine Shaw, 22–41. Aldershot, 2000. Reprinted in *Medicean and Savonarolan Florence*, below, chap. 8.

———. "Lucretius and the Epicureans in the Social and Political Context of Renaissance Florence." *I Tatti Studies* 9 (2001): 11–62.

———. *Medicean and Savonarolan Florence: The Interplay of Politics, Humanism and Religion*. Turnhout, 2010.

———. *The Medici in Florence: The Exercise and Language of Power.* Florence, 1992.

———. "Pierfrancesco de' Medici, 1430–1476: A Radical Alternative to Elder Medicean Supremacy?" *JWCI* 42 (1979). Revised in Brown, *The Medici in Florence,* above, 73–102.

———. "The Revolution of 1494 and its Aftermath." In *Italy in Crisis, 1494,* edited by Jane Everson and Diego Zancani. Oxford, 2000. Revised in Brown, *Medicean and Savonarolan Florence,* above, chap. 5.

———. "Uffici di Onore e Utile: La Crisi del Repubblicanesimo a Firenze," *ASI* 161 (2003): 285–321. English trans. in Brown, *Medicean and Savonarolan Florence,* above, appendix.

———, ed. *Writings.* See Scala, *Humanistic and Political Writings,* below.

Cerretani, Bartolomeo. *Dialogo della mutatione di Firenze.* Edited by Giuliana Berti. Florence, 1993.

———. *Ricordi.* Edited by Giuliana Berti. Florence, 1993.

———. *Storia fiorentina.* Edited by Giuliana Berti. Florence, 1994.

Comanducci, Rita. "Impegno politico e riflessione storica. Bernardo Rucellai e gli Orti Oricellari," in *Ceti dirigenti in Firenze,* ed. Insabato, below, 153–170.

de la Mare, Albinia. "New Research on Humanistic Scribes in Florence." In *Miniatura fiorentina del Rinascimento, 1440–1525. Un primo censimento,* 2 vols., edited by Annarosa Garzelli. Vol. 1, 395–574. Florence, 1985.

Denley, Peter, and Caroline Elam, eds. *Florence and Italy: Renaissance Studies in Honour of Nicolai Rubinstein.* London, 1988.

Draper, James. *Bertoldo di Giovanni.* Columbia, 1992.

Ficino, Marsilio. *Lettere.* Edited by Sebastiano Gentile, 1ff. Florence, 1990–.

———. *Opera omnia.* 2 vols. Basel, 1576. Reprint, Turin, 1962.

———. *Theologia Platonica.* Edited by James Hankins. Translated by Michael Allen. 6 vols. I Tatti Renaissance Library. Cambridge, MA, 2001–2006.

Field, Arthur. *The Origins of the Platonic Academy of Florence.* Princeton, NJ, 1988.

Fonzio, Bartolomeo. *Epistolarum libri III.* Edited by Laszio Juhasz. Budapest, 1931.

Garin, Eugenio. "Ricerche sull' Epicureismo del Quattrocento." In id., *La Cultura filosofica del Rinascimento italiano: Ricerche e documenti,* 72–84. Florence, 1979.

Gentile, Sebastiano, ed. *Firenze e la scoperta dell' America: umanesimo e geografia nell'400 Fiorentino.* Florence, 1992.

Gillespie, Stuart, and Philip Hardie, eds. *Cambridge Companion to Lucretius.* Cambridge, 2007.

Goddard, Charlotte. "Epicureanism and the Poetry of Lucretius in the Renaissance." PhD diss., Cambridge University, 1991.

Godman, Peter. *From Poliziano to Machiavelli: Florentine Humanism in the High Renaissance.* Princeton, 1998.

Godwin, John. *Lucretius.* Bristol, 2004.

Gordon, Cosmo. *A Bibliography of Lucretius.* London, 1962.

Grafton, Anthony. *Bring Out Your Dead: The Past as Revelation.* Cambridge, MA, 2001.

Guicciardini, Francesco. *Storie fiorentine dal 1378 al 1509.* Edited by Roberto Palmarocchi. Bari, 1931.

Hankins, James, ed. *Cambridge Companion to Renaissance Philosophy.* Cambridge, 2007.

———. *Plato in the Italian Renaissance.* 2 vols. Leiden, 1990.

Haskell, Yasmin. "Religion and Enlightenment in the Neo-latin Reception of Lucretius." In the *Cambridge Companion to Lucretius,* edited by Gillespie and Hardie, above, 185–201.

Insabato, Elisabetta, ed. *I ceti dirigenti in Firenze dal gontalonierato di giustizia a vita all' arento del ducato.* Lecce, 1999.

Jenkyns, Richard. *Virgil's Experience: Nature and History: Times, Names and Places.* Oxford, 1998.

Johnson, Monte, and Catherine Wilson. "Lucretius and the History of Science." In the *Cambridge Companion to Lucretius,* edited by Gillespie and Hardie, above, 131–48.

Kidwell, Carol. *Marullus: Soldier Poet of the Renaissance.* London, 1989.

Kristeller, Paul Oskar. *Studies in Renaissance Thought and Letters.* Rome, 1969.

———. *Supplementum ficinianum.* 2 vols. Florence, 1937.

Landino, Cristoforo. *Commentary on Dante.* Florence: Nicholas Alamannus, 1481. Edited by Paolo Procaccioli. 4 vols. Rome, 2001.

Leonardo da Vinci. *Literary Works.* 2 vols. Edited by Jean Paul Richter. London, 1883. Reprint, New York, 1970.

Lucretius. *De rerum natura.* Translated by William Rouse. Revised by Martin Smith. Cambridge, MA, Loeb edition, 1982.

———. *On the Nature of Things.* Translated by Anthony Esolen. Baltimore, 1995.

Machiavelli, Niccolo'. Letters = *Machiavelli and His Friends: Their Personal Correspondence.* Translated and edited by James Atkinson and David Sices. DeKalb, 1996.

———. Opere = *Tutte le opere.* Edited by Mario Martelli. Florence, 1971.

———. Works = *The Chief Works and Others.* 3 vols. Translated by Allan Gilbert. Durham, NC, 1989.

Marchand, Jean-Jacques, ed. *Niccolò Machiavelli: Politico, storico, letterato.* Rome, 1996.

Marsh, David. *Aesopic Fables: Aesopic Prose by Leon Battista Alberti, Bartolomeo Scala, Leonardo da Vinci, Bernardino Baldi.* Tempe, AZ, 2004.

Martelli, Mario. "Il 'Libro delle Epistole' di Angelo Poliziano." *Interpres* 1 (1978): 184–255.

Marullo, Michele. *Hymni et Epigrammata.* Florence: Societas Colubris, 1497.

Masson, John. *Lucretius: Epicurean and Poet* 2 (complementary volume). London, 1909.

Najemy, John. *Between Friends: Discourses of Power and Desire in the Machiavelli-Vettori Letters of 1513–1515.* Princeton, 1993.

———, ed. *Cambridge Companion to Machiavelli.* Cambridge, forthcoming.

———. "Papirius and the Chickens, or Machiavelli on the Necessity of Interpreting Religion." *Journal of the History of Ideas* 60 (1999): 659–81.

Parel, Anthony. *The Machiavellian Cosmos*. New Haven, 1992.

Parenti, Piero. *Storia fiorentina*. 2 vols. Edited by Andrea Matucci. Florence, 1994, 2005.

Parronchi, Alessandro. "The Language of Humanism and the Language of Sculpture." *JWCI* 27 (1964): 108–36. Reprinted as "Il Latino di Bartolomeo Scala e Quello di Bertoldo" in Parronchi, *Lorenzo e dintorni*. 63–105. Florence, 1992.

Pizzani, Ubaldo. "Angelo Poliziano e i primordi della filologia lucreziana." In *Poliziano nel suo tempo*, edited by Luisa Secchi Tarugi. 343–55. Florence, 1996.

Prosperi, Valentina. *"Di soavi licor gli orli del vaso": La fortuna di Lucrezio dall'Umanesimo alla Controriforma*. Turin, 2004.

———. "Lucretius in the Italian Renaissance." In the *Cambridge Companion to Lucretius*, edited by Gillespie and Hardie, above, 214–26.

Rahe, Paul. *Against Throne and Altar: Machiavelli and Political Theory under the English Republic*. Cambridge, 2008.

———. "In the Shadow of Lucretius: The Epicurean Foundations of Machiavelli's Political Thought." *History of Political Thought* 28 (2007): 30–55.

Raimondi, Enzio. "Il politico e il centauro." In id., *Politica e commedia dal Beroaldo al Machiavelli*. Bologna, 1972, reprint, 1998.

Reeve, Michael. [I] = "The Italian Tradition of Lucretius." *Italia medioevale e umanistica* 23 (1980): 27–48.

———. [II] = "The Italian Tradition of Lucretius Revisited." *Aevum* 79 (2005): 115–64.

———. [III] = "Lucretius from the 1460s to the 17th Century: Seven Questions of Attribution." Ibid., 80 (2006): 165–84.

———. "Lucretius in the Middle Ages and Early Renaissance: Transmission and Scholarship." In the *Cambridge Companion to Lucretius*, edited by Gillespie and Hardie, above, 205–13.

Richardson, Brian. "A Manuscript of Biagio Buonaccorsi." *Bibliothèque d'Humanisme et Renaissance* 36 (1974): 589–601.

Rossi, Tribaldo de'. *Ricordanze*. In *Delizie degli eruditi toscani* 23 (Florence, 1786).

Santoro, Mario. *Fortuna, ragione e prudenza nella civiltà letteraria del Cinquecento*. Naples, 1967.

Sasso, Gennaro. *Machiavelli e gli Antichi e altri saggi*. 3 vols. Milan-Naples, 1987–1988.

———. "Qualche osservazione sui Ghiribizzi al Soderino." In *Machiavelli e gli Antichi*, above, 2: 3–56.

Savonarola, Girolamo. *Prediche sopra Amos e Zaccaria*. 2 vols. Edited by Paolo Ghiglieri. Rome, 1971.

Scala, Bartolomeo. *Apologi* [I]: *Apologi Centum* (1481), and *Apologi* [II]: *Apologorum liber secundus* (1488?–1492). Edited by Brown in Scala's *Writings,* below. Edited and translated by Marsh in Scala's *Essays and Dialogues,* below. Reprinted from Marsh, *Aesopic Fables,* above.

———. *Essays and Dialogues.* Edited by Alison Brown and translated by Renée Watkins. I Tatti Renaissance Library. Cambridge, MA, 2008.

———. *On Laws and Legal Judgements.* Translated by David Marsh in Scala, *Essays and Dialogues,* above. Reprinted from *Cambridge Translations of Renaissance Philosophical Texts* 2, edited by Jill Kraye. 174–99. Cambridge, 1997.

———. *Writings: Humanistic and Political Writings.* Edited by Alison Brown. Tempe, AZ, 1997.

Segal, Charles. *Lucretius on Death and Anxiety: Poetry and Philosophy in De rerum natura.* Princeton, 1990.

Verde, Armando. "Il secondo periodo de Lo Studio Fiorentino (1504–1528)." In *L'Università e la sua storia,* edited by Paolo Renzi. 105–31. Arezzo, 1998.

———. *Lo Studio fiorentino, 1473–1503: ricerche e documenti.* Vols. 1 and 2, Florence, 1973. Vol. 3, pts. 1 and 2, Pistoia, 1977. Vol. 4, pts. 1, 2, and 3, Florence, 1985. Vol. 5, Florence, 1994.

Warburg, Aby. *The Renewal of Pagan Antiquity.* 1932. Translated by David Britt, Los Angeles, 1999.

Index

Acciaiuoli, Roberto, 43–44, 48
Adriani, Marcello, viii, xi, xii, 33, 43, 44, 56–57, 71, 77, 90, 108–109, 113
   Commentary and translation of Dioscorides, 61, 64–66, 114
   De rerum natura emendations, 114, 117, 119
   on Horace, 51, 61–62
   lectures, xii, xiii, 44–67, 69, 78
   Nil admirari, 50–56, 67, 69–72, 77, 78, 85, 109
   on poetry, 46
   on rhetoric, 47–48
   use of exempla, 45, 65, 66
Aesop, 33, 36
Africa, viii, 28, 30–31, 89
Alamanni, fra Andrea, 81
Albert the Great, viii
Alberti, Leon Battista, 7, 8, 36, 103
   Apologi Centum, 33
   De re aedificatoria, 7
   Libri della famiglia, 7
   Momus, 7
   Theogonius, 7
Alexander of Aphrodisias, 77
Alfonso II of Naples, 61

alphabet, 29–31, 65, 67
Altoviti, Francesco, 55n
ambition. *See* Lucretius: themes and topics: ambition
America, viii
amulets, 64
Anaxagoras. See *homoeomeria*
animals, 10
   boar, 83, 84, 86
   and men, 7, 30, 36–38, 50, 83–87, 104–106
"anthropology"
   and primitivism, 59, 107
   and religion, 31, 79, 109
antiquity, viii–ix, 57, 77
Appiano, Semiramide d', 104
Aquinas. *See* Thomas Aquinas, Saint
Argyropoulos, Giovanni, 22
Arienti, Francesca degli, 13
Arienti, Giovanni Sabadino degli, 13, 53
Aristippus, 3, 92
Aristophanes, 50
Aristotelian(s), 5, 20
Aristotle, viii, 19, 55, 86
   academy, 66
   De anima, 92

INDEX

Aristotle *(continued)*
  Ethics, 22
  and language, 30
  and law, 28–29
armies, 57, 79, 90. *See also* militarism
artifex, 94
astrology, 49, 64, 72–73, 82, 85
  and the wise man, 59, 72–73
atheism, viii, ix. *See also* religion: unbelief
Athens, plague in, 40
atomism/atoms, vii, xii, 19, 24, 27, 32, 40, 43, 46, 49, 56, 63–66, 67, 106
  punctus, 70
  swerve *(clinamen),* viii, 74–76, 85, 86
Avanzi, Girolamo, 114, 116, 117
Averroism, 6, 68, 76–77

Bajezet II (sultan), 61
Bambello, ser Pace, 54
Barbaro, Francesco, *De re uxoria,* 23
Baroni, ser Francesco, 103
Beccadelli, Antonio (Panormita), *Hermaphroditus,* 4, 6
Becchi, Riccardo, 113
Bembo, Bernardo, 93
Bertelli, Sergio, xii, 68, 70, 101, 113–114
Bertoldo di Giovanni, 108
Bible, 29, 80
Boccaccio, 3–4
  Commentary on Dante, 3
  Decameron, 3
  "Phylostropos," 3
Bonincontri, Lorenzo, 4
Borgia, Cesare, 100
Borgia, Girolamo, 117–118
Borgo San Sepolcro, x
Botticelli, Sandro, 43, 104–105
  Birth of Venus, 104
  Divine Comedy illustrations, 104
  Mars and Venus, 104
  Primavera, 103

Bracciolini, Poggio, 1–2, 4, 6, 8, 9–10, 14, 17, 31
  De infelicitate principum, 8
  De miseria conditionis humanae, 8
  De varietate fortunae, 8, 9–10
  world as theater, 8
Brazil, 31, 109
Bredekamp, Horst, 104
Bruni, Leonardo, 45
  Isagogicon, 5–6
Buoninsegni, Giovanni Battista, 22n, 93
Buoninsegni, Giovanni Lorenzo, 35
Burchiello, 12

Cambano, Andrea, 118
Candido, Pier, 99, 101, 116, 121
cannibalism, 90, 107
Casavecchia, Filippo, 69n
Castilionchio, Lapo, 6, 8
  De curae commodis, 6–7
Catharism, 10, 11
Cavalcanti, Giovanni, 93
Celenza, Christopher, ix
centaurs (and Chiron), 37, 38, 84, 96–97, 104, 105–106, 108
Cerretani, Bartolomeo, 12
Cervini, Marcello (cardinal), 14
chance, 30, 57, 72, 85, 109
  creation, 8, 63, 92–93
  see also fortune (chance)
Christianity, 12, 77, 79–80, 83–84
  and ancient philosophy, viii–x, 3–5, 6, 23, 35, 54–55, 64, 66, 71, 80, 82, 95
  Christ, 83, 84
    Sermon on the Mount, 28, 29
  and non-Christians, 32, 61
  orthodoxy, viii–x, 23, 32, 66
  heterodoxy, ix, x, 10
  unorthodoxy, 8, 12, 64, 84
  Ptolemaic, 109
  see also Church; religion

INDEX

Chrysoloras, Manuel, 9
Church
    career structure, 4–5
    council of 1439, 13
    Lateran council, fifth, 77–78
    papal court, 4, 79
        in Florence, 5, 6–7, 16
    Schism, 5
Cicero, x, 2, 23, 26
    De finibus, 6
    De legibus, 26
    De natura deorum, 21
    Tusculan Disputations, 20–21
Circe, 83
civilization, viii, 7, 36, 37–38, 40, 48, 57, 94–95, 105, 106
clandestine theories. *See* Lucretius: clandestine theories and exempla
clinamen. *See* atomism / atoms: swerve *(clinamen)*
Columbus, Christopher, 89
Compagnacci, 91, 101, 102
Constantinople, 1, 98
Conti, Niccolò de', 10
Correr, Gregorio, 6
Crinito, Pietro, 5, 97, 98, 100–101, 120–121
    De honesta disciplina, 97, 98
    life of Lucretius, 97, 118
cycles (of life and history), 62, 76, 80, 86
cynicism, 33, 36–37

Dante, *Divine Comedy*, 3, 38, 104
Darwinism, viii
Dati, Giuliano, 89
Davidson, Nicholas, ix
Death, xi, 13, 33–34, 60, 109. *See also* fear: of death
de la Mare, Albinia, 95, 116
Della Rovere, Francesco. *See* Sixtus IV (pope)
Della Rovere, Giuliano. *See* Julius II (pope)

Della Stufa, Sigismondo, 96
Del Nero, Francesco, 76–77
Del Pugliese, Francesco, 105
Democritus, 18, 21, 56, 59–60, 62, 64–66
De rerum natura, 39
    circulation, 10, 14, 16, 88–89, 108
    Paraphrase, 101
    prohibition in 1516, 14, 108
    quoted, 17–20, 24, 25, 27, 44, 47, 60, 61–62
    rediscovery, vii, xi
    texts, 1, 113–122
        Carolingian, 2
        in later middle ages, 2
        manuscripts, 1, 30, 45, 68, 70, 85, 94, 95, 96n, 99, 114–117, 119–122
            chapters *(capitoli)* in, 88
            MS Vat. Rossi 884 (R), xii, 68, 69, 74–76, 113–122
            Poggio's discovery, 1, 6, 16
        printed editions, 1
            1486, 74, 114, 115, 120–122
            1495, xiii, 98, 100, 114, 115, 116–118, 119–122
            1500, 114–116
            1512, 99, 101, 114, 116, 119
Diacceto, Francesco da, 58, 91
Diogenes the Cynic, 36, 66
Dioscorides, *De materia medica*, 45, 64, 66, 114
dissimulation, ix, 108
Dominici, fra Giovanni, 12
Dovizi family, 91

Egyptians, religion, 53
Empedocles, 21, 40, 46, 62, 63, 66
Epicureanism / Epicureans, 1, 7–8, 10, 31, 90, 104
    atomism, 19, 24, 63–66, 68, 77. *See also* atomism / atoms
    in circulation, 35
    errors, 92, 101–102

[131]

Epicureanism / Epicureans *(continued)*
   ethics, 24–25, 28, 33, 34–35, 56
   godenti, 91
   highest good, 4, 18, 19
   obstreperous, x, 93–94
   revival, 1
   voluptas, 5. See also love *(voluptas)*
   see also Lucretius: and Epicurus
Epicurus, vii, xi, 2, 3–4, 7, 18, 21, 25, 29, 35,
     46, 63, 102
   Defense of, 5–6
   garden, 66
   on justice, 85
   letter to Menoeceus, 19
   life of. *See* Guasconi, Zanobi; Laertius,
     Diogenes, *Life of Epicurus*
   on marriage, 23–24
   Maxims, 29, 65, 85
Eusebius, 116
evolution. *See* Lucretius: evolution
exploration, 9, 30–31

fables, 33–37
   De rerum natura, 14
   on divine origin of law, 29
fantasia. *See* imagination *(fantasia)*
Farnese, Alessandro, 35
fatalism, 12
fate, 17, 21, 74, 83
fear, 78, 90, 105
   of death, vii, viii, 13, 17, 24–25, 33–34, 40
   of God, 54, 78
   mental, 15
   and religion, 80, 87
   of retribution, 12, 25, 54, 78
   of the unknown, 51–53, 55, 69
Febvre, Lucien, ix
Ficini, Luca, 35
Ficino, Marsilio, x, xi, xiii, 5, 10, 13, 14, 16–
     23, 35, 43, 88, 91–95, 96, 101, 103
   Commentariola in Lucretium, 20, 23, 92

   Commentary on Plato's Convivium (Libro
     dell' amore), 93
   De quatuor sectis philosophorum, 20–22
   De voluptate, 18–20, 92
   Platonic Institutions, 17, 22, 23
   Platonic Theology, x, 23, 92–94
   religious crisis, 23
   villa in Careggi, 22
flexibility. *See* mobility (flexibility)
Florence, xi, 9, 44, 47, 63, 82, 90, 104–105
   Council of 1439, 8, 9–10, 13
   Great Council, 42
   Guelf Party, 16, 26
   intelligentsia, 9
   liberty, political, 47
   maritime affairs, 9, 26–27
   merchants, viii, 9, 10, 13
   new lifestyle, 63
   papal court in, 5, 6, 16
   religion, 10–13, 55
   republican regime, 42, 62, 97
   revolution, 42, 43, 90
   S. Croce, 80
   S. Marco, library, 94, 99
   S. Maria Novella, library, 4
   SS. Annunziata, 35
   synod, 14, 108
   university, xii, 9, 11, 16, 21, 44–47, 50, 69,
     94, 95. *See also* Pisa: university in
   via Larga, 83
Fonzio (della Fonte), Bartolomeo, xi, xiii, 5,
     23, 30, 93, 95–96, 103, 108
Fortini, Clemens, 20
fortune (chance), vii, xi, 6, 10, 47, 51–52, 62,
     69, 71–72, 73, 76, 86, 109
   author of events, 51, 56–57
   fickle, 62
   play of, viii, 8
   power of, 10, 32, 47, 98
   spoils of, 44, 48, 89
   variety of, 9–10, 74
   wheel of, 72, 86

Franceschi, Raffaello, 58, 76, 77, 101–102
    Paraphrase of Lucretius, 101–102
frankincense, 66
free will (freedom), viii, 52, 64, 72–76, 82, 84, 85–86
friars, 12–13, 79–80
    sermons, 10–11, 12–13, 54, 79–80
    see also Savonarola, fra Girolamo
Fridenperger, Paulus (publisher), 117

Gaeta, Franco, 113–114
Gagliano, Filippo, 13, 54
Galen, 64
Garin, Eugenio, 21
Gentiles, 90
Germanus, Donnus Nicolaus, 27, 114
Ghinea, 31
ghiribizzi (musings), 72–73, 83
Ghislieri, Michele, 14
Giovanni, Francesco, 11
Giovanni, Nannina. *See* Michelozzi, Nannina
Giunti (publishers), 64, 114
    De rerum natura, 70, 99, 114, 116, 119, 121
    Dioscorides, 114
God, nature and role of, 51–55, 57, 76, 78, 79, 86, 93, 96. *See also* Lucretius: themes and topics: religion and gods
godenti. *See* Epicureanism/Epicureans: *godenti*; libertines *(godenti)*
Godman, Peter, 45, 47, 56, 58, 59, 66
gods, viii, 4, 8, 20, 21, 24–26, 33, 35, 46, 55, 60, 75–76, 98, 107
Golden Age, 26, 39, 108
Gonzaga, Francesco (cardinal), 35
Gonzaga, Francesco (marquis of Mantua), 99
Gordon, Cosmo, 116
Grafton, Anthony, 45
grammar, 49–50

Gratian, 28
Guasconi, Zanobi, 4
Guelf Party. *See* Florence: Guelf Party
Guicciardini, Francesco, 48, 67, 81, 82, 83, 86, 97, 101, 102
Guicciardini, Luigi
    "Dialogo delle pecchie e ragnateli," 67n
    "Del libero arbitrio," 82, 85n
Guzzarati, 107

Hankins, James, 92, 94
Hebrews, 32, 96
hedonism, 3, 10, 24, 103
Heraclitus, 59–60
heresy. *See* religion: heresy
Hermetic texts, 22, 92, 95
Holmes, George, 5
Homer, 29
homoeomeria, 21, 57, 66
homosexual/-ity, 81, 101–103
Horace, 62, 104n
    Adriani's lectures on, 51, 61–63
    letters, 3, 51, 62n
    Satires, 60n, 61, 62
Hoskier, H. C., 117
humanism/-ists, xi, xiii, 5, 45–47, 50, 88
    chancery, xi, 88
    curial, 6–7, 9, 16

imagination *(fantasia)*, 82–83, 84
immortality, of letters, 34–35. *See also* soul: immortality of
Index of Prohibited Books, 14, 108
Isidore of Seville, 2, 106
Italy, invasions of, 42, 43, 57, 62, 79, 86, 90
Ives, Samuel, 117

Jews, 90
John I of Portugal, 28, 31

[133]

Julius II (pope), 72
justice, 28, 30, 85
Justinian, *Codex*, 28
Juvenal, 23

Kristeller, Paul O., ix, 5

Lactantius, x, 2
Laertius, Diogenes
   Life of Epicurus, 1, 7, 19, 23
      translation, xi, 1–2, 16, 29
   Lives of the philosophers, xi, 1–2, 8, 21, 22
Landino, Cristoforo, 5, 21, 22, 35
   Commentary on Dante, 3, 11, 38
language, origin of, 30, 49–50
law
   divine origin, 29, 78
   and morality, 28, 30–31
   of nature, 28–29, 75
   Roman and canon, 28
   see also Scala, Bartolomeo: *Dialogue on Laws and Legal Judgments*
Leo X (pope), 56, 64, 66, 91
Leonardo da Vinci, 90, 106–107
   fables and prophecies, 107
   paintings and drawings, 106
Leto, Pomponio, textual emendations, x, 74, 94, 97, 100, 115, 117, 118, 120–122
letters *(litterae)*, 34
libertines *(godenti)*, xiii, 102, 103
liberty. *See* Florence: liberty, political
life, flower of, 70
Lippi, Filippino, *Wounded Centaur*, 105–106
Livy, 78
   Decades, 114
love *(voluptas)*, vii, 5, 7, 18–19, 33, 56, 74, 93, 95–96, 103, 104
Lucan, x

Lucian, 33, 36, 106
Lucretius, 15, 17, 77, 93, 102
   attacks on, 14, 92–95, 108
   clandestine theories and exempla, 61, 64–65, 67
   counterculture, 39, 43, 108
   and Epicurus, vii
   "insane," 61–62, 66, 92, 95
   and libertinism, 103
   networks, xiii, 4, 99, 102, 103, 108
   relevance, viii, xi, 17, 41, 44, 48–49
   in Renaissance art, 22, 88, 103–107
   teachings, 75
   themes and topics, viii, 15, 65n
      ambition, 8, 25, 85, 87
      atomism. *See* atomism/atoms
      avoidance of fear, viii, 17–19, 24–25
      evolution, vii, viii, 15, 26, 94, 105
      fortune, viii, 6, 8, 32–33, 93, 109. *See also* fortune (chance)
      free will, viii, 74–75, 84, 86. *See also* free will (freedom)
      highest good, 18, 20
      justice, 85
      language, 49–50
      life *ante legem*, 41, 44, 48, 90
      limits of civilization, 7, 37, 38, 40, 48
      machina mundi, 109
      militarism, 37–38
      nature, 51, 52
      origin of society, 84–85, 105–106
      primitivism (naturalism), vii, 26–27, 28–31, 36–37, 39–40, 43–44, 48, 56–59, 84, 90, 105–109
      religion and gods, viii, 20, 24, 29, 31–32, 33, 55–56, 59–62, 67, 75, 79, 87, 92–93, 108–109
      simulacra, 9
      suave, mari magno, 60, 65
      voluptas. *See* love *(voluptas)*
      world(s)
         chance creation, 8, 32

multiple, viii
novelty of, 52, 71, 90, 94
as theater, 8–9, 82–83, 84
see also animals: and men; *De rerum natura;* world(s): new

Machiavelli, Bernardo, 28–30, 44, 114
 death and bequest, 80–81
 library, 70
Machiavelli, Giovan Pietro, 102n
Machiavelli, Guido di Niccolò, 84
Machiavelli, Niccolò di Bernardo, viii, xi, xii, 33, 39, 50, 56, 67, 68–87, 98, 108
 "good man," man of *virtù,* 69, 86, 87
 last testaments, 82, 109
 philosophy, xii, 69, 72, 74, 76, 80, 85
 physiology, 82
 portrayed, 83, 84
 religion, 69, 71, 78–84, 86–87
 transcription of Rossi 884 (R), xii, xiii, 69, 113–115, 117, 119–122
 writings
  Decennale, 114
  Discourses on Livy, 72, 76, 84–85, 98
  Florentine Histories, 79
  On Fortune, 72
  Ghiribizzi to Soderini, 72–73
  The Golden Ass, 37, 79, 83, 84, 86
  The Prince, 10, 38, 72, 76, 78, 84, 86
Machiavelli, Totto di Bernardo, 76–77, 80
Manetti, Giannozzo, *Adversus iudeos et gentes,* 21
Manuzio, Aldo (publisher), 116
Mappamundi, sphere, 27
marriage, 23–24, 36
Marsuppini, Carlo, 11, 12
Martelli family, 122
Martelli, Braccio, 99
Martelli, Carlo, 100, 118

Martelli, Domenico, 91
Martelli, Piero di Braccio, xiii, 98, 99–100, 102, 106, 118
Martial, *Epigrams,* 37
Marullo, Michele, x, xiii, 4, 31, 39, 41, 43, 91, 97, 98–99, 104
 Epigrams, 39, 43, 98
 Hymni naturales, 39, 43, 98–99
 textual emendations, xiii, 97, 99, 100, 115, 116, 118–122
mask, 82
materialism (matter), viii, 64, 75, 76, 86, 92, 96, 98, 109
McManamon, John, 58
Medici
 Bank, 30, 89, 96
 elder branch, 46, 58–59, 68, 101, 102, 122. *See also* Medici: regime
 library, xii, 22, 26
 palace, 22, 83
  courtyard medallions, 22, 26
 regime, 42, 47, 61, 90, 91, 108
Medici (de') family
 Cosimo, 6, 16, 22, 24–26, 92
 Giovanni di Cosimo, 22, 24, 26
 Giovanni di Lorenzo. *See* Leo X (pope)
 Giovanni di Pierfrancesco de', xiii, 39, 41, 43, 90, 97, 99, 102–103, 122
 Giovanni delle Bande Nere, 83, 86
 Giuliano di Lorenzo (duke of Nemours), 58
 Giuliano di Pierfrancesco, 116, 122
 Lorenzo (Cosimo's brother), 23
 Lorenzo di Pierfrancesco, xiii, 31, 39–41, 43, 89–90, 97–102, 104, 105, 109, 122
 Lorenzo di Pierfranceso (grandson of above), 116, 122
 Lorenzo di Piero (duke of Urbino), 86
 Lorenzo il Magnifico, 33, 34, 36, 39, 42–43, 90–91, 99, 103–104, 116
 Pierfrancesco, 16, 22, 26, 99

Medici (de') family *(continued)*
   Pierfrancesco di Lorenzo (the younger), 101
   Piero di Cosimo, 30
   Piero di Lorenzo, 34, 43, 91, 97, 100, 101
medicine, 53, 57, 64
Memmius, Gaius, 17, 40
Mercati, Michele, 17
Michelangelo, 43, 108
Michelozzi, Nannina *née* Giovanni, 54
Michelozzi, ser Niccolò, 13n, 54
militarism, 36, 37–38. *See also* armies
Minos, 29, 34
miracles
   Christian, 11, 35, 61, 67, 79
   of nature, 52
mobility (flexibility), 51–52, 62–63, 69, 73, 74. *See also* motion
Montaillou, 10
Montepulciano, 32
morality, ancient and Christian, 38, 55. *See also* law: and morality
motion, 74, 75, 76, 106
Moses, 29
Munro, Hugh, 119
Muses, 34, 47
Muslims, 90

Naldi, Naldo, 93
names, 30, 50, 79
Naples, 4, 6, 39, 47, 61, 90, 98
nature, 18, 32, 51, 52, 56–57, 59, 106, 109
   adulteration of, 7
   miracles of, 52
   secrets of, 63, 65, 94–95
   see also law: of nature
necessity, 52, 78, 80
neoplatonism, 37, 42, 91, 95
Nerli, Benedetto di Tanai, 100
Nesi, Giovanni, 5
New World *(mundus novus)*. *See* world(s): new

Niccoli, Niccolò, 1, 6
Nifo, Agostino, 77
Nil admirari. *See* Adriani, Marcello: lectures: *Nil admirari*

Orphism, 98
Orti Oricellari. *See* Rucellai: Gardens *(Orti Oricellari)*
Ovid, x, 26, 104n, 116

Pachierotto, 81
Padua (university), 73
Panormita. *See* Beccadelli, Antonio (Panormita), *Hermaphroditus*
papacy, 5, 82
papal court. *See* Church: papal court
Parmenides, 46
Parronchi, Alessandro, 36
Patarines, 11
Paul III (pope). *See* Farnese, Alessandro
Pavia (university), 6
Persius, 60n
Perugia, 72
Petrarch, Francesco, ix
Piccolomini, Aeneas Silvius. *See* Pius II (pope)
Pico della Mirandola, Giovanni, x, 5, 43
Piero di Cosimo, early man paintings, 105, 106, 107
Pio, Alberto (prince of Carpi), 116
Pisa, 32, 47
   university in, 47, 58, 76–77, 101–102
Pius II (pope), 23, 24
Plato, 17, 19, 23, 28–29, 46, 52, 56, 58, 71, 86–87, 93, 98
   academy, 66
   Convivium, 93
   Dialogues, 22, 92
   Minos, 28
Platonic ideas, 57
Platonic law, 29

Platonic revival, 13
Platonists, 20
pleasure *(voluptas)*. See love *(voluptas)*
poetry, 46–47, 49, 94, 95
Poliziano, Angelo, x–xiii, 5, 43, 46, 49, 69, 88, 91, 92, 94–95, 96, 99, 104, 116
   Nutricia, 94
   Rusticus, 104
   Stanze, 104
   textual emendations, 91, 94, 115, 116, 119–121
Pollaiuoli, Antonio and Piero, 108
Polybius, 78, 85
Pomponazzi, Pietro, 76
Pontano, Giovanni, x, 4, 91, 97, 98, 100
   textual emendations, 75n, 91, 99, 115, 116, 117–122
Portugal, 30, 31, 57. *See also* John I of Portugal
Prato, 44, 47
primitivism, vii, 26–31, 39, 47, 57, 59, 84, 108
   hard, 26
   in paintings, 105–108
   see also Lucretius: themes and topics: primitivism (naturalism)
printing, 1–2, 57, 114. *See also De rerum natura*: printed editions
Priscian, 2
prodigies, 72
prophecy/-ies, 31–32, 53n, 72, 90, 107
Prosperi, Valentina, 108
Ptolemy, *Geography*, 9–10, 26–27, 89
Pucci (cardinal Antonio?), 116
Pulci family, 10, 11
Pulci, Luigi, 11, 12
Pythagoras, 66, 95

Quintilian, 23, 48

Ragazonibus, Theodorus de (publisher), 117
Raimondi, Cosma, *Defense of Epicurus*, 6
Raimondi, Enzio, 97
Ravenna, battle of, 62
Reeve, Michael, ix, 114–115, 117–119
religion, 3, 5, 31, 59, 61, 64, 78–84, 87, 92–93, 96, 109
   ancient Roman, 53, 78, 80
   Egyptian, 53
   heresy, ix–x, 11, 47, 65, 77
   naturalistic, 31–35
   orthodoxy, hetero-/unortho-. *See* Christianity: orthodoxy
   political use of, 29, 78, 80, 87, 93, 109
   popular, 12
   propitiatory, 53–55, 61, 78–79, 84
   skepticism toward, 10–12, 35, 39
   superstitious, 33, 54–56, 59–62, 67, 71, 78, 87, 95, 96
   unbelief, ix, 11–12, 109
   see also Lucretius: themes and topics: religion and gods; Machiavelli, Niccolò di Bernardo: religion; Scala, Bartolomeo: religion
renaissance
   Carolingian, 1–2
   fifteenth-century, 2
Reynolds, Susan, 11
rhetoric, 47–48
Ridolfi, Roberto, 113
Rome, 39
   ancient, 78, 79
Rossi 884 (R). *See De rerum natura*: manuscripts: MS Vat. Rossi 884 (R)
Rucellai family, 99, 101
Rucellai, Bernardo di Giovanni, 91, 97–98, 100–102
   De bello italico, 98
Rucellai, Cosimo di Bernardo, 97–98, 100
Rucellai, Cosimo di Cosimo, 98
Rucellai, Giovanni, 10, 32
Rucellai Gardens *(Orti Oricellari)*, 91, 97, 98, 100

INDEX

Salutati, Coluccio, ix
S. Andrea in Percussina, 81
San Martino at Gangalandi, 8
Sanseverino, Antonello (prince of Salerno), 39, 41, 43, 98
Sassetti, Francesco, 30, 95, 96–97
Sasso, Gennaro, 72n, 73, 77, 83, 115
Savonarola, fra Girolamo, xii, 12, 32, 46, 50, 54, 55–56, 79, 80, 84, 91, 102
   death, 56, 60
   regime, 31, 41, 97
   sermons, 13, 42, 43, 45, 49, 51, 54, 71
Savonarolans, 42, 91, 101, 102
Scala, Alessandra, xiii, 98
Scala, Bartolomeo, vii–viii, x–xiii, 5, 16, 20–41, 43, 44, 69, 97, 99, 102
   house in Borgo Pinti, xii, 5, 36–37
   last testament, 109
   religion, 31–32, 33, 35, 80, 109
   writings
      Apologi (I) and (II), 33–37, 40
      Defense against the Detractors of Florence, 27, 31–33, 43, 80
      "De rebus naturalibus," 27, 40
      De sectis philosophorum, 20–22
      Dialogue of Consolation, 22, 23, 24–26, 30
      Dialogue on Laws and Legal Judgments, 27–31, 50, 80
      Elegy in praise of Pius II, 23, 24
      On Trees, xiii, 7, 39–41, 43, 48, 69, 105, 107
      On whether a Wise Man Should Marry, 23–24
Schism, 5
Scipio Africanus, 85
Seneca, x, 104n
   Letters, 2
Serafico, Antonio, 18
Seville, 89
Sisyphus, 85
Sixtus IV (pope), 53
skepticism, 33, 80, 108–109. *See also* religion: skepticism toward

Socrates, 66
Soderini family, 99
Soderini, Giovan Battista, 72, 83
Soderini, Giovanvittorio, 101n
Soderini, Pagolantonio, 101
Soderini, Piero (life-gonfalonier), 97–98
   regime, 91, 108
Soderini, Tommaso di Pagolantonio, xiii, 100–102
Solaro, Giuseppe, 117, 118
soul, 11–13, 20, 21, 31, 32, 34–35, 76, 81–82, 96n, 107, 109
   All Souls Day, 34
   immortality of, 23, 35, 66, 92–93, 95, 96, 101–102
   mortality of, 3, 4, 14, 77, 82, 107
   unity of, 77
South America, 31, 89
Spini, Doffo di Agnolo, 102–103
St. Augustine, 2
St. Basil, 23
St. Benedict, 61, 67
St. Dominic, 80
St. Francis, 80
St. Jerome, 23
Stoicism/Stoics, 5, 20, 24, 31, 66, 90
Strozzi family, 97
Strozzi, Filippo, 101
Superchio Valerio, of Pesaro, 116
superstition. *See* religion: superstitious
syncretism, x

Terence, *Eununchus*, 113–114
theater, life as, 8–9, 82–83, 84
Themistius, 76–77
Theophrastus, 40
Thomas Aquinas, Saint, viii, 92
Traversari, Ambrogio, 1, 16, 22, 29
trees, 10, 107
   grafting, 7, 107n
   praises of, 40n, 48
   see also Scala, Bartolomeo: *On Trees*
Turkey, justice in, 28

unbelief. *See* religion: unbelief
universe, 76, 82, 86

Valla, Lorenzo, ix
   De voluptate (De vero bono), 6
Vasari, Giorgio, 105
vegetarianism, 105, 107
Venus, vii, 2, 19, 40, 56, 96, 103, 104
Verde, Armando, 45–47, 50, 52, 66
Verino, Francesco, 58, 77
Verino, Michele, 27, 40
Vespasiano da Bisticci, 25
Vespucci, Amerigo, 31, 39, 43, 89–90, 105, 109
   Mundus novus, 39, 89
Vespucci, Bartolomeo, 73
Vespucci, Giorgio Antonio, 89, 105
Vettori, Francesco, 78, 81, 82
Vettori, Pier, 118, 120
Villani, Giovanni, 3
Virgil, 2, 17, 21, 32, 48, 51, 52
   Aeneid, 50
   Georgics, 17, 50, 52, 56

voluptas. *See* love *(voluptas)*
Vulcan, 40
   paintings of, 105

Warburg, Aby, 96–97
West Indies, 89, 109
wonder, 51, 52, 71. *See also* Adriani, Marcello: lectures: *Nil Admirari*
Wootton, David, ix
world(s)
   eternal, 71, 73, 76–78, 82
   new, viii, 52, 57, 71, 80, 89–90, 94, 107, 109
   see also Lucretius: themes and topics: world(s); Vespucci, Amerigo: *Mundus novus*

Zeno, the Stoic, 24
Zodiac, sphere, 27